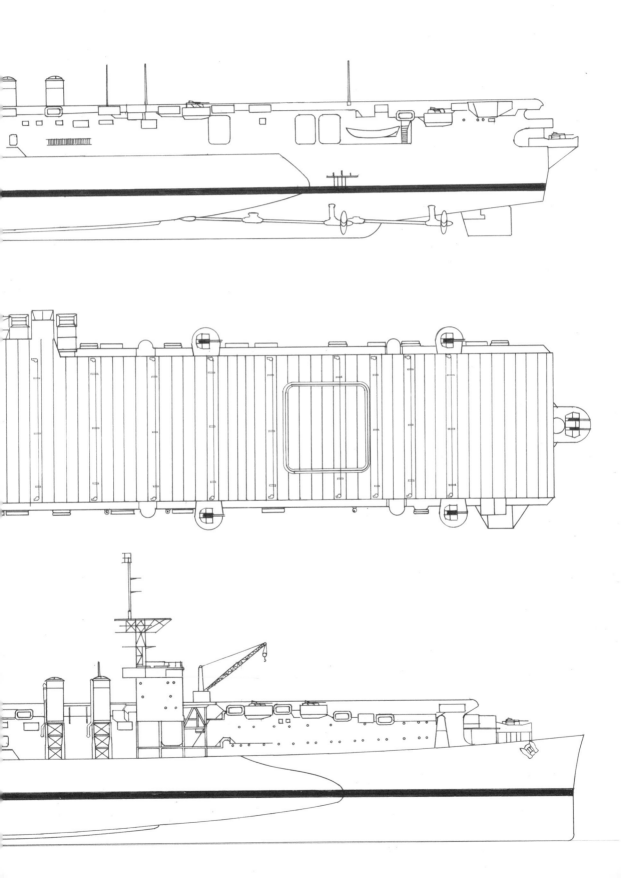

THE *INDEPENDENCE* LIGHT AIRCRAFT CARRIERS

THE *INDEPENDENCE*
LIGHT AIRCRAFT CARRIERS

by ANDREW FALTUM

The Nautical & Aviation Publishing Company of America
Charleston, South Carolina

Library of Congress Catalog Card Number: 2001008208

ISBN: 1-877853-62-3

Printed in the United States of America

                        Library of Congress Cataloging-in-Publication Data

Faltum, Andrew, 1947-
    The Independence light aircraft carriers / Andrew Faltum.
          cm.
Includes bibliographical references and index.
    ISBN 1-877853-62-3 (hardcover)

    Aircraft carriers—United States—History—20th century. 2.
Independence (Aircraft carrier : CV 22) 3. World War, 1939-1945—Naval
operations, American. 4. World War, 1939-1945—Aerial operations,
American. 5. World War, 1939-1945—Campaign—Pacific Area. I. Title.
    V874.3 .F3523 2002
    359.9'4835'097—dc21

                                                                        2001008208

Picture credits:
Unless otherwise noted, all photographs are official United States
Navy
Edited by Pamela Ryan
Book design by James M. Faulkner

Contents

Acknowledgments

I wish to express my appreciation to the many individuals and organizations who have given generously of their time and advice, and for their assistance and encouragement in writing this book: the staffs at the National Archives and the Naval Historical Center, particularly Ed Finney of the Photographic Branch and Mark Evans of the Naval Aviation History Branch; Peter Mersky and Norman Polmar for reviewing my drafts; Tom Walkowiak from The Floating Drydock for help with camouflage and drawings; various ship's veterans groups, especially Ed Hudson of the *Cabot* and Al Hiegel of the *Independence;* and the staff of The Nautical & Aviation Publishing Co. Finally, I would like to thank my wife Sherryl and my sons James, Chris, and Dave, who have put up with me while I struggled with this book.

Preface

When I was a boy, I would haunt a local used book store looking for books and old magazines on anything related to ships, airplanes, and naval subjects. One of my prize finds was an old copy of the August 1945 issue of *National Geographic*, which included an article titled *"The Saga of the Carrier Princeton"* by Captain William H. Buracker, USN. The dramatic story of the *Princeton* fired my imagination and, as I learned more about carrier aviation and the battles of World War II, it struck me that I didn't know much more about this ship than what I had read in this one article. Later, as an adult, a chance comment to a fellow naval reservist led to writing my first book, *The Essex Aircraft Carriers*. (Nautical & Aviation, 1996). In the course of researching the Essex book, I came across a lot of material related to the *Independence*-class light aircraft carriers. Once the first book was completed, it seemed only natural to tell the story of the light carriers that were such a vital part of the fast carrier task forces of World War II. As a class

of warships, their contributions were ignored in many ways, probably because they were viewed, both then and now, as a wartime expedient. I hope this book helps to redress this neglect.

As in the previous book, I have avoided technical explanations so that the average reader is not weighed down by jargon. Also, the conventions used in this book are the same: dates and times are given in military fashion, that is 31 January 1942, rather than January 31, 1942, and 1300 instead of 1:00 p.m. Distances are given in nautical miles unless stated otherwise. Since this book is a compilation from many sources, some with conflicting information, I have tried to resolve these issues whenever possible and any errors in judgment are ultimately mine. Professional historians may notice that a lot of the material presented here duplicates more general histories of fast carrier operations in World War II. This was a deliberate choice on my part, as I wanted to keep the story of the

1

Independence class within context for readers who may be unfamiliar with the subject. The follow-on class of light carriers, the *Saipan* class are included in an appendix. While their story is not really a part of the main narrative of World War II light carrier operations, I felt that they deserved at least some coverage.

In the course of writing this book, I have come to appreciate the contributions of those who served in the *Independence*-class light carriers and hope that it, in some small way, adds to the record of their wartime achievements and sacrifices.

Introduction

The aircraft carrier evolved following World War I, as the world's navies sought a means of taking aircraft to sea. A few naval officers had envisioned a role for aircraft in naval operations as early as 1909, and in November 1910 a civilian pilot, Eugene Ely, became the first to fly an airplane successfully from the deck of a ship. Using a Curtiss biplane, he took off from a makeshift flight deck built on the cruiser *Birmingham* anchored in Hampton Roads, Virginia. Two months later, he became the first to land an aircraft on a ship when he landed aboard another cruiser, the *Pennsylvania*, in San Francisco Bay.

In World War I, the British began experimenting with aircraft operating from ships and by the end of the war had developed an aircraft-carrying ship with an offensive strike capability. However, they never got the opportunity to prove its full potential and only after the war did Britain, the United States, and Japan develop true aircraft carriers.

During the 1920s and 1930s, governments were swept up in a rising tide of public sentiment for disarmament. At the same time, aviators in the Army and Navy struggled with conservative leaders for greater recognition of the role of air power. A growing disillusionment with America's participation in World War I led the public to view armaments, particularly such expensive symbols of naval might as dreadnought battleships, as unaffordable. At the Washington Naval Arms Limitation Conference, which opened in November 1921, America offered to scrap many thousands of tons of ships then under construction. Great Britain, the United States, Japan, France, and Italy were the major players in the conference and the treaties signed in February 1922 established the famous 5:5:3 tonnage ratio between the U.S., Great Britain, and Japan (with 1.75 ratios for France and Italy) for battleships and aircraft carriers, a ten-year holiday on building capital ships, and a restriction on individual battleships

3

of no more than 35,000 tons. The *Lexington* and *Saratoga,* originally part of a class of battle cruisers then under construction, could be completed as carriers, although at 33,000 tons, both exceeded the 27,000-ton limit for individual aircraft carriers. The total tonnage allowed the U.S. for aircraft carrier construction was 135,000 tons.

In 1919, the Navy had ordered the conversion of the collier *Jupiter* to an experimental aircraft carrier. A few years later, partly in response to the challenge of air-power advocate Brigadier General Billy Mitchell and partly in response to air power advocates within the Navy itself, the Navy began expanding its aviation capabilities. The Bureau of Aeronautics (BuAer) was created in August 1921. BuAer was responsible for the development of aircraft- and aviation-related ship equipment, such as catapults and arresting gear, and was unique in that, unlike the other bureaus in the Navy Department (Construction & Repair, Engineering, Ordnance, and Navigation), it had a lot of authority over operational doctrine and personnel assignments. The establishment of BuAer was followed by the addition of an Assistant Secretary of the Navy for Air, which indicated the growing importance of naval aviation.

The *Langley* was commissioned in 1922 as CV-1, the U.S. Navy's first "flattop." Her ungainly appearance earned her the nickname "The Covered Wagon," and she pioneered many aspects of carrier aviation that became standard features of all later carriers. As the *Lexington* and *Saratoga* neared completion, the *Langley* and her aviators developed the methods, tactics, and doctrine that all future carriers would follow.

Commissioned late in 1927, the *Lexington* (CV-2) and *Saratoga* (CV-3) were the largest carriers in existence. Their 180,000 shaft horsepower (SHP) turbo-electric drive propulsion plants gave them high sustained speed (33 knots), and their size (888 feet overall length) allowed ninety aircraft to be carried. They were armed with eight 8-inch guns mounted in four twin turrets fore and aft of the large island structure, and twelve 5-inch guns along the edge of the flight deck, three at each quarter. As the first real American aircraft carriers, the *Lexington* and *Saratoga* pioneered the use of aircraft carriers in an offensive role.

In the "cruiser bill" passed in 1928, Congress also provided for one aircraft carrier. The *Ranger* (CV-4), was the first American ship built as an aircraft carrier from the keel up. In designing the *Ranger,* the Navy wanted the greatest aircraft carrying capacity possible for a given hull size. Based on tonnage allowed, the Navy decided to build five medium-size carriers rather than only four or fewer larger ones. With a standard displacement of 14,500 tons and a length of 769 feet overall, the *Ranger* was too small to be a satisfactory fleet carrier. Although she could carry eighty-six aircraft, her lack of speed and protection limited her practical usefulness. Because of her size, she had difficulty operating in heavy seas, reducing her capability even further. Although she played a role in the Atlantic during the early part of World War II, she was not suitable for fast carrier operations and was soon relegated to training duties.

Franklin D. Roosevelt, former Assistant Secretary of the Navy in World War I, became president in 1933. He was not only an advocate of sea power, but of air power as well. The *Yorktown* (CV-5) and *Enterprise* (CV-6) were part of the National Industrial Recovery Act of 1933, which aimed to create employment. The *Yorktown* class applied the lessons learned by practical experience with the *Lexington* and *Saratoga*, and the design proved large enough to be useful in carrier operations, with a good blend of size, speed, and aircraft carrying capacity. The *Yorktown* and *Enterprise* were laid down in 1934 and commissioned in 1937 and 1938 respectively. At 19,900 tons and 769 feet overall length, they could operate a hundred aircraft. Both had eight 5-inch guns (two at each quarter along the flight deck edge), underwater protection against torpedoes, and protective decks over the machinery spaces. They were a highly successful design and formed the basis of what would become the *Essex* class.

The *Wasp* (CV-7) was laid down in 1936 and commissioned in 1939. At 14,700 tons, she used the remaining tonnage allowed under treaty. Although similar to appearance to the *Yorktown,* she suffered many of the same shortcomings as the *Ranger,* such as lack of speed, but was the first carrier to use a deck-edge aircraft elevator. The deck-edge elevator allowed more flexibility in handling aircraft on the hangar deck than conventional centerline elevators, and due to its success on the *Wasp,* was incorporated into the design for the *Essex* class.

In May 1938, a 20-percent expansion program of the 1934 Vinson-Trammel Act added 40,000 tons to the original treaty limit of 135,000. This allowed for the construction of two 20,000-ton carriers. Because of the urgent need for aircraft carriers, the

Hornet (CV-8) was built to the *Yorktown*-class design, although with some changes and slightly greater displacement. Commissioned in 1941, the *Hornet* was the last carrier finished before the outbreak of war. The other carrier became the *Essex* (CV-9), the first of a class of ships that formed the backbone of American carrier task forces through the latter half of World War II and on into the Korean and Vietnam wars. Although designed after the lifting of treaty limitations, the *Essex* class was developed from the earlier treaty-bound *Yorktown* class. The *Essex*-class design, however, started where the *Hornet* left off. At 27,500 tons and 872 feet overall length (888 feet in "long hull" ships), these ships were armed with twelve 5-inch guns, eight quad 40mm mounts (up to eighteen in later ships), and forty-six 20mm cannon (up to sixty in later ships) and were capable of handling large air groups of the latest aircraft. The original *Essex* design was funded under the Fiscal Year 1940 (FY 40) program for construction beginning in FY 41. By the time the first ship was ordered, however, it became clear that more would be needed. The passage of the "Two Ocean Navy Act" of June 1940, provided for three more carriers, CVs 10-12, that had already been ordered under a Chief of Naval Operations directive of 20 May 1940. These became the new *Yorktown* (CV-10), *Intrepid* (CV-11), and the new *Hornet* (CV-12). After the fall of France in June, Congress voted an additional seventy-percent expansion and another seven carriers, CVs 13-19, were ordered under a 16 August 1940 directive:*Franklin* (CV-13), *Ticonderoga* (CV-14), *Randolph* (CV-15), *Lexington* (CV-16), *Bunker Hill*

(CV-17), *Wasp* (CV-18), and *Hancock* (CV-19). Just after the outbreak of war, on 15 December 1941, two more, CVs 20-21, were added to the original series, *Bennington* (CV-20) and *Boxer* (CV-21). With America's entry into World War II, their construction was greatly accelerated and by the end of the war, seventeen of the twenty four *Essex* class carriers eventually completed were in service. In the dark days of early 1942,

however, more fleet carriers were needed as soon as possible.

Because of the great need for fleet carriers, the Navy ordered the conversion of light-cruiser hulls into light carriers in 1942. The *Independence* class of light carriers, CVLs 21-30, supplemented the Essex class and allowed for a much more rapid expansion of the carrier force. This book is the story of these carriers.

Chapter 1

A Wartime Expedient

"An aircraft carrier is a noble thing. It lacks almost everything that seems to denote nobility, yet deep nobility is there. A carrier has no poise. It has no grace. It is top-heavy and lop-sided. It has the lines of a well-fed cow.

"It doesn't cut through the water like a cruiser, knifing romantically along. It doesn't dance and cavort like a destroyer. It just plows. You feel it should be carrying a hod rather than wearing a red sash.

"Yet a carrier is a ferocious thing, and out of its heritage of action has grown its nobility. I believe that today every Navy in the world has as its No.1 priority the destruction of enemy carriers. That's a precarious honor, but it's a proud one."[1]

These words, written in 1945 by the famous war correspondent Ernie Pyle, were based on his experiences aboard the *Cabot*, one of the nine *Independence* -class light aircraft carriers to serve in World War II. Explaining his choice, he said, "I had asked to be put on a small carrier, rather than a big one. The reasons were many. For one thing, the large ones are so immense and carry such a big crew that it would be like living in Grand Central Station. I felt I could get the 'feel' of a carrier more quickly, could become more intimately a member of the family, if I were to go on a smaller one."[2]

These proud ships were a successful gamble to provide carrier air power to the fleet at a critical point in the war. They were not the best carriers possible–they were a wartime expedient that would not be repeated in the postwar Navy. But they all entered service quickly and contributed more to victory than if they had been completed as the light cruisers that served as their point of origin. Their story begins in the period of rearmament just before America's entry into the war.

From Concept to Commitment

President Roosevelt, who had become a strong advocate for naval aviation while serving as Assistant Secretary of the Navy under Josephus Daniels in World War I, was the driving force behind two kinds of aircraft carriers built as emergency war designs in World War II. The first of these were the converted merchant ship hulls, which became escort carriers for both American and British service. The president had first proposed a merchant-ship conversion for convoy antisubmarine protection in October 1940. A few months later, the Chief of Naval Operations (CNO), Admiral Harold R. Stark, held a series of conferences to discuss merchant-ship conversions and by early January 1941, two diesel-powered C-3 merchant ships, the *Mormacmail* and the *Mormacland*, were selected for conversion. "The president, who considered U.S. entry into the war imminent, [threw] out any plan which would take more than three months..."[3] The real issue was accepting what was "good enough" instead of what the Navy wanted, which was something close to a full carrier. The *Mormacmail* was taken over in March and emerged on 2 June 1941 as the *Long Island* (AVG-1, aircraft tender, general purpose). Her designation was later changed to ACV-1 (auxiliary aircraft carrier) and eventually to CVE-1 (escort carrier). She was the first of many to follow.[4]

Like the escort carrier, the light carrier was to bring sea-based air power into the war as quickly as possible, using resources already in the pipeline. The Navy had studied cruiser-sized aircraft carrier designs during the 1930s, but too often competing requirements limited their ability to operate as efficiently as larger fleet units. As in the case of the escort carriers, the president, who had proposed in August 1941 a conversion of cruisers already on order, wanted the Navy to discard peacetime

"gold plated" standards in the interest of producing these ships quickly.[5] The Bureau of Ships (BuShips), responsible for ship design, objected to the proposal. (BuShips had been created in 1940 by combining the ship design functions of Construction & Repair with the machinery and radio design functions of Engineering.) BuShips Preliminary Design section opposed the project because "it would upset the orderly construction of this series of cruisers, and would produce small, costly aircraft carriers of limited effectiveness [not much, if at all] earlier than the large *Essex* class now building." (The scheduled completion date of the *Essex* was March 1944, but she was finished much sooner, being commissioned on the last day of 1942.) Also, the Bureau of Aeronautics (BuAer) felt the design "has a number of undesirable aeronautical features which combine to jeopardize seriously the probable usefulness of these vessels...flight operations would be both hazardous and difficult."[6] On 13 October, the Navy's General Board rejected the president's idea. But Roosevelt, probably with the experience of the first escort carrier in mind, was not put off. On 25 October, he asked for a new cruiser conversion study. The Navy had left a loophole in its assessment: if a smaller flight deck, fewer aircraft, or less effectiveness were acceptable, the conversion could, of course, be completed sooner. This was exactly the point. After the Japanese attacked Pearl Harbor on 7 December 1941, the Navy came around to the president's way of thinking as America mobilized for wartime production. Warships of all kinds were needed as quickly as possible and aircraft carriers received the highest priority.

Designing for Wartime

The Navy had ordered thirty-six of the 10,000-ton *Cleveland* class light cruisers in 1940 and 1941. Originally authorized in 1934 as a follow-on to the *Brooklyn* class light cruisers, they were armed with twelve 6-inch guns in four triple turrets, twelve 5-inch guns in six twin-mounts, twenty-eight 40mm cannon in seven quad-mounts, plus varying numbers of 20mm cannon. They were the largest single class of cruisers in U.S. Navy history. Because of the numbers available, and the fact that they were considered the smallest hulls that could be adapted as aircraft carriers to provide a useful aircraft capacity with the speed required for fleet operations, they were the logical choice for conversion.[7] On 2 January 1942, the CNO, Admiral Stark, wrote to BuShips to confirm that one of the *Cleveland* class light cruisers would be converted to an aircraft carrier. BuShips started work the next day, at first using their earlier plans, but soon shifting to a design based on the *Sangamon*-class escort carriers. The *Sangamon* class CVEs, built on fleet-oiler hulls, were larger and more capable than the C-3 merchant-ship conversions and comparable in dimensions and displacement to light cruisers, so the two designs had essentially the same flight deck.[8] In designing the *Independence* class, the original cruiser main deck, with its camber and sheer, would have posed problems as a hangar deck, which should be flat to allow easy movement of aircraft. The designers solved this problem by adding a flat hangar deck, which ran between the forward and after aircraft elevators, four feet above the original cruiser main deck. This also avoided the problem of weakening the hull by cutting holes in the main deck (which was a "strength deck" that carried part of the structural load) for the elevator pits. A hangar clearance height of seventeen feet four inches, comparable to that found in a fleet carrier, was achieved by using flight deck girders which were only three feet deep. This was possible because the requirement for carrying spare aircraft from the overhead of the hangar bay, as in fleet carriers, was waived. Unlike previous fleet carrier designs, the sides of the ship were closed up to the flight deck; ventilation was provided by light steel roller door openings in the sides at the ends of the hangar.

The stability problems of the previous cruiser conversion studies, that would have required 400 tons of ballast, were solved by adding a 315-ton blister, increasing the beam by five feet. This had the added benefit of providing space for an additional 635 tons of fuel storage to the original cruiser design, allowing 225 tons for aviation gasoline (avgas). The cruising radius, 10,000 miles at fifteen knots, was better than the *Cleveland*-class cruisers, but only two-thirds that of the larger *Essex*-class carriers.[9] Although the blister decreased top speed by 1.5 knots to 31.6 knots, this was good enough to operate with larger fleet carriers. Overall, the standard displacement rose to 11,000 tons and the draft increased by one foot to twenty-six feet.[10]

The blister, however, caused problems with the armor belt. Since Class A cruiser armor could not be used (it was too difficult to cut and weld in attaching it to the blisters), Class B armor was needed. This added another 360 tons to the displacement, another three inches to the draft, and cut down the top speed by another quarter knot. Due to expected delays in the delivery of Class B armor, the first two ships carried no side armor in order to save time. The original ammunition magazines were converted to bomb storage and a space aft of the hangar was created to store twenty-four torpedoes, which rode the aft aircraft elevator to the flight deck. To protect this vulnerable area, 15-lb. Special Treatment Steel (STS) about 0.38 inch thick was applied to the side of the hangar aft by the torpedo storage and exposed control spaces. Bomb elevators and ammunition hoists were protected with 25-lb. and 30-lb. STS. (Unlike armor steel, STS could be used to provide structural strength as well as armor protection. It came in a variety of thicknesses; the designations 15-lb., 25-lb., etc. refer to the weight per square foot.)[11]

As the design evolved, changes were made. The original main propulsion machinery of the *Cleveland* class-geared turbines producing 100,000 shaft horsepower (SHP) was retained, but disposing of stack gas was a problem. Different arrangements were considered, but in the end four simple smoke pipes, arranged in pairs on the starboard side, were used. The *Independence* class light carriers, along with the C-3 merchant and *Sangamon* oiler escort carrier conversions, were originally intended to have flush decks. In February 1942, however, based on early British operational experience, all three classes received essentially the same small island, actually no more than a small open bridge, six feet wide, four feet from the starboard edge of the flight deck near the forward end. The island was equipped with the captain's and navigator's sea cabins, a chart room, an open bridge, and sky lookout platforms extending four feet to either side.[12] As small as it was, the island still had to be counterbalanced with eighty-two tons of concrete added to four blister compartments below the second platform deck level on the port side.[13]

In World War II, radar became a significant factor in naval operations and answered the problem of carrier fighter defense that existed before the war. Air-search radars provided long-range detection of incoming enemy raids, allowing defending fighters to intercept them before they could attack the carrier task forces. Early wartime experience in the Pacific had shown the need for a backup air-search radar on fleet carriers, in case the first broke down or was damaged in combat. The original flush-deck design of the *Independence* class called for an air-search radar mounted on a mast, which could also act as a kingpost for the aircraft crane, but when the island was added, it provided a site for a second air-search radar. The primary air-search radar, the SK, had a large seventeen-foot by seventeen-foot "mattress" antenna with IFF (Identification Friend or Foe) antennas attached to the top edge. It had a range of a hundred miles under normal conditions, and was mounted atop a stub mast located just forward of the after pair of smoke uptakes. The secondary air-search radar was the smaller SC-2, which had a range of about eighty miles. Besides the SC-2, the island carried an SG surface-search radar and the YE aircraft homing beacon.[14] Because of the separation of the radars, the *Independence* light carriers actually suffered fewer of the mutual interference problems experienced by their larger *Essex* cousins. The Combat Information Center (CIC) and radar rooms were located on the gallery deck forward of the hangar bulkhead, with air plot forward of the CIC at the same level.[15]

In the end, the aviation handling facilities were better than predicted in the earlier design studies, although at 215 feet long and fifty-eight feet wide, the hangar bay was smaller than even the *Sangamon* CVEs. The flight deck was 552 feet long and ended before it reached the slender cruiser bow. Like the CVEs, the *Independence* class had two aircraft elevators, but they had a faster cycle. As the first ship was fitting out, extensions were added to the flight deck between the stacks to allow "duds" to be moved out of the way. Another improvement was an extension of the flight deck on the port side next to the forward elevator, which allowed aircraft to bypass the elevator well and also served as a jettison ramp for damaged aircraft. An H 2-1 hydraulic catapult was installed on the port side of the flight deck. Later, a second was added to the starboard side.[16] An aircraft crane of 14,000-pound capacity was added forward of the island to load aircraft or other large items of equipment. To counteract these and other necessary additions, topside weight was reduced wherever possible, such as substituting simple cloth curtains for doors in officers' quarters.

The armament on the first two ships included two single 5-inch dual-purpose guns–one mounted on the bow and the other on a sponsor at the stern–plus eight 40mm twin mounts

and sixteen 20mm single mounts arranged around the edge of the flight deck. The two 5-inch guns were soon replaced by two quad 40mm mounts, because it was recognized that, apart from the close-in antiaircraft defense provided by the 40mm and 20mm guns, the light carriers would have to rely on their escorts and their own aircraft for protection. Later, another 40mm twin mount and 6 more 20mm guns were added. Some ships ended the war with nine 40mm twin mounts and five 20mm twin mounts (six in *Monterey*).[17]

Construction

On 10 January 1942, the *Amsterdam* (CL-59), which had been laid down in May 1941 as a light cruiser, was reordered for conversion to an aircraft carrier as the *Independence* (CV-22). The next month, on Valentine's Day, the new CNO, Admiral Ernest J. King, reviewed the conversion plans and added two more. The *Tallahassee* (CL-61), laid down in June 1941, was reordered as the *Princeton* (CV-23) and the *New Haven* (CL-76), laid down in August 1941, as the *Belleau Wood* (CV-24). On 27 March, three more were added. The *Huntington* (CL-77) became *Cowpens* (CV-25), *Dayton* (CL-78) became *Monterey* (CV-26), and *Fargo* (CL-85) became *Crown Pointe* (CV-27). Later, on 2 June, the final three ships of the class were ordered: *Wilmington* (CL-79) as *Cabot* (CV-28), *Buffalo* (CL-99) as *Bataan* (CV-29), and *Newark* (CL-100) as *Reprisal* (CV-30). Three of the ships, CV-27, CV-29 and CV-30, were not yet laid down as cruisers when they were reordered as carriers, greatly speeding their "conversion." In

January 1943, the *Reprisal* was renamed *San Jacinto* to honor the *Houston* (CA-30), which was lost in March 1942 in the Sunda Strait of the Java Sea. The people of Houston had collected money during a war bond drive to pay for the construction of a new *Houston* (CL-81) and when the drive ended, there was enough money left over to fund the construction of a light carrier. Since aircraft carriers were, at the time, named for battles or other famous ships, the name was chosen to commemorate the 1836 battle in which Sam Houston won independence for Texas.[18] Similarly, in May 1943, the *Crowne Point* became the *Langley* to honor the Navy's first aircraft carrier. The original *Langley* was converted to a seaplane tender (AV-3) in 1937 and was lost in the Java Sea in February 1942. All the conversions were in the same hull number sequence as for fleet carriers, but they were redesignated as light carriers or CVL (for "aircraft carrier, small") on 15 July 1943.[19]

All of these ships were built by the New York Shipbuilding Corporation at Camden, New Jersey. A company representative from the builder even attended the initial meeting in January 1942 and much of the conversion design work was done by the builder.[20] The company, established at the turn of the century by Henry G. Morse with financial backing by Andrew Mellon and Henry Frick, was originally to have been located on Staten Island, hence the name. When Morse decided that Camden, which offered better land, rail facilities, and access to a great number of experienced shipyard workers, was a better location, the new shipyard was built there, but the name was kept.

The shipyard opened in 1900 and,

by World War I, had become the largest shipyard in the world and a major builder of U.S. Navy warships. New York Ship, as it was also known, operated according to five principals. First, it used the template system, with fabrication and assembly being done separately. Second, all major parts were prefabricated. Third, overhead cranes connected all parts of the yard, allowing easy movement of parts. Fourth, the shipbuilding ways were roofed to avoid delays caused by bad weather. Fifth, many tasks usually completed during outfitting were completed before launching instead. During World War II New York Ship would supply 26 heavy combatant ships for service in the U.S. Navy, which included 2 destroyer tenders, 3 seaplane tenders, 1 repair ship, 8 light cruisers, 2 battle cruisers and 1 battleship. This does not include the 44 other ships that were on active duty prior to America's entry into the war. In all, 70 ships originally built by New York Ship saw service during World War II–quite an impressive production record. But among the many warships built, the shipyard workers were especially proud of the nine light carriers of the *Independence* class and they were referred to collectively in wartime company advertisements as the "sunsetters" for their role in the defeat of Japan, the "land of the rising sun."

There are significant milestones in the life of a naval warship. The first is when the keel is laid down, and the structure that will become a ship begins to take form. At this point the ship is primarily the concern of her builder. The second milestone occurs when the hull structure is essentially complete and she is christened at her launching.

During the launching ceremony, it is Navy tradition that a woman sponsor christens the ship with a bottle of champaign or other spirits broken across the bow as the ship slides down the ways. The occasion is also a time for speeches by attending dignitaries expressing the hopes for the new ship's future career. In the urgency of war-time, these speeches often conveyed a sense of grim determination and national purpose. In the case of the *Bataan,* the first ship named to com-memorate a battle of World War II, there was an added element of commit-ment to victory. Secretary of the Navy Frank Knox predicted that the ship "...has a rendezvous with destiny that shall not be denied." President of the Philippine Commonwealth, Manuel Quezon, expressed the faith and hope of Filipinos and Americans alike that "...the valor of the American and Filipino fighting men who battled through the long months on Bataan will serve as an inspiration to the men of this fine new ship."[21]

After launching, the ships of the *Independence* class were towed from the New York Shipbuilding Corporation's yard across the river to the Philadelphia Navy Yard, where there was still much work to be done as they neared com-pletion. At this point, the crews began preparations for the third milestone: commissioning as a fighting ship in active service. The complement of an *Independence*-class carrier was 140 officers and 1,321 enlisted men, but as wartime requirements led to demands for more men to operate added weaponry and equipment, this later increased to a total of 1,561. This was slightly more than half the crew of the larger *Essex* class and accommodations

were always tight. Initially only a small group, perhaps 300 or so, reported aboard as part of the fitting out detail, while others were quartered ashore at the Philadelphia receiving station or attended specialized training else-where. The ships of the *Independence* class often did not receive their final drafts of men until just before commis-sioning. The difficulties of learning to operate and maintain a large and com-plex ship were compounded by the need to transform a body of officers and men into a cohesive team that could fight and win. Many of the skills needed were taught ashore at various schools and training centers, but experi-enced crew members were a precious commodity. Some of the carriers put to sea with seventy percent of their enlist-ed and half of their officers without prior sea experience, many never hav-ing been aboard an ocean going vessel of any kind.[22] For "old salts" this could be unsettling, as Lou Mitnich, an expe-rienced fireman first class learned. Expecting leave after his transfer from a heavy cruiser, he was instead ordered to report to the *Belleau Wood* as she was nearing completion in Camden: "I rushed in a chit for leave, but the offi-cer, after looking through some papers, said, 'You're just the man we are look-ing for. B division has been waiting weeks for a fireman like you.' I retired wearily...and prepared to hit the sack. ...After breakfast [the next morning] I met the chiefs and some of the boys and was ready to get my first glimpse of the *Belleau Wood*...Suddenly some-body yelled, 'That's her!' You could have knocked me over with a feather. All the time I had thought the *Belleau Wood* was one of the big *Essex*-class car-riers, but there she was, a little ugly flattop and with a starboard list to boot. For a moment I wished I'd joined the Army."[23]

Commissioning

The *Independence*-class carriers were all commissioned in 1943, the first in January and the last in December. Due to the press of wartime, the commissioning ceremonies themselves were often brief and businesslike. The February commissioning of the *Princeton*, for example, was held on the flight deck in the early afternoon. The Philadelphia Navy Yard band played the National Anthem, the new skipper, Captain George R. Henderson, made a brief speech, and Chief Boatswain R. C. Hawk piped his boatswain's mates and set the watch, signifying that the ship was now under the control of her crew. In a sense, this is the point when a ship becomes alive and is no longer an inanimate object. To celebrate her new status, Dr. Harold W. Dodds, president of Princeton University, presented the ship with a silver punch bowl, and a representative of the New York Princeton University Club presented a Currier & Ives print of the old gunboat *Princeton*, the new ship's namesake.[24] Commissioning, however, did not mean the ships were ready for combat. Problems with equipment or construction defects often caused ships to be in a Navy Yard for days or weeks until they could be corrected.

Shakedown

As each of the new *Independence*-class carriers was commissioned, the demanding process of working up for combat, known in the Navy as the "shakedown," began. The captain held absolute responsibility for the combat readiness of his ship and for the safety, well-being, and efficiency of the crew. His ability, experience, and leadership often determined what kind of "personality" the ship would develop. The new captains were of varied backgrounds. The captain of the *Belleau Wood*, Captain A.M. "Mel" Pride, for example, was a "mustang" who had worked his way up the ranks from machinist mate 3rd class to captain, having earned his wings of gold in World War I.[25] By the end of the war he was a rear admiral and later an admiral. Captain Robert P. McConnell of the *Cowpens,* had been the captain of the old *Langley* (AV-3) when she was sunk south of Java in 1942.[26] Most would go on become successful commanders, but a few would not measure up to the leadership demands of carrier combat.

In practice, the captain delegated the duties of the ship through the executive officer, often referred to as the "exec" or "XO," the department heads, and the officer of the deck (OOD). The XO was next in line of command and, by long tradition and practice, responsible for matters relating to personnel, routine, and discipline of the ship. Major functions aboard ship were delegated to departments, with an officer in charge responsible for the organization, training and readiness of all the men in the department. Departments, in turn, were made up of divisions with varying numbers of men assigned. Aboard the *Independence*-class light carriers, the Gunnery Department normally had six divisions. Typically the First, Second and Fourth Divisions manned the 40mm mounts, while the Marines of the Fifth Division (the Marine detachment might have two officers and about forty enlisted Marines) manned the 20mm battery. The Third Division provided lookouts and the Sixth Division manned the fire direction equipment, magazine and armory, as well as maintaining the aerial torpedoes. Engineering had the A, B, E, and M Divisions, and Supply had the S-1 and S-2 Divisions. The rest of the departments were all organized into single divisions – Communication (K), Navigation (N), Hull (R), Medical (H), and Executive (X). But aircraft carriers also have an Air Department headed by the Air Officer, known as the "air boss." The Air Department took care of the aviation functions – the V-1 Division served on the flight deck and was responsible for the arresting gear, the catapults, the Landing Signal Officer (LSO), aircraft handling and servicing, and firefighting, among other things. The V-2 Division performed similar functions on the hangar deck, especially aircraft maintenance. V-3 handled the Combat Information Center (CIC), air control, intelligence, aerology, and the photo lab.

The Air Group
The primary weapon of the light carriers would be their aircraft and during shakedown, the ship and her air group learned to work as a team for the first time. The *Independence* and *Princeton* began their shakedowns with air groups that were scaled down versions of those of their larger cousins: one fighter squadron (VF) of twenty-four Wildcats and one composite squadron (VC) of twelve Dauntless dive bombers and nine Avenger torpedo bombers.

The stubby little mid-winged

Grumman F4F Wildcat was the Navy's first line fighter when World War II began. With its reliability and rugged construction, and the skill and superior tactics of its pilots, it held its own against the superb Japanese Zero in the first year of Pacific combat. The F4F-4 version was armed with six .50 caliber machine guns and was the first model to have folding wings. The Eastern Aircraft Division of General Motors later took over production of both the Wildcat and Avenger to allow Grumman to concentrate on producing the Hellcat; these aircraft were designated FM-1 and TBM-1, respectively, and were identical in most respects to their Grumman-built counterparts. The Wildcat would be replaced by the F6F Hellcat before any of the *Independence*-class carriers entered combat.

The Douglas SBD Dauntless, the Navy's workhorse in the Pacific, was the deciding factor in the Battle of Midway, the turning point in the war against Japan. This two-place dive bomber was slow and vulnerable, but its ruggedness and dependability kept it in service long after its planned replacement by the Curtiss Helldiver. Although the Dauntless served with the fast carrier forces until June 1944, none flew in combat from the *Independence* class.

Another Grumman product, the TBF Avenger was designed as a replacement for the aging TBD Devastator torpedo bomber and became operational in 1942. A large, mid-wing airplane with a crew of three, the Avenger was powered by a 1,700 horsepower Wright R-2600 Cyclone engine and armed with one forward firing .30 caliber machine gun in the nose cowling (synchronized to fire through the propeller arc), one .50 caliber machine gun in a power-operated dorsal turret at the end of the long greenhouse canopy, and a flexible .30 caliber machine gun firing through a ventral tunnel aft of the large internal torpedo bay. Later versions of the Avenger had two forward firing .50 caliber machine guns. With a wingspan of fifty-four feet two inches, the wings had to be folded back hydraulically. Besides carrying torpedoes, the Avenger was used as a level bomber. It was a stable airplane but, although faster than its predecessor, was too slow and heavy on the controls to be used as a dive bomber. The Avenger was known affectionately by its crews as the "turkey."

When the new, larger F6F Hellcat replaced the Wildcat, fewer fighters could be carried, so in October 1943, the authorized complement for CVL air groups was established at twelve fighters, nine dive bombers and nine torpedo bombers.[27] Looking like the Wildcat's younger but bigger brother, the F6F Hellcat was unmistakably a product of the Grumman "iron works." It was chubby and angular, but rugged and powered by a magnificent engine, the 2,000 horsepower Pratt and Whitney R-2800 Double Wasp. With a wingspan of forty-two feet ten inches and a gross weight of nearly seven tons, the Hellcat was a lot of airplane, but steady as a rock when coming aboard a carrier. The Hellcat was the first Navy fighter designed on the basis of combat experience with the Zero, and matched or exceeded the Zero's performance in nearly every category except maneuverability. The Hellcat's heavy armament of six .50 caliber machine guns could easily tear apart a Zero, and its self-sealing tanks, armor

plate, and sturdy structure made it more survivable than its opposition.

As the air groups worked up for combat, experience soon showed that the composite squadron of SBDs and TBFs was unworkable–the Dauntlesses did not have folding wings and were hard to manage on the narrow flight deck and in the cramped hangar. They were eventually eliminated and the light-carrier air group complement was revised to twenty-four Hellcats and nine Avengers, and remained at that level throughout the war, despite recommendations from the fleet for the light carriers to have all-fighter air groups. These air group changes were made official in November 1943, but when the first of the *Independence* -class carriers arrived at Pearl Harbor in the summer of 1943, their air groups were reshuffled by sending the Dauntlesses ashore and adding detachments of Hellcats. The original VC composite squadrons were later redesignated as torpedo (VT) squadrons.[28]

Because of their smaller size, the pilots of a light carrier air group had more to contend with than pilots on the larger *Essex* carriers. As Arthur Hawkins, at the time navigator and gunnery officer of VF-31 aboard the *Cabot*, recalled:

"At that time, I had not operated from an *Essex* - class carrier, so to me it was routine to operate off a smaller CVL. The deck was much narrower. You had to be lined up coming in; there was no way to be off center and make your landing. So the length of the ship had nothing to do with difficulty of landing aboard, since the landing area was about the same length as the landing area on an *Essex* - class carrier. But the width was certainly much less on a

CVL, since a CVL was built on a cruiser hull. With all that flight deck added on top of it, it had a tendency to roll much more than the *Essex* - class, so in rough seas, you were fighting a pitching and rolling deck."

But he also noted that there were advantages to a smaller ship and air group: "The operations were different in that, since we were a smaller unit, the air group knew the shipboard people, whereas on the *Essex* you could be there for a year and not know the first lieutenant. But, in our case, it just seemed that you knew you were more of a family-type affair than aboard the larger ships; the camaraderie was much better, I thought, than on the *Essex* - class. Other than that, a CVL pilot was always a CVL pilot; they were proud of it. A CVL pilot would come in on an *Essex*-class carrier and would ask which runway to use–just to put the needle into them, you know. 'Right or left runway? Which one?'"[29]

After shakedown operations in Chesapeake Bay and the Caribbean, the light carriers proceeded by way of the Panama Canal to the Pacific, where they became members of a larger team, the fast carrier forces of the Pacific Fleet.

Holding the Line in the Pacific

While the new *Essex* and *Independence* carriers were being built, the carrier forces available at the outbreak of war had to hold on in the Pacific. After their brilliant carrier attack on the American battleships at Pearl Harbor on 7 December 1941, the Japanese ran up an impressive string of victories in the first six months of 1942,

landing in the Philippines and overrunning the British in Malaya and Singapore. By the time resistance ended in the Philippines in May, the British were on the retreat in Burma and the Japanese had defeated British naval forces in the Bay of Bengal. The Dutch East Indies, the Bismarks, the northern Solomons, the Gilberts, Guam, Wake, and most of the northern coast of New Guinea were under Japanese control. But the Japanese had failed to sink any of the three carriers assigned to the Pacific at Pearl Harbor and, even before the outer defensive perimeter of their newly conquered territory was in place, they were concerned with the buildup of Allied forces in Australia and the threat posed by the remaining naval forces of the American Pacific Fleet.

Of particular concern were the American aircraft carriers, which launched a series of raids on Japanese-held outposts in early 1942. In April, the Doolittle force of sixteen Army B-25 Mitchell twin-engined bombers took off from the carrier *Hornet* to attack Tokyo and other Japanese cities. Although the raid inflicted little real damage on their homeland, the Japanese realized their vulnerability and embarked on another strategic offensive to extend their defensive perimeter further into the Pacific. By pushing into the southern Solomons, southern Papua, New Guinea, Midway, and the Aleutians, the Japanese hoped to force the Americans to commit their fleet to a "decisive battle" while the balance of strength was still in their favor.

In early May 1942, an attempt to take Port Moresby on the southeastern side of New Guinea, resulted in the Battle of the Coral Sea, the first naval battle in history fought entirely by carrier aircraft. Although tactically a draw–the *Lexington* was lost and the *Yorktown* damaged in exchange for the light carrier *Shoho*–it was an American strategic victory. The Japanese expedition to Port Moresby was turned back and air strikes against Australia were prevented.

The turning point of the Pacific war came at the Battle of Midway, fought in early June 1942, when the Japanese decided to force a major fleet engagement by assaulting Midway. Unknown to the Japanese, the Americans had cracked the Japanese codes and knew their intentions. Admiral Chester W. Nimitz, in command of the Pacific Fleet since January, concentrated his three carriers-the *Enterprise, Hornet* and *Yorktown*-to defend Midway.[30] The Japanese lost all four of their fleet carriers in the Carrier Striking Force: the *Akagi, Kaga, Hiryu* and *Soryu,* while the Americans lost the *Yorktown*, which had been hurriedly repaired at Pearl Harbor following the Coral Sea battle.

Throughout the rest of 1942, action centered on the South Pacific and Southwest Pacific areas. With the arrival of the *Wasp* from the Atlantic and the return of the *Saratoga* from repairs on the West Coast, American carrier strength immediately after the Battle of Midway was superior to that of the Japanese. Offensive operations were now possible and in control of the Japanese stronghold of Rabaul on New Britain became a major American objective.

The Marines landed on Guadalcanal in August, marking the beginning of a desperate struggle which seesawed back and forth for several months. Several hard-fought air and naval engagements took place in and around the waters of the Eastern Solomons. The Japanese lost the light carrier *Ryujo* to American carrier aircraft in the Battle of the Eastern Solomons in August. The *Wasp* was sunk by three torpedoes from a Japanese submarine in September. The *Hornet* was sunk by Japanese carrier aircraft during the Battle of the Santa Cruz Islands in October. Under the command of Vice Admiral William F. Halsey since mid-October, the South Pacific forces slowly turned the tide. By the end of the year, an American victory was assured, but only the *Enterprise* and *Saratoga* remained.[31]

As 1943 began, both sides took a breather to regroup and rebuild their forces. New fast carriers, battleships, and other warships flowed from American shipyards throughout 1943, as a buildup of naval forces in the Pacific began. How this new naval strength would best be used to defeat Japan became the center of a strategic debate. On the one hand, General Douglas MacArthur, commander of the Southwest Pacific forces, advocated a series of landings up the northern coast of New Guinea aimed at the eventual liberation of the Philippines. On the other hand, Admiral Nimitz favored a drive across the islands of the Central Pacific. In the end, both drives would be conducted in parallel until they converged on the Philippines later in 1944. MacArthur's war complemented the Central Pacific drive and, occasionally, Central Pacific forces were called in to help MacArthur's forces. The stage was set for an American offensive across the vast distances of the Pacific and the *Independence* class carriers would play their part.

Chapter 2
The Central Pacific

As new warships arrived in the Pacific in the spring and summer of 1943, naval planners mapped out a drive across the Pacific. Taking the islands of the Central Pacific would be very different from MacArthur's jungle campaigns in New Guinea. Instead of short amphibious thrusts in support of what was essentially a land campaign, the Central Pacific targets were small atolls and islands separated by vast expanses of ocean. The drive westward would begin in the Gilberts, an island group straddling the equator just west of the international dateline, about 2,400 miles southwest of Hawaii. Beyond the Gilberts, to the north and west, are the Marshalls. Further west are the Carolines, strung out westward toward the Philippines. North of the central Carolines lie the Marianas, and above them, in a line aimed in the general direction of Japan, lie the Volcano and Bonin island groups.

In March 1943, Vice Admiral Raymond A. Spruance, commander at the Midway victory and currently Nimitz's chief of staff, was named commander of the Fifth Fleet.[1] A cool, calculating professional, he was thoroughly "regulation" and regarded as a "battleship admiral" by aviators, but was known for meticulous planning and the careful weighing of risks. In the upcoming campaigns, Spruance would be methodical and cautious. The two main targets in the Japanese occupied Gilberts, Tarawa and Makin, would not be given up easily. Before these islands could be assaulted, forces had to be gathered from the United States, Hawaii, New Zealand, and the South Pacific. In the meantime, the fast carrier forces would have to learn how to use their new ships, aircraft, and weapons. Their leaders and crews would be in a learning status–"makee learn" as the old Navy expression goes.

In August, Commander Air Force Pacific Fleet (ComAirPac) decided to augment the fighter complements on the light carriers. The *Independence, Princeton,* and *Belleau Wood* left their SBD Dauntless dive bombers ashore and welcomed detachments from the veteran VF-6 aboard. The detachment aboard the *Independence* was led by the commander of VF-6, Lieutenant Commander Edward H. "Butch" O'Hare, who had won fame and the Medal of Honor for saving the old *Lexington* in February 1942, and included Lieutenant (jg) Alex Vraciu, who would go on to become an ace with nineteen victories. The *Cowpens*, which arrived at Pearl Harbor in mid-September, received a similar Hellcat detachment from VF-6 for the upcoming Wake Island strikes. These detachments would continue through the invasion of the Gilberts in November.[2]

The Marcus Strike

On 23 August 1943, Task Force 15 formed north of Hawaii. Under the command of Rear Admiral Charles A. "Baldy" Pownall, Task Force 15 included the *Essex*, the *Yorktown*, the *Independence*, the fast battleship *Indiana*, two light cruisers, and ten destroyers. Pownall flew his flag from the *Yorktown*. The task force was supported by a fleet oiler and, at Pownall's suggestion, a submarine was standing by in the target area to pick up any downed fliers. The ships cruised in a circular formation, the three carriers in the center surrounded by the battleship and cruisers, with destroyers in an outer ring. The plan was to refuel the big ships before the strike and on retirement, with the destroyers topping off from the big ships every third or fourth day.

On 27 August, after going far to the north, the task force began two days of refueling and followed a weather front all the way into the launch area. Before dawn on 31 August, task force radars

picked up a returning Japanese search plane. The task force easily followed the search plane back to Marcus, since the Japanese had not changed their patrol patterns since the Halsey raids of 1942.

In the predawn darkness of 1 September, the sea was dead calm and the sky was clear. The big-gun ships gave the carriers sea room while the destroyers swung out in front, marking a horizon with their lights for the pilots' reference. The carriers maneuvered at up to thirty knots, chasing any breeze, trying to give their aircraft enough wind over the deck to launch. At 0422, the first Hellcat rolled down the *Yorktown's* deck. In the cold gray dawn the planes caught the Japanese "with their pants down" according to Pownall in his after-action report. On the first sweep, strafing fighters destroyed seven parked twin-engine Betty bombers while the bombers hit the airstrip and buildings. The TBFs carried 2,000-pound general purpose bombs and the SBDs carried 1,000-pound fragmentation "daisy cutters." Five deck-load strikes were flown, two each from the *Essex* and *Yorktown* and one from the *Independence*. Flak was heavy at first and claimed three aircraft. The submarine *Snook* stood by to assist, but could not locate any of the survivors, and they were later captured. The task force had closed to within ten miles of the target while rearming and refueling its aircraft, but fortunately, there were no Japanese air or submarine attacks.

Aboard the *Independence*, Captain George Fairlamb, however, did not hold up under the strain of combat. Marcus was deep in enemy territory,

2,700 miles from Pearl Harbor, but only a thousand miles from Japan, and the tension proved too much for him. He had lost his composure, and his breakfast, on the bridge during the operation and was relieved when Task Force 15 returned to Pearl Harbor on 8 September. The executive officer of the *Independence,* Commander Rudolph L. Johnson, replaced him on 27 September shortly after his departure.[3]

Pownall's action report included a number of recommendations for future operations, such as multi-carrier formations and regularly assigning submarines as "lifeguards" to pick up downed aviators, which were soon adopted as standard practice. However, his recommendation to remove the TBF Avenger torpedo bombers from the light carriers and use thirty-six Hellcat all-fighter air groups was rejected.[4] Unfortunately, although an experienced aviator and personally likable, Pownall was unsuited for the command of a carrier task force. He had shown signs of nervousness and irritability during the operation which would eventually lead to his relief as commander of the fast carriers.

The Occupation of Baker Island

Pownall, as the ranking naval aviator, commanded during the Marcus operations. For the occupation of Baker Island on 1 September, the ranking battleship officer in the Pacific, Rear Admiral Willis A. "Ching" Lee, led a force that, ironically, included no battleships. Air cover for Task Force 11 was provided by the *Princeton* and *Belleau Wood* under Rear Admiral Arthur W. "Raddy" Radford. Although

the landing was unopposed, this operation marked the first aerial combat for the F6F Hellcat when large Japanese reconnaissance flying boats, code named "Emily" by the Allies, were encountered and shot down by *Princeton* Hellcats. The gun cameras of the Hellcats also provided the fleet with the first photographs of this type of aircraft.

The *Princeton* and *Belleau Wood* were to alternate providing cover for the landings, but *Princeton* seemed to have better luck. The first Emily intercept was by VF-6 pilots north of Howland Island on 1 September. The next day the *Princeton* refueled while the *Belleau Wood* spent an uneventful day patrolling. The following day, VF-6 pilots encountered a second Emily twenty to fifty miles southwest of Baker Island and shot it down in a running fight. As Commander Henry L. "Hank" Miller, commander of *Princeton's* Air Group 23, remembered:

"It looked as though the Japs were very regular and prompt about arriving over the same area on odd days about 1300 hours. Consequently, everyone wanted the noon flight, and the *Belleau Wood* fighter squadron indicated they thought the *Princeton* squadron was being favored. The admiral allowed the *Belleau Wood* pilots to take the Baker Island patrols. As luck would have it, on September 8–an even day–two Princeton pilots, Lt. Harold Funk and Lt. (jg) Leslie Kerr, were patrolling the offshore area miles from Baker when lo and behold, a Jap plane approached from a different direction than the earlier two. Number three hit the water in short order."

Air cover was provided through 14 September before Task Force 11 returned to Pearl Harbor.[5]

The Tarawa Raid

The plan for the Tarawa raid was similar to that for the Marcus operations, except that Seventh Air Force land-based bombers would hit Tarawa the night before (17-18 September), and photographs were to be taken for the landings scheduled for November. Task Force 15 included the *Lexington, Princeton,* and *Belleau Wood* and Pownall, who flew his flag from the *Lexington,* again displayed signs of nervousness and irrationality. He countermanded the plans of his operations officer to make a key navigational turn before dawn on the day of the strike, so that the task force was almost on top of the target at first light. Although the Japanese were expected to launch strikes on the task force from Kwajalein, only three enemy aircraft appeared and these were shot down by the defending Hellcats. The carrier strikes destroyed several enemy aircraft and small boats, but camouflage spoiled the effectiveness of the bombing on the installations. Good oblique photographs were taken of the beaches, but the aircraft carrying the vertical cameras was one of two friendly aircraft shot down by flak. Pownall refused to send another photo aircraft.[6]

The Wake Raids

For the Wake raids, Rear Admiral Alfred E. "Monty" Montgomery, commander of Task Force 14, experimented with different cruising formations of the six carriers involved: *Essex, Yorktown, Lexington, Independence, Belleau Wood* and *Cowpens.* He tried a single formation of six carriers, two groups with three carriers each, and three groups with two carriers each.

Task Force 14 launched its first strikes in the pre-dawn darkness of 5 October. For the first time, the carrier aircraft met enemy fighters, about thirty Zeros, over the target and the escorting Hellcats shot down most of them. An interesting aspect of the Hellcat's early combat career was an attempt at operational deception by Lieutenant Leland Johnson, skipper of VF-22, who had his men paint wheels on the undersides of their new Hellcats. The idea was to fool the Japanese into thinking they were older F4F Wildcats.[7] Three times as many bombs hit Wake as either Marcus or Tarawa, but the Japanese responded with two flights of six bombers and six fighters each from the Marshalls. Combat air patrol (CAP) fighters intercepted them and drove them off. The Japanese landing at Wake escaped to the Marshalls later that night. Between the flak and enemy fighters, twelve carrier aircraft were lost, although six survivors were picked up by the submarine *Skate.* The cruisers shelled Wake on both days. Virtually all the techniques of ship handling for a multi-carrier force found their origins in the Wake Island strikes and the three-carrier formation was adopted for Operation Galvanic, the invasion of the Gilberts, in November. After the Marcus-Wake series of raids, Task Force 14 returned to Pearl Harbor.

The *Cowpens,* called "Mighty Moo" by her crew, seemed to have a run of bad luck. During her shakedown peri-od back in July, she had run afoul of an anti-submarine net while returning to the Norfolk Navy Yard and had to spend a day in drydock for repairs.[8] On 17 October, her bad luck continued while she was conducting night carrier-landing operations off Hawaii; she was rammed in the starboard side aft by the destroyer *Abbott*, sending her into dry-dock for another nine days. To add insult to injury a gasoline fire broke out while she was in drydock, but fortu-nately it was soon under control and no serious damage was done.[9]

The build-up in the Central Pacific continued as the new *Essex*-class carrier *Bunker Hill* arrived at Pearl that fall, along with the *Monterey* and the refur-bished *Enterprise.* These ships would play an important role in the invasion of the Gilberts, but in the meantime, the fast carriers were needed to support Admiral Halsey's operations in the South Pacific.

On 1 November, Halsey's forces had landed on Bougainville in the northern Solomons. The Japanese responded by sending a cruiser force from their base at Rabaul, on the north-ern end of New Britain, as well as pro-viding additional aircraft from the Imperial Japanese Navy's First Air Fleet, to threaten Halsey's landings. After the cruiser action of the Battle of Empress Augusta Bay on 2 November, search aircraft discovered that addition-al Japanese heavy cruisers had arrived at Rabaul from Truk, hence the need for fast carriers to knock out another Japanese counterstrike before it could leave Rabaul.

The Rabaul Strikes

The *Saratoga* and *Princeton*, organ-ized as Task Force 38 under Rear Admiral Frederick C. "Ted" Sherman, had been loaned to Halsey by Nimitz to support the Bougainville landings. The *Princeton's* catapult had broken down during the strikes on Makin and Tarawa and she returned to Pearl Harbor for repairs, causing her to miss the Wake operation. She left Pearl Harbor 11 October, just as the Wake task force was returning. After pilot-qualification training off Hawaii, *Princeton* headed south to join Halsey's forces at Espiritu Santo, arriving 20 October.[10] *Saratoga* and *Princeton* launched strikes on the Buka-Bonis airfields at the northern end of Bougainville on the day of the landings, and struck again the next day, after which the task force withdrew to the south.

On 4 November, Task Force 38 was ordered north to knock out or disable as many cruisers at Rabaul as they could. Halsey hated to send surface ships into an area within range of land-based aircraft, but he had little choice. Task Force 38 ran in to the launching point, some 230 miles southeast of Rabaul, at twenty-seven knots. Luckily, rain squalls and poor visibility covered the task force from Japanese search air-craft. At 0857 on the morning of 5 November, fifty-two Hellcats, twenty-two Dauntlesses, and twenty-three Avengers from *Saratoga* and *Princeton* launched, while air cover over the car-riers was provided by land-based fight-ers from New Georgia. Leader of the strike was Commander Howard H. Caldwell of *Saratoga's* Air Group 12, who was flying an Avenger. The fight-ers were led by Lieutenant Commander

J.C. "Jumpin' Joe" Clifton, who kept sixteen of his VF-12 Hellcats only 800 to 1,000 feet over the bombers, while his "exec," Lieutenant Commander R. G. Dose, took a like number 3,000 feet above that. Commander Hank Miller, of *Princeton's* Air Group 23, maintained high cover with sixteen Hellcats from VF-23 above that. Two Hellcats, one from VF-12 and one from VF-23, would cover Caldwell's Avenger, from which he would select targets and photograph the attack.

The bombers, covered closely by Hellcats, flew up the St. George Channel, circling left and holding formation despite intense flak. The Japanese had put up fifty-nine Zeros, but they held off, expecting the Americans to break formation when the flak began. When they realized their mistake, it was already too late to catch the leading Dauntlesses and Avengers. Clifton's disciplined pilots stuck with the bombers until they were into their dives, despite the temptation to chase after groups of Zeros. The Dauntlesses of VB-12 split into sections to dive on the seven cruisers below, which were trying to get underway to Rabaul's outer harbor, Blanche Bay, and escape. The Japanese fighters would overshoot the dive bombers, who were slowed by their dive brakes, and only the last section was attacked. Five of the six cruisers attacked were either hit or took damaging near misses.

The Avenger torpedo bombers dropped beneath the Dauntlesses in a high speed glide. Then they broke into sections, singled out assigned targets, and slowed to 150 knots to drop their torpedoes. Some sections used scattered low hanging clouds, typical of the tropics, to cover their approach. The Avengers went mostly for the heavy cruisers, but despite claims of several hits (most of which were probably "prematures" from the still unreliable Mark 13 torpedoes) only two hit and only one exploded, badly damaging the new light cruiser *Noshiro*.

The Japanese were determined not to let the Americans get away unscathed, and attacked single Dauntlesses and Avengers when they could find them. But Clifton's fighters broke into four-plane divisions and weaved above the bombers, ready to knock down any pursuing Zeros. Only one Dauntless was lost to the defending fighters, but the rear gunners of several others exchanged fire with the Zeros, claiming two shot down at the cost of two gunners killed and eight wounded. (One Dauntless pilot had shot down a Zero with his forward-firing machine guns during the initial attack.) The Avengers were hit hard; four were lost as the Zeros pursued them out into the St. George Channel. Caldwell and his escorting Hellcats tangled with eight Zeros, and his Avenger was hit repeatedly, wounding his two gunners and killing the photographer, as they weaved constantly to ward off repeated runs. The pilot of one of his escorting Hellcats, Lieutenant H. M. Crockett from VF-23, was also wounded and his flaps shot out, but he made it back to the *Princeton* with 277 bullet holes in his F6F. Clifton's fighters claimed eleven Zeros destroyed and fourteen probables against a loss of four Hellcats. Air Group 23 had been hit hard–three of the four fighters and all four of the torpedo bombers lost were from the *Princeton*. The Japanese tried to send a strike out to find Task Force 38, but by that time it had headed south, out of range.[11]

The strike had achieved its purpose, severely damaging four heavy cruisers and damaging two light cruisers and a destroyer, but Halsey wanted a follow-up strike as soon as possible. After considering Halsey's needs for carrier support, Nimitz had also sent Task Group 50.3 under Montgomery with *Essex, Bunker Hill,* and *Independence* to the South Pacific. Although the task group arrived 5 November, Halsey's cruiser and destroyer forces were stretched to the limit, so the task group stayed at Espiritu Santo for three days while more escorts were rounded up. This time Task Force 38 would hit Rabaul from the north while Task Group 50.3 would strike from the south. With the attack finally set for 11 November, Halsey pointed out that "five air groups . . . ought to change the name of Rabaul to Rubble."

Task Force 38 launched at 0830 and the strike aircraft bucked heavy weather on the way to Simpson Harbor. The Japanese, alerted by radar, scrambled sixty-eight Zeros to intercept, while ships in the harbor headed for the cover of local rain squalls. The Avengers and Dauntlesses missed the heavy cruisers *Maya* and *Chokai,* hidden by rain in the inner harbor, but caught the new light cruiser *Agano* with a torpedo hit. When the strike returned to the task group, Sherman decided to cancel a planned second strike because of poor weather over the target.

Thirty-five minutes after the first strike, aircraft from Task Group 50.3 struck, first Air Group 9 from the,

Essex, then Air Group 17 from the *Bunker Hill,* and finally Air Group 22 from the *Independence.* As the strike approached Simpson Harbor from the northeast, the defending Zeros looped and rolled above them, trying to lure away the defending Hellcats, which weaved over the bombers. The Japanese even tried a bizarre new weapon, phosphorous bombs that sent streamers of smoke across the paths of the Helldiver bombers, which were making their combat debut with VB-17 from the *Bunker Hill.* In the meantime, the Avengers had dropped down in high-speed glides for torpedo attacks. Despite claims that a heavy and a light cruiser were hit, the Japanese actually lost the destroyer *Naganami,* which sank after being hit by a torpedo, and the destroyer *Suzunami,* which was sunk near the harbor entrance with bombs. About ninety fighters ran into sixty-eight Zeros and shot down six. Six of the strike aircraft were lost to flak and the Zeros.

The Battle of the Solomon Sea

The Japanese retaliated with strikes by about 120 aircraft. The task group had only the guns of the carriers and the destroyers for antiaircraft defense, since the cruisers had been detached to support Halsey's beachhead. The fighter direction officers, or FDOs, in the *Essex* and *Independence* had three land-based Navy fighter squadrons-two F4U Corsair squadrons and an F6F Hellcat squadron-plus a division of Hellcats from VF-23, to cover the task group. The combat air patrol intercepted the first enemy bombers forty miles from the task group and the inexperienced

Hellcat pilot who spotted the incoming Japanese blurted out, "Jesus Christ! There are millions of them! Let's go to work!"[12] The CAP tore into the Japanese, but went mostly for the escorting Zeros, not the following Val and Kate bombers, which went into their attacks largely unmolested. The early afternoon action lasted 46 minutes, with the carriers driving off over two dozen enemy aircraft as the carrier skippers skillfully maneuvered to avoid bombs and torpedoes. Bombs fell close–five near misses showered the *Bunker Hill* with shrapnel, while others punctured the *Essex's* hull, and the *Independence* took four near misses. In a freak, and lucky, occurrence, a 40mm round detonated a fifth bomb aimed at the *Independence* in mid-air. The FDOs had made mistakes in allowing the Kates and Vals a "free ride," but expert ship handling and effective antiaircraft fire had saved the day. Eleven aviators were lost, but the Japanese had lost more experienced naval aviators in the Rabaul meat grinder.

The Rabaul strikes, and those of the Army's land-based Fifth Air Force, convinced the Japanese that Rabaul was unsafe for shipping. With the landings on Bougainville, Rabaul now lay within range of Halsey's land-based fighters. Admiral Koga, who replaced Yamamoto as Commander in Chief of the Combined Fleet, recalled his remaining carrier planes on 13 November. Of the 173 aircraft sent to Rabaul from Carrier Division One, half the fighters and almost all the attack aircraft were lost, including many experienced flyers. On 11 November, Task Force 38 was redesignated Task Group 50.4 and along with Task Group 50.3,

proceeded north to rejoin the Central Pacific Force. Task Group 50.1 and Task Group 50.2 rendezvoused with their oilers and escorting battleships north of the Phoenix Islands before the final approach to the targets for the Gilberts operation.

The Gilberts–Operation Galvanic

The Gilberts invasion involved three task forces: a Southern Task Force to take Tarawa, a Northern Task Force to take Makin, and the Fast Carrier Force under Pownall. Under Spruance, the carriers, much to the disgust of the aviators, would be limited to defensive sectors. Task Group 50.1 under Pownall made up the Carrier Interceptor Group with *Yorktown, Lexington,* and *Cowpens.* Radford commanded the Northern Carrier Group, Task Group 50.2, with the veteran *Enterprise, Belleau Wood,* and *Monterey.* Montgomery commanded the Southern Carrier Group, Task Group 50.3, with *Essex, Bunker Hill,* and *Independence.* Sherman commanded the Relief Carrier Group, the newly redesignated Task Group 50.4, with the old *Saratoga* and *Princeton.*

The softening up of the target beaches on Makin and Tarawa began several days before by Navy land-based aircraft from SoPac. Task Group 50.3 hit Tarawa 18 November and Task Group 50.1 hit airfields at Mili and Jaluit in the southern Marshalls. Task Group 50.2 bombed Makin and Task Group 50.4 destroyed Japanese air power at Nauru. While the other three task groups stayed on station, Task Group 50.4 turned east to escort garrison convoys to the objective. The surface ship bombardment of Tarawa began on 20 November, less than three hours before the assault, augmented by planes from the escort carriers and the fast carriers. The inexperienced pilots thought they had destroyed Tarawa's defenses, but when Marine casualties began to mount, everyone realized the bitter truth. That evening, the Japanese struck back. The task groups had each sent special radar picket destroyers 30,000 yards ahead to detect incoming enemy aircraft, but the only carrier with night capability was *Enterprise.* It would not be enough. At around 1800, in the gathering dusk, a group of fifteen to thirty long-range Japanese Betty bombers from Kwajalein and Maloelap attacked Task Group 50.3 off Tarawa, coming in very low and fast over the water, avoiding radar detection. CAPs from *Essex, Bunker Hill,* and *Independence,* along with antiaircraft fire, brought down nine of them, but the *Independence* did not escape.

The Independence is Torpedoed

Aboard the *Independence,* preparations were being made to recover her antisubmarine patrol (ASP) when one of her patrolling TBFs reported sighting a large group of strange aircraft, "This is 85 Victor 435. Fifteen Bettys just barreled past me low on the water, not more than twenty miles from you. I say again . . ." This was followed almost immediately by the sighting, from the bridge, of fifteen Bettys on the starboard beam on the horizon. The "Indy" just barely had time to go to battle stations and man her guns. Six of the Bettys singled out the *Independence,* the others went for the *Essex* off her port quarter and the *Bunker Hill* off her port

beam. One of the Bettys went into the sea in a column of flame, then another, then a third. All this time the helm was hard starboard, as she snaked away from the attack. Another enemy plane was almost upon her when a burst of 40mm fire turned it into a ball of orange flame. During the action, the wakes of several torpedoes were seen in the water. Three passed astern, crossing the ship's wake, and one passed close aboard on the starboard side on a parallel course.

Three torpedoes struck the starboard quarter, but only the one that hit the after mess deck exploded, just forward of the after elevator and only thirty feet from where seven torpex-loaded torpedoes were stored in racks on the starboard side of the hangar. The ship trembled, heaved up and settled back down as a billowing geyser of oil settled back into the sea-she had been hit in the fuel oil blister. The explosion had wiped forty feet of her starboard side clean, leaving no 40mm gun sponsor, no gun crew, and no catwalk. A fighter was lost when it was bounced over the side, and the aft flight deck was covered with oil, but planes which had just been spotted forward, in anticipation of recovering the ASP, were not at risk.

The *Independence* began to list, water roaring through the gaping hole, and one engine room flooded. The explosion set off several fires and the concussion knocked out the generators, leaving her with no radar or communications of any kind. Her speed dropped from thirty-five knots to fifteen, then to ten, and then to three.

Damage control and engineering crews battled to save their ship; the fires were contained and the water tight compartments held the flooding to the after messing compartment. Topside, planes were shifted to the port side to help correct the list. Suddenly from the bridge came the call: "Periscope off the port bow." The gunners on the port side opened up, but no one knew for sure if there really was a Japanese submarine there or not. Below decks the engineering crew, working by battle lanterns, had the one good screw churning faster. The heavy cruiser *Pensacola* stood by to tow, but the *Independence* had never gone completely dead in the water and was soon able to withdraw under her own power, working up to 13.5 knots within a half hour. Eighteen men were dead or missing and about thirty more were badly burned, mostly from the initial explosion. Casualties below decks were low–three mess cooks who had not cleared the messing compartments were the only engineering ratings killed, in spite of the rapid flooding of the after engine room and fire room. Captain Johnson attributed this not only to luck, but also to the superb engineering and damage control work done by his crew. (He later received the Silver Star medal and fourteen officers and men were recommended for Distinguished Service Medals.)

No one aboard slept that night as the "Evil I" withdrew from the combat area, escorted by two destroyers and the cruiser *Salt Lake City.* Around midnight, someone finally remembered that all hands had missed dinner, so the storekeepers broke out oranges and cans of Spam. The next day, the chaplain held services for the dead on the fantail. As the morning wore on, it became evident that the *Independence,*

still trailing a telltale streak of oil in her wake, would make it without a tow and the *Salt Lake City* turned back to rejoin the task force. Captain Johnson got on the "bull horn" and called the crew together to announce that they were headed for Funafuti, in the Ellice Islands, for preliminary inspection of the damage and that "we're going there like the sleek fighting ship we are." All hands turned to with swabs and buckets to scrub off as much oil as possible. By the time she arrived on 23 November, there was, as one crewman remembered, a lot of grumbling about "housemaid's knee" or "scrub woman's back," but their ship was as squared away as possible.

After temporary repairs, she departed on 7 December for Pearl Harbor and then on to San Francisco, where she arrived on 2 January 1944. She would be out of action for six months. When she emerged from the drydocks at Hunters Point in June, she sported a second catapult, making her the first of her class to have two catapults. She would return to the war in July, ready to take on a new role as the Navy's first night carrier.[13]

Meanwhile, as the *Independence* left the combat area, Japanese air strikes continued and two small strikes were destroyed by Task Group 50.3 on 23 and 24 November. In the pre-dawn hours of 24 November, a Japanese submarine *(I-175)* torpedoed the escort carrier *Liscome Bay,* which sank with the loss of 644 men, including her commander, Captain I.D. Wiltsie, and a promising carrier group commander, Rear Admiral Henry M. Mullinix. The loss of the *Liscome Bay* emphasized the danger inherent in tying carriers down to beachheads.

The major Japanese tactic turned out to be night torpedo attacks. A single Japanese aircraft, called "Tojo the Lamplighter" by the nervous carrier crews, arrived over Radford's Task Group 50.2 off Makin. On the night of 26 November, about thirty torpedo bombers flew in from the Marshalls to attack, but Butch O'Hare's night team from the *Enterprise,* made up of two Hellcats and an Avenger torpedo bomber equipped with primitive radar, was ready. Two Bettys were shot down by the TBF before it rendezvoused with the Hellcats and the Japanese attack broke up in the confusion, but O'Hare's aircraft was lost. A few more air actions took place, but attacks ended on 28 November, the same day organized resistance ended on the islands. Seventy-one Marshalls-based planes had been shot down, including several more staged from Truk. The last thirty-two Japanese carrier fighters had been sent to the Marshalls, where most were shot down. American losses totaled forty-seven aircraft, but the submarine *Plunger* picked up several pilots in the Gilberts.

North to the Marshalls

Spruance ordered Pownall to leave *Bunker Hill* and *Monterey* north of the Gilberts under Sherman, while the rest were ordered to hit Kwajalein in the Marshalls. With Pownall's Task Group 50.1 were the *Yorktown, Lexington,* and *Cowpens,* while Montgomery's Task Group 50.3 was reshuffled to include *Essex, Enterprise,* and *Belleau Wood.* (*Princeton* had developed an intense shaft vibration while operating off

the Gilberts and had to return to Pearl Harbor for repairs, arriving 7 December. Leaving Air Group 23 in Hawaii, she headed for the West Coast for repairs and overhaul. On 3 January 1944, she departed Bremerton, where a second catapult and more antiaircraft weapons had been added, and returned to the forward area.[14]) Pownall approached the area from the northeast on 4 December. The early results of the bombing and strafing attacks against the installations and ships were poor. During the forty-five-minute strike, Task Force 50 destroyed four merchant vessels and fifty-five aircraft, twenty-eight of them in the air. As the strike returned, many Bettys were spotted on an airfield at nearby Roi, but Pownall would not launch a second strike. About noon, two flights of four Kates each attacked the task force and were shot down.

After recovering the Wotje strike, Task Force 50 headed for friendly waters, but heavy seas slowed the task force down. Everyone knew the Japanese would make night torpedo attacks. Cruising at eighteen knots, Task Force 50 prepared for a night attack. Shortly after 2000, it came. Under a bright moon, thirty to fifty Bettys, guided by snooper aircraft that had shadowed the task force, attacked. The task force broke up into two task groups as Pownall relied on independent evasive ship maneuvers and antiaircraft fire. (The task force no longer had night fighter capability following O'Hare's death.) The attack was erratic, sometimes heavy, sometimes only threatening. Thirty minutes before midnight, parachute flares silhouetted the *Lexington,* and ten minutes later she was hit by a torpedo to starboard, which knocked out her steering gear. Settling five feet by the stern, she began circling to port amidst dense clouds of smoke pouring from ruptured tanks aft. She had lost steerage, but by varying the speed of her shafts, she could maneuver enough to escape. The last attack was beaten off by the ships' fire and the increasing darkness as the moon set around 0130 on 5 December. Intelligence later reported that Japanese aircraft had withdrawn to Nauru.

Kavieng

Sherman reported back to Halsey with *Bunker Hill* and *Monterey* as Task Group 37.2. On Christmas day, Task Group 37.2 struck Kavieng, New Ireland (north of Rabaul). Several snoopers were shot down by *Bunker Hill* CAP during the day, but it was apparent the enemy knew the task group's position and night attacks were expected. Radar plot picked up bogies at dusk and for nearly an hour the task group eluded night torpedo attacks by an estimated fifteen enemy aircraft by rapid maneuvering and laying down a smoke screen. Aboard the *Monterey*, the gun crew of the 40mm quad mount on the fantail spotted a plane heading directly for the ship. First the 40mm opened fire, then the 20mm guns on the fantail, finally the whole starboard battery. The plane was hit but kept on coming, enveloped in flames. Passing over the flight deck from starboard to port, it crashed into the water 200 yards off the port beam. A cheer went up from everyone topside as the *Monterey* claimed her first enemy aircraft brought down by her own guns.

The task group retreated to the southeast that evening and the crews enjoyed a belated Christmas dinner the next day. Refueling over the next few days, the task group continued toward Espiritu Santo until Halsey passed the order, on New Year's Eve, to repeat the strikes on Kavieng–there were reports of shipping concentrated in Kavieng Harbor. Kavieng was hit again on New Year's Day and Halsey ordered a third strike for 4 January. Although several enemy aircraft were shot down and Task Group 37.2 had suffered little damage, targets, unfortunately, were few. With the last strike aircraft recovered, the task group again retired from enemy waters. Late that morning, the *Monterey's* CAP brought down a snooping Betty and in the midafternoon the *Monterey* FDO directed the CAP to a group of bogies sixty miles out. The CAP spotted the bogies–six Zeke fighters escorting one Nell bomber–and within sixty seconds all seven were shot down. The task group proceeded to Espiritu Santo without further incident.[15]

CHINA

KOREA

Tokyo

JAPAN

Honshu

Shikoku

Kyushu

RYUKYUS

EAST
CHINA
SEA

Formosa

PHILIPPINE

SEA

PHILIPPINES

LUZON

Manila

Mindoro

Panay

Samar

Leyte

Mindanao

Celebes

CELEBES
SEA

BANDA SEA

JAVA SEA

ARAFURA
SEA

AUSTRALIA

NEW
GUINEA

Port Moresby

CORAL SEA

ADMIRALTY IS.

BISMARCK
ARCH.

Kavieng

New Ireland

Rabaul

New Britain

SOLOMON ISLANDS

Bougainville

Guadalcanal

CAROLINE

ISLANDS

Palau

Yap

Truk

BONIN IS.

Iwo Jima

MARIANA
IS.

Saipan

Tinian

Marcus

Wake

PACIFIC

OCEAN

Eniwetok

Wotje

Kwajalein

MARSHALL
ISLANDS

Makin

GILBERT
IS.

Tarawa
Betio

Abemama

Nauru

Midway

400

0

Statute Miles

The Central Pacific

Chapter 3
Task Force 58

The early months of 1944 marked the beginning of a new phase in the fast carrier offensive. Although Task Force 50 had been the first actual fast carrier force, it had lacked an effective commander. That situation changed when, on 13 January 1944, Rear Admiral Marc A. "Pete" Mitscher hoisted his flag aboard the *Yorktown* as Commander, Task Force 58. An early naval aviator, Mitscher was quiet and soft-spoken, but he was a leader's leader who held the respect of all his carrier group commanders. Mitscher commanded twelve fast carriers–the *Langley* and *Cabot* were new, the *Cabot* had arrived late in November and the *Langley* on Christmas Eve, 1943–plus 650 aircraft, eight fast battleships, and numerous cruisers and destroyers.

When Task Force 58 departed from Pearl Harbor late in January 1944, it marked the last time the fast carriers operated from Hawaii, which had become a rear area. The objective of Operation Flintlock was to capture Kwajalein, the most important of the western Marshall Islands. Kwajalein

Atoll is the world's largest–about sixty-five nautical miles across on its longest axis–and is roughly triangular in shape, with the islands of Roi and Namur on the northernmost tip and Kwajalein Island on the southernmost tip. The strongly fortified eastern Marshalls –Wotje, Maloelap, Mili, Jaluit, and Nauru–would be neutralized by air attacks and left to "wither on the vine." For Operation Flintlock, Task Force 58 was given the opportunity to knock out Japanese strength before it could be used against the invasion forces. The carriers conducted practice exercises en route and pre-attack briefings assigned specific targets for each crew. Unknown to U.S. naval intelligence, however, the last of Japan's best navy pilots had been lost in the Rabaul meat grinder–virtually no experienced carrier pilots remained. When the Japanese learned that Task Force 58 was at sea, Admiral Koga withdrew most of his major units to Palau in the western end of the Carolines, leaving about 150 aircraft, including many Betty bombers, to defend the Marshalls.

Between 29 January and 6 February, the four task groups struck daily at targets in the Marshalls, virtually destroying Japanese sea and air power in the area.

The Marshalls

On 29 January 1944, Task Force 58 launched strikes against the Marshalls. Rear Admiral John W. "Black Jack" Reeves' Task Group 58.1, with *Enterprise, Yorktown,* and *Belleau Wood,* hit Maloelap; Rear Admiral Samuel P. "Cy" Ginder's Task Group 58.4, with *Saratoga, Princeton,* and *Langley* bombed Wotje; Rear Admiral Montgomery's Task Group 58.2, with *Essex, Intrepid,* and *Cabot,* attacked the airfield on Roi, while Sherman's Task Group 58.3, with *Bunker Hill, Cowpens,* and *Monterey* hit Kwajalein Island. The few Japanese aircraft airborne over Roi were shot down by Hellcats from *Essex, Intrepid,* and *Cabot,* which then strafed parked aircraft on the airstrips. To ensure the Japanese did not stage through Eniwetok, Task Group 58.3 shifted to Eniwetok for the next three days, while Task Group 58.4 moved to Maloelap for two days and joined Task Group 58.3 at Eniwetok on the third day. Task Group 58.2 spent the next five days hitting Roi and Namur in close support. Task Group 58.1 spent the same five days on Kwajalein, while Navy land-based air worked over Mili and Jaluit. The fast carriers lost seventeen fighters and five torpedo aircraft to enemy action, and twenty-seven other aircraft operationally.[1]

From 31 January to 3 February, the carrier aircraft took directions from the air support commanders in hitting Japanese defensive positions. Com-bined with the land-based strikes, the more than 4,500 sorties resulted in lower resistance than in the Gilberts. In spite of the improved air support arrangements, the tendency of pilots to ignore the signals of friendly troops continued to be a problem. After Kwajalein fell on 4 February, Task Groups 58.1, 58.2, and 58.3 headed for the newly occupied Majuro Atoll while Ginder's Task Group 58.4 continued strikes against Eniwetok.[3] Later, after the Marines had landed there, the carriers of the task group provided direct support to the landing forces.

Captain Bill Buracker, aboard the *Princeton,* would listen in to the pilots' radio conversations. "When things got slack, I went down to the information center to listen to the radio. It was fascinating to hear the ground forces talking to each other in combat. A tank commander would shout against the static of gunfire, 'Look out for that Jap gun on the right!' or an aviator would tell a pal what he had hit. It was like listening to an Army-Navy football game, but much more exciting. The wonderful teamwork among the air, sea, and ground forces was strikingly brought out by these radio conversations."[4]

As the Central Pacific war moved on, the four atolls where the Japanese had airbases–aluit, Mili, Maloelap, Wotje–and Nauru, too, became practice targets for new carriers, or veterans returning from overhaul, on their way to the forward area.

Majuro

Majuro Atoll, 2,000 miles west of Pearl Harbor, allowed commercial tankers to bypass Hawaii, cutting down on transit times to the forward area. From there, service squadrons provided logistic support for operational forces in the Pacific. Servron 4, which had fueled the carriers for Operation Galvanic, merged with Servron 10 when the latter, formed for Operation Flintlock, arrived at Majuro. Servron 10 supported the fast carrier forces exclusively for the rest of the war. Early in 1944 escort carriers joined the Servron to provide antiaircraft and antisubmarine protection, and to ferry replacement aircraft to the fast carriers.

After most of Task Force 58 enjoyed a brief lull at Majuro, which included some command changes, the next target for Task Force 58 was the fabled Japanese bastion of Truk, the "Gibraltar of the Pacific," located to the west of the Marshalls in the center of the Caroline Islands chain.

The Raid on Truk

Truk had long been held by the Japanese and threatened any future American moves in the central Pacific. It would have to be neutralized for the invasion of Eniwetok and before the Marianas could be attacked. The task force sailed from the anchorage at Majuro on 12 February 1944. Mitscher headed for Truk with three task groups.[5] When the aircrews heard that they were going to attack Truk, there were serious misgivings. Not much was really known about Truk and everything they had heard was bad. A land-based reconnaissance mission flown from the Solomons on 3 February had shown some twenty naval vessels in Truk lagoon, but the major Japanese naval units had departed on 10 February.

Mitscher tried some new tricks for the Truk strike, including tighter task group formations and following under rain squalls on the way into the launch area. The first aircraft off would be a fighter sweep to clear the area of Japanese aircraft that might interfere with the bombers. Another tactic used 1,000-pound delayed action bombs on the last runway strikes on to make repairs during the night more difficult. Also, strikes against oil storage sites were saved for last to keep the flame and smoke from obscuring other targets.

The attack was launched at 0600 on 17 February, when the task force was a hundred miles northeast of Truk. As the fighter sweep moved in, about fifty Japanese aircraft tangled with the seventy-four Hellcats of the fighter sweep. In half an hour, the Americans had dealt with most of the opposition, some of whom were tough veterans of previous battles. Within an hour and a half, no more Japanese aircraft rose to challenge the attackers, and when the bombers arrived at 0930, there were no Japanese aircraft to interfere with their bombing runs. Some bombers carried fragmentation bombs in 100-pound clusters, while others carried incendiary bombs and went after service installations on the air fields. Then came the dive bombers with 1,000-pound bombs, moving in to hit the shipping in the Dublon anchorage.

Most of the Japanese warships had gone, but some merchantmen and a pair of cruisers remained. The bombers hit a merchantman and made a near miss on a cruiser in the first pass. With the bombers came more fighters, who strafed antiaircraft positions that were firing at the strike aircraft. The bombers attacked repeatedly, setting a tanker on fire, hitting a small carrier, and hitting the merchantmen. In mid afternoon a strike went after the other anchorages. One aircraft found a destroyer trying to escape and dropped four 500-pound bombs on it. The first landed astern, but the other three hit the destroyer squarely from stem to stern, leaving her dead in the water and engulfed in a mass of flame and smoke. A strike later in the day dropped the delayed action 1,000-pound bombs on the bomber airfield at Moen. A strike at the end of the day hit the revetments on the airfields, spoiling a potential night attack. The Japanese fighters reappeared and tangled with the strike aircraft.

That night the Japanese were out looking for the task force. From around 2100 until midnight, small groups of bogies appeared on task force radars. *Yorktown* launched a night fighter to drive off the snoopers, but a small group of radar-equipped Japanese aircraft moved in on the *Intrepid,* scoring a torpedo hit on her starboard side aft. Five men were killed in the explosion and her rudder was jammed hard to port. She fought off her remaining attackers and made her way to Majuro at twenty knots, accompanied by the *Cabot* and other escorts.[6]

On the same night the *Intrepid* was torpedoed, the *Enterprise's* VT-10 launched the first night carrier strike of the war with radar-equipped Avengers, sinking two tankers and five freighters and damaging five others.[7] The smoke was still rising over the lagoon when the morning fighter sweep arrived the following day. Not a single Japanese fighter rose to challenge the fighters

and they resorted to strafing the already burning ships and airfields. There were three more strikes which hit other ships and sank two destroyers. The total score was two light cruisers, four destroyers, three auxiliaries, two sub tenders, two sub chasers, an armed trawler, a plane ferry, twenty-four merchant ships (five of them tankers), and 250 Japanese aircraft destroyed. The carriers lost twenty-five aircraft, but most of the crews had been picked up by submarines and seaplanes. The Truk strike had achieved its primary objective, to ensure that the Japanese would not interfere with Operation Catchpole, the capture of Eniwetok, and opened the way for carrier strikes further west into Japanese territory.[8]

The Marianas Strikes
Following the Truk strike, the task force stayed at sea, replenishing underway on 19 February before moving on to strike the Marianas. Spruance and Servron 10 returned to Majuro. With the departure of *Intrepid* and *Cabot,* and the later departure of the *Enterprise,* which bombed bypassed Jaluit on 21 February, Task Group 58.2 was reshuffled to include the *Essex, Yorktown,* and *Belleau Wood,* while Task Group 58.3 was now made up of *Bunker Hill, Monterey,* and *Cowpens.*

The Marianas stretch for some 425 miles in a rough arc beginning about 335 miles southeast of Iwo Jima down to Guam, 250 miles north of the Carolines. The four biggest of the islands–Saipan, Tinian, Rota and Guam–are all at the southern end of the chain. On the night of 21-22 February, a Japanese Betty bomber spotted Task

Force 58, but Mitscher was undeterred, saying, "We'll fight our way in." The task force fought off night attacks on the run in to the launch point. The strikes were launched from a hundred miles west of Saipan and Tinian before dawn. Most of the seventy-four intercepting aircraft were shot down. A new airfield discovered on Guam was attacked–168 Japanese aircraft were destroyed and several transports sunk against six American aircraft lost. Task Force 58 retired to Majuro on 22 February.

In March 1944, Mitscher was officially made Commander, Fast Carrier Forces Pacific Fleet and promoted to vice admiral, while Spruance became a full admiral. Mitscher hoisted his flag aboard the recently returned *Lexington* and, in line with a new policy that non-aviator commanders would have aviators as chiefs of staff, and vice versa, Captain Arleigh Burke was assigned as his new chief of staff.[9]

Palau

Task Force 58 left Majuro 22 March 1944, heading for Palau in the western Carolines. Although the task force swung to the south to avoid Truk-based search aircraft, it was spotted on 25 March. Thus alerted, the Japanese withdrew their fleet units to Singapore, Borneo, and Japanese waters. On the night of 29 March the Japanese made their usual night torpedo attacks, which were driven off by antiaircraft fire.

At dawn on 30 March, Task Force 58 launched a fighter sweep from ninety miles south of the target, eliminating thirty airborne Zeros. The fighters then joined the bombers in attacking the

large amount of merchant shipping. A Japanese destroyer was sunk by torpedoes and other torpedo bombers mined Palau waters. This turned out to be the first and only time mines were dropped by planes from the fast carriers during the war. It proved too dangerous for the low and slow Avengers, and was thereafter left to long-range land-based bombers. During the strike, the *Cabot* was assigned to provide CAP and ASP for Task Group 58.2. One of her fighter pilots, "being confused" joined a strike from another carrier and upon his return reported shooting down two Zekes.[10]

That night, another sixty enemy aircraft flew into Palau, and the following day at dusk, the *Cabot's* fighter director officer (FDO) directed the CAP to intercept nine Japanese dive bombers. Seven were shot down in short order and the remaining two were chased down and destroyed soon after.[11] On 31 March, Task Groups 58.2 and 58.3 hit Palau again while Task Group 58.1 hit Yap to the northeast. All three task groups hit Wolei on 1 April. A few aircraft visited Ulithi, northeast of Yap, but most of the targets were on Palau. Along with the dozens of aircraft shot down, about 130,000 tons of Japanese shipping was lost to bombing and delayed action mines. Of forty-four aircrew ditching at sea during this series of strikes, twenty-six were picked up by submarines, seaplanes, and destroyers.

When the fighting in the South Pacific ended in March 1944, there was no longer any reason for Nimitz to split his operations. The title "Central Pacific Force" was abolished in April in favor of "Fifth Fleet" (which had been the administrative title of the Central

Pacific Force), while all the forces under Halsey became the "Third Fleet." Spruance shifted his flag to Pearl Harbor to begin planning the invasion of the Marianas, leaving Mitscher on his own until June.

Hollandia

The Hollandia operations briefly brought together the Central and Southwest Pacific forces. Following the neutralization of Japanese air forces in the Palaus, Task Force 58 provided close air support for MacArthur's Hollandia landings on 22 April. Massive Army land-based air attacks on 30 March and 3, 5, and 12 April largely eliminated Hollandia as a Japanese air base and the carrier strikes of 21 April turned out to be anticlimactic. Task Force 58 had sailed from Majuro 13 April under Mitscher's direct command, with three task groups under Reeves, Montgomery, and Rear Admiral J.J. "Jocko" Clark, who had replaced Ginder.[12] (He was relieved and replaced by Clark upon Task Force 58's return to Majuro.) The task force feinted toward Palau, then hit New Guinea 21 April. Only snooper aircraft from the west harassed Clark's Task Group 58.1. The operation went smoothly as the Japanese offered only token resistance. Mitscher used his night fighters to watch for enemy night torpedo attacks and to keep the Japanese troops awake. On 24 April, the task force withdrew to the new fleet anchorage at Manus in the Admiralties, at the northwestern end of the Bismarck Archipelago. Later landings at Wakde, Biak, Noemfoor, and Sansapor carried MacArthur's forces to the northwestern point of the

New Guinea Vogelkop, 550 miles west of Hollandia, in a little more than three months.

The Second Truk Strike

Meanwhile, a daylight land-based B-24 raid on Truk from SoPac was surprised on 29 March by a force of ninety Japanese fighters. The bombers shot down twenty-one and lost two. Truk was back in business. Nimitz passed the word to Mitscher at Manus and Task Force 58 hit Truk again. A predawn fighter sweep on 29 April began the second carrier battle over Truk. *Langley's* VF-32, led by Lieutenant Commander Eddie Outlaw, was to score half of its total for their combat tour during this sweep. Outlaw personally shot down five Zekes, while his pilots claimed sixteen more. Three of these were shot down by Lieutenant Hollis Hills, a former RCAF pilot who had scored his first victory against a Fw 190 while flying a Mustang over Dieppe in 1942.[13]

The fighter sweep had stung the Japanese into action and they immediately launched a torpedo plane attack on Task Force 58. Lieutenant (jg) Arthur R. "Ray" Hawkins had just catapulted from the *Cabot* when a Japanese torpedo plane appeared in his sights. He promptly shot it down though he had only been airborne for fifteen seconds.[14] It was his first kill. As he recalled later, "I was on standby, in the cockpit on the catapult. A flight of torpedo bombers came in from Truk to hit the ships. They came in low on the water, and CIC [Combat Information Center] didn't pick them up until they were about fifteen miles out. I was on the starboard catapult, and, as they launched me, the ships opened up with antiaircraft fire. As I went off the cat, I turned into the flight coming in, and there I was head-to-head with a Judy coming in. So I opened up on him and splashed him there, then pulled up in sort of a quick chandelle, getting my gear up and what have you, and turned and followed the remainder of the raid on through the force while eighteen destroyers, two battleships, and four carriers were firing at these planes coming through, and here I was following them. It was one flight I'll always remember; let's put it that way."[15]

Antiaircraft and combat air patrols drove off the attackers, while Japanese antiaircraft fire over Truk was equally intense. Although sixty Zeros challenged the Hellcats, the quality of Japanese pilots had deteriorated and, by midmorning, Task Force 58 controlled the air over Truk. The next day, more were destroyed on the ground, bringing the total to ninety aircraft. The Americans lost twenty-six aircraft, but over half of the forty-six aircrew were picked up, twenty-two by the submarine *Tang* alone. The Japanese could no longer maintain Truk as a major airbase, even though heavy antiaircraft and a few aircraft remained. Mitscher detached heavy surface ships for shelling; cruisers shelled Satawan on 30 April, while Vice Admiral Lee formed the battle line to shell Ponape on 1 May. Mitscher headed for Majuro with Task Groups 58.2 and 58.3 and assigned Clark's Task Group 58.1 to give the battleships air cover. Lee and Clark then headed for Eniwetok, which was being used as an auxiliary anchorage to relieve the load on Majuro.

In May 1944, some air groups were changed during the breather before the next series of operations. Back in January, ComAirPac had scheduled rotations for six to nine months, but with the tempo of operations, this was shortened to six months in April. Altogether, six air groups were rotated home and more carriers reported for duty–*Essex* returned from overhaul and *Wasp* and *San Jacinto,* the last of the *Independence* class to enter service, were new. The *Bataan* returned to Kwajalein 14 May with a damaged elevator. Since it could not be repaired in the forward area, she continued on to Pearl Harbor for repairs. She rejoined Task Force 58 at Majuro on 2 June.[16] A new task group, Task Group 58.6, under Monty Montgomery was formed for training and included *Essex, Wasp,* and *San Jacinto.* The task group departed Majuro 14 May and divided as it approached Marcus. *San Jacinto* steamed north and west searching for enemy picket boats while *Essex* and *Wasp* attacked Marcus on 20 May. Heavy antiaircraft fire made accurate bombing difficult and negated the use of rockets, which required a long gliding approach. Weather interfered the next day, so Montgomery broke off the attack. *San Jacinto* rejoined, and on 24 May, all three carriers hit Wake.

Operation Forager–Capture of the Marianas

Although most of Japan's remaining carrier aircraft and their experienced crews had been lost in the defense of Rabaul, enough new aircraft and crews were available by the spring of 1944 to raise Japanese hopes of luring the Americans into one big, decisive battle. In May, Admiral Toyoda, the new Commander-in-Chief of the Combined Fleet, launched Operation A-Go to lure Spruance into the waters between the Palaus, Yap, and Woleai, where Japanese land-based and carrier aircraft would annihilate the American fleet.[17] The Japanese First Mobile Fleet comprised the bulk of the surface forces left in the Combined Fleet. Despite the losses of the previous months, it was still a formidable force of seventy-three surface ships, including 9 carriers (6 fleet carriers and 3 light carriers), 5 battleships, 7 heavy cruisers, 34 destroyers and 6 oilers. Admiral Jisaburo Ozawa had commanded the First Mobile Fleet since relieving Admiral Nagumo in November 1943, and was a formidable opponent for Mitscher. Carrier Division 1 included the *Shokaku, Zuikaku,* and the new 33,000-ton *Taiho.* Carrier Division 2 had the *Hiyo, Junyo,* and *Ryuho.* Carrier Division 3 had the *Chitose, Chiyoda,* and *Zuiho.* Ozawa could muster over 400 aircraft aboard the carriers and was counting on land-based aircraft from other Japanese bases to take part in the coming battle.[18]

Ozawa's forces rendezvoused at Tawi Tawi, the westernmost island of the Sulu Archipelago off the northeast coast of Borneo, on 16 May, but were spotted by the U.S. submarines *Bonefish* and *Puffer.*[19] Admiral Toyoda had intended to send a powerful naval force, including the super battleships *Yamato* and *Musashi,* to repulse MacArthur's forces at Biak off the northwest tip of New Guinea, but by mid-June it was apparent that the Central Pacific forces under Spruance would strike in the Marianas. On 13

June the Japanese fleet departed from Tawi Tawi and headed for the Marianas.

Operation Forager, the capture of the southern Marianas, would provide bases 3,000 miles farther west than Pearl Harbor, and enable the Army Air Force's new long-range B-29 bombers to reach Japan. The strikes of February had provided photographic coverage of the islands, but the Joint Chiefs of Staff had not made the decision to invade the Marianas until March. The target date for the invasion of Saipan was 15 June. While Guam, the southernmost island in the chain had been an American possession for nearly forty years before the war, Japan considered Saipan home territory. Its loss would be regarded as a breach of Japan's inner lines of defense.

Saipan, Tinian, Rota and Guam

Task Force 58 departed Majuro 6 June 1944 and refueled from Servron 10 two days later. At Mitscher's disposal were six *Essex*-class carriers, the *Enterprise,* and eight *Independence*-class light carriers. Together these carriers operated a total of 448 Hellcats, 174 Helldivers, 59 Dauntlesses, and 193 Avengers (plus 27 Hellcat and Corsair night fighters).[20] The strikes were scheduled for 12 June, but Mitscher decided to change the pattern of strikes launched at dawn and moved the fighter sweep up to the afternoon of 11 June. During the day, Japanese reconnaissance aircraft were shot down during the task force's approach to the targets and Lieutenant Commander John C. Strange, commander of *Bataan's* VF-50, brought down a Judy, the first of seven snoopers. This was the first of what would become 870 enemy aircraft destroyed by Hellcats in the two-month campaign.[21] The task force launched from 192 miles east of Guam. The first strike by 208 Hellcats and eight Avengers hit the airfields on Saipan and Tinian, destroying thirty-six Japanese aircraft. After strafing Guam and Rota, aircraft from Clark's Task Group 58.1 met about thirty Japanese fighters and shot them down. Antiaircraft fire was thick.

Over Tinian, VF-28 Hellcats from the *Monterey* entered a landing circle of Betty's, which they quickly shot down. Three Zekes, plus three more probables, and nine Bettys were destroyed in the air and one Zeke and three Bettys were probably destroyed on the ground.[22] The CAP also shot down an enemy plane forty miles west of the formation. *Cabot's* VF-31 "Meataxers" also scored well over Tinian, claiming thirteen kills.[23] Aircraft from Task Groups 58.3 and 58.4 faced smoke pots at Saipan. The Hellcats strafed and bombed the airfields, claiming 150 aircraft destroyed, mostly on the ground. Eleven Hellcats were shot down;three of the pilots were rescued.

The next day, a torpedo wake was spotted approaching the port bow of the *Cabot*. An emergency turn was executed while flight deck crewmen nervously watched the torpedo pass by. The task force continued to be harassed by submarine contacts and a few days later, *Cabot* planes on morning antisubmarine patrol spotted a periscope, which they bombed with no visible results.[24] On the three days before the Saipan landings, the task force worked over the Marianas; antiaircraft fire con

tinued to be heavy. The TBMs used rockets again, since Mitscher wanted to save bombs for a possible naval battle. On 12 June, Lieutenant Commander Robert H. Price, skipper of Air Group 25 on the *Cowpens,* was shot down. He was spotted in the water and a life raft dropped, but night fell before he could be picked up. Searches the next day failed to locate him. Eleven days later, he was picked up by Jocko Clark's Task Group 58.1. He was hungry, but otherwise alright.[25]

The pre-landing strikes also hit some shipping. While strafing Pagan, aircraft from Rear Admiral William K. "Keen" Harrill's Task Group 58.4 found a convoy to the north and attacked it on 12 and 13 June, sinking ten transports and four small escorts. A *Hornet* fighter located another convoy to the east of Guam on the 12th, and on 13 June Clark's Task Group 58.1 sent twenty Hellcats with bombs escorted by two radar-equipped night fighters to attack it at long range. The night fighters located the ships, but the fighter pilots had so little bombing experience that they damaged only one vessel. On the night of 15 June, Montgomery's Task Group 58.2 beat off a small torpedo plane attack from Yap with a combination of antiaircraft fire, maneuvering, and night fighters. As Captain Buracker of the *Princeton* observed, "It was a superb spectacle, a hundred Fourth of July's rolled into one. All around us scores of ships seemed on fire as their guns put up an AA screen. Weaving tracers, flares, and bursting shells spangled the skies. Once I saw six flaming Jap planes falling like meteors around us."[26]

The fast battleships of the task force

shelled Saipan on 13 June with poor results. The old battleships and escort carriers under Turner arrived the next day to join the fast carriers in hitting the island. Resistance on Saipan, despite all the pre-landing strikes, was tenacious and the landings on Guam had to be postponed.[27]

The Iwo Strikes

Spruance knew, through decoded intercepts of Japanese message traffic, that the Japanese were staging aircraft through the Bonins and Volcanos to the north, principally Iwo Jima and Chichi Jima. He directed Mitscher to send two task groups north to neutralize the threat. Mitscher sent Clark's Task Group 58.1 and Harrill's Task Group 58.4.[28] The two task groups rendezvoused north of the Marianas, refueling on the 14th. In the meantime, Spruance had received word that night that the Japanese fleet had left Tawi Tawi, and decided that the strikes should be cut to one day, 16 June, to allow both task groups time to rejoin Task Force 58 before the Japanese struck. Clark raced north to get in an attack on 15 June to allow the two days of strikes that he felt were needed, while Harrill tagged along. A pair of Japanese vessels were unlucky enough to cross the path of the oncoming carriers. First, a sampan was sunk by *Langley* planes around mid-morning, and about an hour later, a freighter was sighted only about thirty miles ahead of Clark's task group. Antisnooper and ASP teams from the *Bataan* pounced on the victim with depth charges and strafing. Although a depth charge from an Avenger blew the maru's bow off,

destroyers had to be called in to sink her with 5-inch gunfire.[29]

About 135 miles from Iwo Jima on the afternoon of 15 June, Clark and Harrill launched their aircraft toward Iwo, Chichi and Haha Jima. Task Group 58.4 sent twenty-two planes on a sweep and fifty-nine planes on a strike against Iwo, while Task Group 58.1 launched a sweep against Iwo and two deckload strikes for Chichi and Haha Jima. The main target was Iwo, where the best airfields were located. More than a hundred aircraft, mostly Zeros, were on Iwo's airfields, and when the first sweep arrived, three dozen Zeros were airborne to challenge them. The Hellcats cleared the air, and the strike aircraft then successfully bombed shipping and installations at Iwo, Chichi, and Haha Jima. By putting two night fighters over the target area, Clark prevented the Japanese night aircraft from taking off, keeping them grounded the next day.

As the strikes returned late that afternoon, the weather had already made recovery difficult. About 1712, one of *Belleau Wood's* fighters crashed into the port catwalk. Almost two hours later, another fighter took the barrier. Then a third Hellcat sliced through the barrier at 1920 and smashed into the island, bursting into flames. The mobile crane was knocked overboard, and the island and radars damaged. For nearly a half hour, the crew battled the fire on a wet and pitching deck before it was put out. The damage prevented air operations the next day.[30]

The task groups turned east-southeast as the weather worsened. On the morning of 16 June the weather forced

The Independence *underway early in 1943, when she was still armed with single 5-inch guns at the bow and stern.*

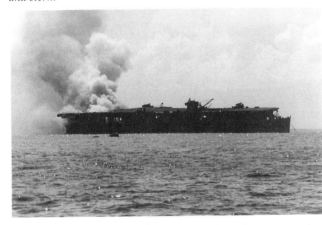

Independence *on fire following the Bikini atomic tests, July 1946. Test "Able" was an air burst that had exploded off the ship's port quarter.*

Another view of the damaged Independence.

Test personnel approach the Independence *to conduct evluations during the Bikini atomic tests.*

Launching of the Princeton, *18 October 1942.*

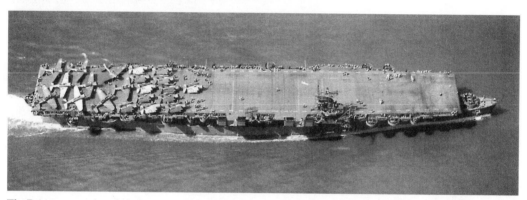

The Princeton *on her shakedown cruise, May 1943.*

The Princeton *on fire, but still underway, about twenty minutes after being hit by Japanese air attack, 24 October 1944.*

The Princeton *on her shakedown cruise, May 1943.*

The Princeton *explodes with the* Birmingham *alongside.*

The Birmingham *comes alongside the buring* Princeton *to assist with fire fighting.*

Crewmen on the Birmingham *spray fire hoses on the* Princeton *as their ship comes alongside to assist with the damage.*

The Belleau Wood *underway, December 1943.*

A Japanese bomber crashes near the Belleau Wood during an attack on Task Group 58.2 off the Marianas, 23 February 1944.

While operating off the Philippines, Belleau Wood *was hit by a kamikaze on 30 October 1944. Flight deck crewmen are moving undamaged TBM torpedo bombers away from the flames as others fight the fires aft. The* Franklin, *also hit by a kamikaze, burns in the distance.*

The Belleau Wood *entered French service as the* Bois Belleau. *She is seen here off Norfolk Naval Base December 1953.*

A Hellcat bursts into flames as it approaches the Cowpens *for landing, 24 November 1943.*

As the burning F-6F lands, the pilot, Lieutenant (jg) Alfred W. Magee, Jr., is unaware of the fire.

The Cowpens *underway, July 1945.*

As Lieutenant (jg) Magee walks off the wing to safety, firefighters rush forward, putting out the flames in a minute and a half. There were no casualties.

The Cowpens *at sea, 31 August 1944.*

The Monterey *maneuvers to recover her planes, March 1994.*

TBMs take off from the Monterey *to strike Tinian, June 1944.*

Lieutenant Ronald P. "Rip" Gift relaxes with other pilots in the ready room aboard the Monterey, *20 June.*

Monterey *catapults a Hellcat during operations in the Marianas, June 1944.*

Future president, Gerald Ford (jumper at left) playing basketball in the forward elevator well aboard the Monterey.

A pilot hurries to man his Avenger aboard the Monterey, *July 1944.*

Lieutenant Commander Rodger W. Mehle, Commander Air Group 28, reports to the Monterey's *skipper, Captain Stuart H. Ingersoll, June 1944.*

A Hellcat in the forward elevator well aboard the Monterey, *June 1944.*

A Hellcat lands "high" on the Langley *during operations in the vicinity of the Nansei Shoto, 10 October 1944. Task Force 38 hit targets in the Okinawa area on that day.*

three more strikes against Iwo.[31] That evening, both task groups turned south to rejoin the rest of the task force.

Task Force 58 broke off support of the beachhead on 17 June, leaving the escort carriers to provide close air support to the Marines, while Spruance ordered the amphibious shipping to a position east of the landing area in anticipation of a Japanese attack. The stage was set for the coming naval battle with the Japanese fleet.

Chapter 4
Philippine Sea

When Admiral Toyoda learned of the Saipan landings on 15 June, he activated A-Go, but there was no hope of luring the American's south–the Americans would have to be destroyed in the Marianas. Spruance, however, was alerted on the evening of 15 June by a report from the submarine *Flying Fish* that a Japanese carrier force was heading in his direction from the San Bernardino Straits. An hour later, the submarine *Seahorse* reported a battleship force heading northeast of the Surigao Strait. To Spruance, the possibility of two separate forces seemed likely and raised concerns about the possibility of an "end run" by the Japanese if his forces were pulled too far away to cover the Saipan landings, his primary mission. Between 15 and 18 June, the two forces searched each other out. On the morning of the 16th, Spruance seemed ready to take the initiative and ordered his flagship, the heavy cruiser *Indianapolis*, out to join the carriers. On the afternoon of 17 June he issued a battle plan calling for the carriers to first knock out the Japanese

carriers and then attack the battleships and cruisers. Then the battle line could come up and finish off any stragglers or cripples and engage the Japanese fleet if they decided to fight it out. He would leave the tactical operational details to Mitscher and Vice Admiral Willis A. "Ching" Lee, commander of the fast battleships of Task Force 58.

That evening a position report of "fifteen or so large combatant ships" heading east came in from the submarine *Cavalla*. The Japanese appeared to be about 800 miles away, but, based on Mitscher's calculations, the opposing forces would close on each other enough to allow the Americans to strike if the task force headed west. Since Spruance had left tactical matters up to Mitscher and Lee, subject to his overall direction, Mitscher sent a message to Lee: "Do you desire a night engagement? It may be we can make air contact this afternoon and attack tonight. Otherwise we should retire eastward." Lee, who had never trained with his battle-line commanders as a unit and who was well aware of

Japanese skill in night combat from the Guadalcanal days, responded, "Do not, repeat NOT believe we should seek night engagement. Possible advantages of radar more than offset by individual difficulties of communications and lack of training in fleet tactics at night. . ." While willing to take on a damaged or fleeing enemy, even at night, Lee was not ready to take on the Japanese at night if they were undamaged and attacking. Instead of heading west toward Ozawa, the task force turned south and then east toward Saipan.

On the morning of the 18th, Spruance issued an order intended to prevent the task force from being drawn too far away to cover the landings. The task force would advance westward during the day and retire eastward at night to cut down on the odds of being "flanked" during the night. Because of air operations and the need to conserve fuel, an advance of only about a hundred miles was made to the west during the day of 18 June. Ozawa, however, after finding the task force that afternoon, turned south and maintained a distance of about 400 miles between his carriers and the Americans. He intended to launch his attacks on the American fleet at dawn the next day. In order to coordinate his attacks with land-based aircraft and to prepare the airfields in the Marianas to receive his strike aircraft on their shuttle missions, Ozawa sent Admiral Kakuta, commander of the Japanese land-based air forces in the Marianas, a coded message on the evening of 18 June.

Although the American land- and carrier-based air searches had not found the Japanese fleet, high

frequency radio direction finding (HF/DF or "huff-duff") stations in the Aleutians, at Pearl Harbor, and in the South Pacific picked up the transmission. Nimitz' intelligence officers at CincPac headquarters triangulated Ozawa's position and relayed it to Spruance. Mitscher estimated that if the fleet turned westward at 0130, Task Force 58 would be in a position to strike the enemy at 0500. Unfortunately, Spruance also received a late message from ComSubPac stating that a dispatch from the submarine *Stingray* had been garbled in transmission. The last known position of the *Stingray* was considerably different from that given by the CincPac intercept and it was not known if the Japanese were jamming the *Stingray's* message. When Mitscher requested permission to turn westward that night, Spruance chose to place more credence in the garbled transmission, responding: "Change proposed does not appear advisable. Believe indications given by *Stingray* more accurate than that determined by direction finder. If that is so, continuation at present seems preferable. End run by other carrier groups remains possibility and must not be overlooked."

Although Ozawa's force was inferior to Spruance's in every ship category except heavy cruisers, he did have some tactical advantages. He had nearly a hundred land-based aircraft at Guam, Rota, and Yap, and the Japanese carrier aircraft could search out to 560 miles, allowing Ozawa to find Task Force 58 while remaining out of range. Mitscher's search aircraft could reach out to a maximum 350 miles. Navy land-based air searches covered out to

600 miles, but Ozawa was careful to remain out of their search areas. Using the Japanese held islands, Ozawa could launch strikes on shuttle missions while remaining out of reach of the American carrier strikes. Ozawa also had the "weather gauge," meaning that the prevailing easterly winds allowed the Japanese carriers to close the distance to their targets while launching into the wind, whereas Mitscher had to turn eastward away from the Japanese to launch and recover aircraft.

The American forces facing them included fifteen fast carriers and eleven escort carriers in a fleet that totaled more than 800 surface ships and twenty-eight submarines. Spruance was aware of the Japanese advance, but search planes had not sighted the Japanese on 18 June or on the morning of 19 June. At dawn on the 19th, the *Lexington*, flagship of Task Force 58, was about ninety miles northwest of Guam and about a hundred miles southwest of Saipan. Task Force 58 was arrayed in the shape of a giant backward letter "F." In a line from north to south about twelve nautical miles apart were Clark's Task Group 58.1 with *Belleau Wood, Bataan, Hornet,* and *Yorktown;* then Reeves's Task Group 58.3 with *Princeton, Enterprise, Lexington,* and *San Jacinto,* and Montgomery's Task Group 58.2 with *Cabot, Wasp, Monterey,* and *Bunker Hill.* Harrill's Task Group 58.4 with *Cowpens, Langley,* and *Essex* was twelve nautical miles west of Clark. Ching Lee's Battle Line, Task Group 58.7, with the fast battleships *Washington, North Carolina, Iowa, New Jersey, South Dakota,* and *Alabama,* was fifteen nautical miles west

of the middle task group, Reeves's Task Group 58.3. Radar picket destroyers were stationed to the west of the battleships.

Although expecting the Japanese from the west, the first attack came from two Judy dive bombers and six Zero fighter bombers flown from Guam, which had been reinforced during the night. On Tinian, Admiral Kakuta had received Ozawa's message and had brought up aircraft from Truk and other areas to Guam and Tinian and launched a strike at dawn. A Zero appeared suddenly out of a cloud and dropped a bomb on the picket destroyer *Stockham.* The bomb missed and the Zero was shot down by the destroyer *Yarnell.* Either that fighter or a Judy shot down by a Hellcat warned the Japanese on Guam of the American fleet's location, for thirty minutes later, task force radars picked up several blips. The *Belleau Wood's* combat air patrol was vectored ninety miles out and arrived over Guam's Orote airfield about 0630 to discover considerable air activity. The Japanese opened up with their antiaircraft fire, but at 15,500 feet, the aircraft were too high and the bursts exploded 2,000 feet below them. Planes from the *Cabot, Hornet,* and *Yorktown* arrived and the sky was soon full of vapor trails, an unusual occurrence in the Pacific war. The action continued as another group of reinforcing enemy aircraft heading toward Guam from the southwest was picked up on task force radars just after 0800. Mitscher ordered three task groups to send fighters, and about three dozen Hellcats were soon heading for Guam, arriving about one hour later. Planes from the *Bunker Hill* arrived to find many Japanese aircraft landing and taking off. Some of the Hellcats went down to strafe while others provided top cover. The strafing Hellcats ran into some experienced Japanese fliers and, while downing fifteen aircraft in the air and several more on the ground, lost one of their own. To prevent further shuttle attacks through Guam, Mitscher ordered bombers and fighters to hit the airfields again.

"The Marianas Turkey Shoot"

Meanwhile, Ozawa had not been idle. At dawn the First Mobile Fleet started an intensive search for the American carriers with forty-three planes, launched in three groups at half-hour intervals. A sighting was made around 0730, and a strike made up of sixteen Zero fighters, forty-five Zero fighter-bombers (older models fitted to carry bombs), and eight Jill torpedo bombers from Carrier Division 3, which was a hundred miles ahead of the main Japanese force, was launched at 0830. At 1003, the battleship *Alabama* picked up a radar contact at a range of 130 miles, a remarkable performance for an air search radar of that time. The contact was quickly verified by the *Cabot* in Task Group 58.2 and the *Enterprise* in Task Group 58.3. Soon after it was detected, the Japanese formation started to circle as their commander briefed his inexperienced pilots over the radio. The delay proved fatal, and doubly so as a Japanese language interpreter aboard the *Lexington* monitored the conversations and passed on the translations to the Task Force

Fighter Direction Officer. The flight decks were cleared, additional fighters were launched, and the airborne combat air patrol was vectored to intercept. At the time, Task Force 58 had fifty-nine Hellcats on CAP and another twenty-three on a fighter sweep over Guam. As soon as it was recognized as a major raid, the old circus call for help "Hey Rube" (meaning to return to the task force immediately), was passed to the squadrons over Guam. Mitscher also ordered all available fighters scrambled and the bombers flown off to orbit west of Guam, allowing the fighters to be recovered, rearmed, and launched as fast as possible. The fifteen carriers turned in to the wind at 1015 and two minutes later, the first aircraft of the scramble was launched off the *Cowpens*. Within the next fifteen minutes, 140 Hellcats were launched to bring the total facing the Japanese to just under 200. Hellcats from VF-15 from the *Essex* were vectored out to meet the incoming Japanese, followed in rapid succession by more from *Hornet's* VF-2, *Princeton's* VF-27, *Cowpens'* VF-25, and *Monterey's* VF-31.

At 1035, the eight *Essex* Hellcats tallyhoed the Japanese force while it was still fifty-five miles from the task force and promptly attacked, followed within fifteen minutes by fourteen Hellcats from VF-25 and VF-31. The raid began to break up after twenty-five minutes of wild dogfighting, as more Hellcats from *Cabot's* VF-28, *Monterey's* VF-31, and *Bunker Hill's* VF-8 arrived. The surviving Japanese had scattered, but were still closing on the task force. At 1120, six Hellcats from *San Jacinto's* VF-51 found ten survivors ten miles from the fleet and destroyed six of them. [1] Minutes later Hellcats from *Enterprises's* VF-10 attacked Zero fighter bombers as they prepared to attack Task Group 58.7. A few uncoordinated single plane attacks were made and the battleship *South Dakota* was hit. When the Japanese survivors made their way back to their carriers, eight of the fourteen Zero fighters, thirty-two of the forty-three Zero fighter bombers, and two of the seven Jills were lost. Against forty-two Japanese aircraft lost, three Hellcats were missing in action. Among them was Lieutenant Commander Earnest Wood, commander of Air Group 27.[2] Wood was an accomplished pianist who was always the center of a happy group gathered around the *Princeton's* wardroom piano, and his loss was keenly felt.

While the first strike was on its way, Ozawa launched his second strike of forty-eight Zero fighters, fifty-three Judy dive bombers and twenty-seven Jill torpedo bombers from Carrier Division 1.[4] The second strike was detected around 1100 at 115 miles, and again the Japanese circled and regrouped before attacking. Not counting the aircraft that had intercepted the first raid, Task Force 58 had 129 Hellcats available in the air and another thirty-three were scrambled shortly after the second raid was detected. Again the Japanese were met by Hellcats from VF-15, this time led by Commander David McCampbell, the commander of Air Group 15 . VF-15 had the formation all to itself for six minutes before they were joined by twelve fighters from *Wasp's* VF-14 and eight from *Princeton's* VF-27. By this time the scattered Japanese began their let down to attack the battleships of Task Group 58.7, where a division of *Bataan's* VF-50 was vectored out and caught two of them. *Yorktown's* VF-1 also joined in about three different actions in the confused battle and between all the squadrons involved, not much was left of the second raid. Between 1145 and 1210, a few Japanese aircraft carried out small attacks against three of the five task groups. Only the battleship *Indiana* was damaged when a Jill crashed into her heavily armored waterline. The *Alabama, South Dakota,* and *Iowa* were attacked, but not hit. In Task Group 58.2, six Judys attacked and a phosphorous bomb exploded over the *Wasp,* killing one man and wounding twelve. Two dove on the *Bunker Hill,* where a near miss killed three, wounded seventy-three, and started a few small fires. One of the attacking planes, starting to smoke from the antiaircraft fire, turned toward the *Cabot.* The *Cabot's* gunners shot its tail off and it started burning. Spinning dangerously and ablaze, it crashed into the water astern.[5] A few Jills reached Task Group 58.3 to launch torpedo attacks against the *Enterprise* and *Princeton.* Antiaircraft fire from the two ships brought down one Judy and, immediately afterward, two Jills making torpedo runs off *Princeton's* starboard beam were shot down by her gunners. A third Jill attacked on her starboard side and the "Peerless P" made a hard starboard turn into the torpedo track. A ships gunner shot a wing off the Jill, which crashed into the sea ahead of the ship. Although a torpedo had been seen to drop, no hits were scored.[6] The Japanese lost ninety-four aircraft in the second raid; only twenty-three of the 117 attacking aircraft survived. The Americans lost only four Hellcats in combat; three of the pilots were missing in action, but the fourth was later rescued from his life raft.

Between 1000 and 1015, Ozawa's third strike of sixteen Zero fighters, twenty-six Zero fighter-bombers and seven Jills was launched from Carrier Division 2. There was some confusion among the Japanese, and only about twenty aircraft found the American carriers. (One of the Japanese scout aircraft had forgotten to apply compass deviation in reporting the position of the American task force earlier that morning, leading to a significant error.) After the third raid was launched, it was directed to another location, but only the covering fighters apparently got the message.[7] This strike was also intercepted and seven Japanese aircraft were shot down.

An hour after the third raid was launched, the fourth strike was sent off from Carrier Division 2 plus the *Zuikaku* and included eighty-two planes. Part of this strike did not find the carriers and turned back, another group stumbled upon a search team from the *Lexington* and was intercepted purely by chance, and another group headed for Rota on Guam. On their way they stumbled across Task Group 58.2 and made ineffectual glide bombing attacks on the *Bunker Hill* and *Wasp* as they were recovering aircraft. The *Cabot* shot down one in flames and two others were seen to hit the water burning. The *Wasp* was straddled, but not

hit. The task group commander, Montgomery, sent a message to the *Cabot* congratulating her on her shooting: "You are tops in the league today."[8] Arriving over Orote airfield, the survivors were set upon by Hellcats from the *Cowpens, Essex, Hornet,* and *Enterprise.* Altogether, the Japanese lost seventy-three of the eighty-two strike aircraft in the fourth raid.

By that afternoon, the Japanese had lost a total of 253 carrier planes against a loss of twenty-nine from Task Force 58. Aboard the *Lexington,* one excited pilot was overheard saying, "Hell, this is like an old time turkey shoot!" The name stuck, and the lopsided aerial victory has been known ever since as "The Marianas Turkey Shoot." The losses in aircraft and their crews were not all the Japanese suffered, they also lost the *Shokaku* and the *Taiho.* The *Shokaku* had been hit by three torpedoes from the submarine *Cavalla* just before noon. By the time stragglers from Ozawa's first strike had returned, *Shokaku* was ablaze, forcing her aircraft to land on other carriers. The veteran of the Pearl Harbor attack blew up later that afternoon. The *Taiho,* torpedoed earlier, had a ruptured gasoline storage tank and fumes spread throughout the ship. The damage control officer decided that the best way to clear up the fumes was to open all the ventilation ducts and blow them away, but this only served to spread them throughout the ship. Eventually the vapors reached a spark that ignited an explosion. One explosion followed another, and the *Taiho* was lost late in the afternoon with heavy loss of life. Ozawa had to transfer his flag to the cruiser *Haguro.* With only about a hundred planes left, Ozawa withdrew to the northwest to regroup.

Task Force 58 Strikes

When it became clear that the "turkey shoot" had stripped the Japanese carriers of much of their offensive capability, Spruance released Mitscher to finish Ozawa. But the Japanese were too far out of range and American air searches could not locate them. Although the aviators must have felt that they had destroyed or damaged every Japanese aircraft in the Marianas, the Japanese had already brought up replacement aircraft. Spruance ordered night sweeps over the Marianas and Harrill's Task Group 58.4 was detached to cover them while Mitscher went after Ozawa. Four night fighters from the *Essex* worked over Guam and Rota that night, shooting down three aircraft at dawn the next day, 20 June. The task group hit Guam at daylight and destroyed another forty planes on the ground, effectively eliminating the last Japanese air strength in the Marianas. The other three task groups recovered their aircraft that evening and Mitscher headed west at 2000 on the 19th. Although searches went out to 325 miles the next morning, they found nothing. Neither did land-based air searches or the submarines. At noon, a search by Hellcats equipped with drop tanks went out to 475 miles, the longest American carrier search of the war, but again found nothing. An afternoon search from the *Enterprise* had detected the Japanese near the limit of its range and radioed a report

back to the task force around 1540. The radio transmissions alerted the Japanese, but because the original transmission was garbled, Mitscher did not receive a corrected report until 1600. A few quick calculations indicated that there would only be a half hour of daylight for the attack, followed by a return trip after sunset. Mitscher did not hesitate. He informed Spruance he was going ahead and launched fifty-one Helldivers, twenty-six Dauntlesses, fifty-four Avengers, and eighty-five Hellcats. All of the large carriers in the three task groups launched aircraft and all of the light carriers launched except the *Princeton,* which was to join in a second strike.[9] Task Force 58, heading westward in the general direction of the enemy, turned eastward into the wind to launch. After the strike was launched and on its way in a long fuel saving climb, the task force again turned westward. As the strike aircraft were en route, corrected position reports placed the enemy sixty miles further west. It would be close. The Japanese were near the extreme limits of striking range and the returning aircraft would be coming back in darkness with little fuel remaining. Only a handful of the pilots had any significant night training.

The sun was just touching the horizon as the strike aircraft reached the Japanese fleet. There was no time to coordinate and no margin for error. Ozawa, who had shifted his flag to the carrier *Zuikaku,* sent up his remaining aircraft, many of which were promptly shot down by the escorting Hellcats. *Belleau Wood's* VT-24 was the only torpedo squadron loaded with torpedoes, the others were armed only with bombs. Lieutenant (jg) George Brown led his Avengers against the light carrier *Hiyo* at about 1820. Japanese antiaircraft fire hit Brown's aircraft, forcing his gunner and radio man to bail out, but Brown kept going until the slipstream put out the fires. Instead of breaking off after dropping his torpedo, he turned his plane in toward the carrier and flew straight down the length of the ship to draw the antiaircraft gunners attention from the following Avenger, flown by Lieutenant (jg) Warren Omark. Whether Brown's torpedo hit is unknown, but Omark's went "straight to the mark" and the *Hiyo* burst into flames. She blew up at 1930 as Brown's crew watched from the water, where they were rescued the next day. Brown, wounded and flying a crippled plane, turned back to the task force, riding his Avenger into the sea on the return flight.[10]

Junyo, another of the light carriers, took two bombs and six near misses which buckled her plates, but she survived. The light carriers *Ryujo* and *Chiyoda* were damaged by near misses and a battleship and a cruiser were hit. Two of the supply ships were sunk. Now the long trip back began. As the striking aircraft headed for home about twenty of the remaining Japanese aircraft followed them for a time, but were kept at bay by the escorting Hellcats.

"Turn on the Lights"

Straggling back to the carriers in the dark, damaged aircraft dropped behind, many to be lost. Others ran out of fuel before they reached the carriers.

Darkness had fallen before 2000 and the sky was overcast, further hampering the pilots. When the strike aircraft were about seventy miles out, Mitscher increased the speed of the task force to close the distance. As the first planes returned around 2030, there was mass confusion. With more and more aircraft running out of gas, Mitscher weighed the possibility of a Japanese submarine attack against the loss of more of his aviators. "Turn on the lights," he said, and the task force lit up, sending searchlight beams and star shells into the overcast sky. As it became apparent that many more would be lost if they did not land quickly, he added, "Tell 'em to land on any carrier." Pilots headed for any carrier they could find. There were many deck crashes as air discipline broke down. Some desperate pilots ignored waveoffs and dived for the deck, often with tragic consequences. Other aircraft ditched alongside ships of the task force.

Amidst the confusion, there were some bizarre moments, and even a few humorous situations. Aboard the *Cabot,* for instance, only two of the nine aircraft landed that night were her own, including two of the big SB2C Helldivers–a type considered too big to operate from a CVL.[11] One *Cabot* pilot, VT-31's Lieutenant (jg) John B. "Beast" Russell was not enthusiastic about landing his big Avenger on his own ship and decided to pick out the biggest carrier he could find. After searching for a few minutes, he found a likely candidate and landed. As he climbed out of the cockpit, a member of the deck crew said, "That was a beautiful landing, Mr. Russell–just like daytime." Surprised, Russell asked, "What ship is this?" The answer came back, "Why the *Cabot* of course! What did you think it was?" "That's all I wanted to know!" replied Russell and bent down to kiss the deck.[12]

The *San Jacinto* also received her share of "guests" that night, one of which was an SBD Dauntless from the *Lexington*. Ensign John F. Caffey of VB-16 found that the deck crew had little familiarity with the SBD. He was told to fold his plane's wings, and when he tried to explain that the Dauntless did not have folding wings, he was told "God damn it, fold 'em anyway!"[13] Even stranger was the report that a Japanese aircraft, either a Judy or a Val, tried to land on the San Jock. As the ship later reported, "It is worth of note that only the studied refusal of the pilot to lower his hook prevented this ship from capturing a wandering Jap 'Val' who thrice attempted to land on board."[14]

By 2230 that night, the last of the strike aircraft were recovered. Of the 216 attacking aircraft only a hundred landed that night. Only about twenty were casualties of the battle, the rest were lost into the sea or in deck accidents. Mitscher recommended heading the task force toward the last location of the Japanese fleet at sixteen knots. The next morning at 0600, Mitscher launched another strike toward a position reported by Saipan based night patrol planes, in addition to search planes carrying only extra fuel tanks. The strike aircraft did not find the enemy, but the search aircraft did. They found a force of battleships and destroyers, and farther ahead, three small carriers. The Japanese were heading toward Okinawa at twenty knots. Spruance, aboard the *Indianapolis*, steamed out to join the battleships, which were out ahead of the task force under the cover of the *Bunker Hill* and *Wasp*.[15] The task force did not find any cripples and Spruance called off any further pursuit later that day. The task force retired toward Saipan, picking up floating aviators en route. In the end, all but sixteen pilots and twenty-two crewmen were saved. The overall results of the two day Battle of the Philippine Sea included American losses of 130 aircraft and seventy-six aviators against Japanese losses of three carriers, 480 planes and nearly the last of their trained carrier pilots.

Most of the task force retired to Eniwetok, while Task Group 58.4 remained off Guam. Clark's Task Group 58.1, ordered to bomb Pagan en route, received permission to detour north to hit the Bonins. On 24 June, Task Group 58.1 aircraft took off in heavy seas to strike the Jimas. The morning fighter sweep claimed sixty-eight aircraft destroyed, with Lieutenant (jg) Everett G. Hargreaves of *Bataan's* VF-50 claiming top honors with five victories.[16] The other carriers involved were the *Hornet* and *Yorktown*. Another sweep in marginal weather later in the afternoon resulted in a further forty-eight enemy aircraft brought down. The Japanese sent three strikes against the task group, all of which were intercepted and repulsed. The last two strikes managed to reach the task group, but antiaircraft fire helped drive them off. The Japanese had lost many aircraft and, for the time being, were unable to attack the Americans off Saipan and Guam. Task Group 58.1 reached Eniwetok on 27 June, the last of the three task groups to arrive.

The Summer of 1944

As the last days of June wore on, Task Group 58.4 remained off Guam and Rota to soften them up for the upcoming landings. The composition of the task group changed as carriers rotated to Eniwetok for rest, command changes, and air group transfers. On 30 June, Clark's Task Group 58.1 and Task Group 58.2, now under the command of Rear Admiral Ralph E. "Dave" Davison, were sent to hit the Bonins again, which they did on the 3rd and 4th of July, resulting in claims for another ninety-two enemy aircraft destroyed. Lieutenant (jg) Cornelius N. Nooy of *Cabot's* VF-31, accounted for four of that total on his way to becoming the top scoring ace from the light carriers.[17] After hitting the Bonins, the task groups followed Task Group 58.4 to Eniwetok, which had retired the day before. On the way south, Task Group 58.1 and Task Group 58.2 hit Guam and Rota and rotated between the islands for a week of strikes. On 9 July organized resistance on Saipan ended. Guam and Tinian would be next. Task Group 58.3 and Task Group 58.4, now commanded by Rear Admiral Gerald W. "Gerry" Bogan, joined in the pre-landing bombardments on the 13th. On 21 July the Marines landed on Guam and the next day, Mitscher left Bogan's Task Group 58.4 behind to cover the beaches while he headed for the Palaus with Task Group 58.1, Task Group 58.2, and

Task Group 58.3.[18] Between 25 and 28 July, Task Group 58.2 and Task Group 58.3 worked over the Palaus, while Task Group 58.1 hit Yap, Ulithi, Fais, Ngulu and Sorol, which were also photographed for possible use as fleet anchorages. On 4 and 5 August, Task Groups 58.1 and 58.3 hit the Bonins yet again, with the cruisers shelling the islands the following day. On 9 August, Task Force 58 anchored at Eniwetok for a two week rest period. It had been a long grind and there was more to come.

On 12 August organized resistance on Guam ended. Ted Sherman returned to relieve Montgomery as commander of Task Group 58.3 that same day. There were other changes and additions as the fast carrier forces prepared for the next phase of the Pacific war. The new *Franklin, Ticonderoga,* and *Hancock* reported to the Pacific. Until the Saipan operations, each carrier returned to Pearl Harbor to pick up a new air group and engage in a ten-day training period. Beginning that summer, all new air groups trained aboard available aircraft carriers at San Diego or Hawaii and were ferried to their ships at advanced anchorages just before going into combat.[19]

Night Carrier

After the *Enterprise* pioneered night operations with Butch O'Hare's "bat" teams in the Gilberts, similar teams were formed on other carriers and, beginning in early 1944, specially trained and equipped Corsair and Hellcat night fighter detachments were placed aboard the larger *Essex* carriers.

This gave the fast carriers a minimal defensive capability. The *Enterprise* had also pioneered night attacks with Bill Martin's VT-10 night strike at Truk. Although ComAirPac had issued a directive requiring all carrier pilots to be night qualified following the harrowing experiences of the Battle of the Philippine Sea, this would not be enough to give the fast carriers a true night combat capability–attack as well as defense. A dedicated night carrier task group was needed. Accordingly, Admiral John Towers, one of the original naval aviators and now Nimitz's deputy, decided early in July that the recently repaired *Independence* would become the Navy's first night carrier "as soon as possible."[20] The *Enterprise* would also become a night carrier, but would continue as a day carrier until the end of her current tour. Late in July, it was decided that *Bataan* would also be converted into a night carrier. Matt Gardner, former captain of the "Big E," was promoted to Rear Admiral in August and would become commander of the new night-carrier task group. In the meantime, the old *Saratoga* and *Ranger* trained for night operations off Hawaii. All these changes would take time, and it wasn't until the end of the year that a two-carrier night task group was formed.

In order to get *Independence* operational quickly, Lieutenant Commander Turner F. Caldwell, a veteran of Guadalcanal and the Solomons who was regarded as the "ring leader" of night fighting tactics, assembled several night fighter and torpedo plane detachments at Pearl Harbor in the first week of July to form a night air group with

nineteen F6F-5N Hellcats and eight TBM-1D Avengers. The fighters were all equipped with the APS-6 air intercept radar and the TBMs carried the ASD-1, which could detect a carrier-sized target at forty miles. Prior to reporting aboard, training consisted entirely of that required for proficiency in night operations. The *Independence*, now commanded by Captain Edward C. "Eddie"Ewen, departed Pearl Harbor for Eniwetok on 17 August with Air Group (Night) 41 aboard.[21]

As part of the Navy's first official night carrier, the men of the *Independence* and her air group faced many challenges. All naval aviators are highly skilled, but a night flyer is the cream of the crop. In Commander Caldwell's words:

"He is the best instrument pilot in combat–he has to be, for his life hangs on his instrument board. The night flyer must be an individualist, for he works alone and safety of the fleet often rests on his decisions. The day fighter attacks at high speed with a youthful, 'jump anything' exuberance. The night fighter must be cool, precise, methodical, self-confident and persevering. Night interceptions against a violently 'jinking' opponent often drag on for three quarters of an hour or more. These are a few reasons why a night flyer must train for two years before cutting his teeth in combat."[22]

Night flying requires learning to see all over again. In the retina at the back of the eye are "rods" and "cones," so called because of their shapes. The cones are concentrated in the fovea, the "bullseye" area of the retina, and are used for seeing color, detail, and far away objects. Surrounding the cones are the rods, which are much more sensitive to light. They are used for peripheral vision and are adapted for detecting motion. At night, staring directly at an object causes it to seemingly disappear and night flyers have to train themselves to scan over an object in order to see it. Also, night flyers have to allow their eyes to adjust to darkness for about a half hour and thereafter avoid "white" light. To preserve their night vision, red instrument lights were used, which do not affect the sensitivity of the rods.

The challenges of landing on a carrier in the dark added to the complexities of night flying. Caldwell's night flyers spent a month practicing before they began to develop confidence in their skills. As one of the ship's stewards, who was watching their efforts, observed, "Man was never made to fly, nohow. And if he was made to fly, he was never made to fly off a ship. And if he was made to fly off a ship, he was never made to fly off a ship at night."[23] Taking off was one thing, landing aboard safely on a narrow, moving flight deck was something else again. This was accomplished by the teamwork of three individuals–the pilot, the landing control officer operating from the bridge, and the landing signals officer, or LSO, stationed on a platform on the aft end of the flight deck on the port side. The pilot returning to the ship would be directed by the landing control officer by radio to the point where he could enter the "racetrack" landing pattern around the carrier. As he came around into the "groove" astern, he would be guided by the LSO. For night operations the LSO wore a "zoot suit" of highly reflective fluorescent satin and used paddles to direct the pilot, just as in day operations. The suit and paddles were illuminated by ultraviolet "footlights" to make the LSO highly visible and dim flight deck "dustpan" lights directed aft helped the pilot line up properly. These lights seemed dim enough to the aviators trying to thread their way in the dark, but to the torpedo-conscious ship's company they seemed to "have all the gaudy brilliance of a community Christmas tree donated by Commonwealth Edison."[24]

While the night fliers adjusted their sleep habits to accommodate night operations, the ship's company had to operate around the clock, as the Japanese were never accommodating enough to leave the *Independence* alone during daylight attacks. The engineering department usually had to operate all boilers nearly continuously and the ship's organization had to be revised as well. Often the executive officer, Commander Edwin J.S. Young, had to take over from Captain Ewen.[25] During night flight operations, the *Independence,* accompanied by two destroyers, operated as a detached unit of Task Group 38.2. This often created difficulty remaining close to her parent task group when the wind was from a different direction than the base course.

Her first operations were principally as a day carrier, participating in the Palau strikes of 6-8 September. The only action by her aircraft was the downing of two Bettys by a search team and one Dinah by a dusk CAP. She also participated in the Mindanao and Visayas strikes of 9-14 September. Off Palau, 16-18 September, her air group was converted to a day group by adding twelve day fighters and subtracting four night fighters. Participating in CAP, ASP, searches, and fighter strikes and sweeps from the 17th through the 24th, her flyers shot down two fighters, three bombers, a floatplane and a transport, destroyed fourteen other aircraft on the ground in the Clark Field area, and hit an oiler from masthead height during the Coron Bay strike. In October she would be reconverted to night operations and would finally have the chance to demonstrate what her crew had trained so hard to do.[26]

Chapter 5
Halsey and the Third Fleet

Of all the changes occurring late in August 1944, the change in fleet commanders was most profound. On 26 August Vice Admiral William F. Halsey, Jr. relieved Vice Admiral Raymond A. Spruance as commander of the Central Pacific forces. The Fifth Fleet became the Third Fleet and Task Force 58 became Task Force 38 as part of the "two platoon" system of rotating fleet command. Known as "Bull" to correspondents, but "Bill" to his friends, Halsey was the opposite of Ray Spruance. Where Spruance was cautious and methodical, Halsey was bold and brash. Halsey was the first carrier admiral to follow the doctrine of risk. Early in the Pacific war, while other carrier admirals avoided confrontation with the Japanese to preserve precious carriers, Halsey went looking for trouble, beginning with his raid in the Marshalls in February 1942. It was Halsey who had commanded the naval task force that launched the Doolittle Tokyo raid in April 1942, and it was his leadership of the South Pacific forces that culminated in the successful drive

up the Solomons chain. When Halsey effectively worked himself out of a job in the South Pacific, which had become a backwater area, he was ready to take on the Japanese wherever he could find them. A late comer to naval aviation, Halsey was an aggressive commander charging into the enemy like a raging bull, but he could also be the "bull in the china shop" who could be his own worst enemy. Unlike Spruance, Halsey would be the real commander of the fast carriers and, for many, the terms "Third Fleet" and "Task Force 38" were synonymous.

Vice Admiral John S. "Slew" McCain had been sent from Washington to the Central Pacific a few months earlier to learn the ropes. Like Halsey, he was one of the latecomers to naval aviation. Fearless and aggressive, McCain had many colorful traits and was generally well liked, but could be sloppy in the way he conducted operations. For the time being, he was in "makee learn" status and commanded one of the fast carrier task groups.[1] This lasted longer than he wanted, since

Mitscher would stay in command of the fast carriers for several more months.[2]

On 28 August Task Force 38 departed Eniwetok. Ralph Davison's Task Group 38.4 with *Franklin, Enterprise,* and *San Jacinto* hit Iwo and Chichi Jima from 31 August to 2 September before moving on to the western Carolines. Among the aircrews taking part in the strikes was a future president of the United States, who would experience one of the most dramatic events of his life–one which would give him a "sobering understanding of war and peace."

George H.W. Bush had joined the Navy as a seaman second class in June 1942, after he graduated from high school. In less than a year, he completed flight training and was commissioned as an ensign. For a time the youngest pilot in naval aviation, he flew TBM Avengers with VT-51 aboard the *San Jacinto,* eventually flying fifty-eight strike missions. On 2 September Lieutenant (jg) Bush's target was a Japanese radio station on Chichi Jima. Before 0900, Bush catapulted off *San Jacinto* with other bomb-laden VT-51 aircraft, as well as a number of VF-51's F6F Hellcats. His crew included his regular radioman, Radioman Second Class John Delaney, and his friend, the squadron air combat intelligence officer (ACI), Lieutenant (jg) William White. Ordnanceman Second Class Leo W. Nadeau, Bush's regular gunner, had flown with him on all but two of his missions. "I was replaced by Lieutenant (jg) White at the last minute," he remembered. "As intelligence officer, White wanted to go along to observe the island." The day before, Bush,

Nadeau and Delaney had flown into Chichi Jima and destroyed an enemy gun emplacement. "The antiaircraft (AA) fire on that island was the worst we had seen," Nadeau said later. "I don't think the AA fire in the Philippines was as bad as that." Another former VT-51 pilot recalled that "Chichi was a real feisty place to fly into. As I remember, it had gun emplacements hidden in the mountain areas. In order to get down to the radio facility, you had to fly past the AA batteries, which was risky business."

As soon as the strike was over the island, black puffs of flak appeared. As he approached the target and dove on it, Bush's plane was hit. He nevertheless continued his dive toward the target and dropped his load. The four 500-pound bombs exploded, causing damaging hits. Bush maneuvered the Avenger over the ocean, hoping to make it back to *San Jacinto,* but the plane began to burn, and clouds of smoke soon filled the cockpit. Choking and gasping for air, Bush and one crewman made it out of the plane and jumped from about 1,500 feet. The other crewman, dead or seriously injured from the blast, went down with the Avenger. Bush parachuted safely into the water, dangerously close to the shore. Unfortunately, the other crewman fell to his death because his parachute failed to open properly. No one ever knew which one–White or Delaney–bailed out with Bush. Once in the water, Bush inflated his yellow life raft, crawled in, and paddled quickly out to sea. The Japanese sent out a boat to capture him, but a fellow VT-51 Avenger pilot strafed the boat, stopping it.

Circling fighters transmitted Bush's position to the submarine *Finback*, patrolling fifteen to twenty miles from the island. A few hours later the submarine had spotted him about seven miles away from Chichi Jima and surfaced to pick him up. "I saw this thing coming out of the water and I said to myself, 'Jeez, I hope it's one of ours,'" Bush recalled years later. "I thought being rescued by the submarine was the end of my problem," Bush added, "I didn't realize that I would have to spend the duration of the sub's thirty remaining days on board." Bush, along with four other rescued pilots were put on watch as lookouts during the remainder of the *Finbacks's* war patrol. The aviators got a real taste of submarine warfare–being bombed and depthcharged. "I thought I was scared at times flying into combat, but in a submarine you couldn't do anything, except sit there," Bush said. "The submariners were saying that it must be scary to be shot at by antiaircraft fire and I was saying to myself, 'Listen brother, it is not really as bad as what you go through.' The tension, adrenaline and the fear factor were about the same (getting shot at by antiaircraft fire as opposed to being depthcharged). When we were getting depth charged, the submariners did not seem overly concerned, but the other pilots and I didn't like it a bit. There was a certain helpless feeling when the depth charges went off that I didn't experience when flying my plane against AA." Besides being bombed and depth charged, Bush was aboard when *Finback* sank two enemy freighters which were trying to get supplies into Iwo Jima.

At the end on her patrol *Finback* discharged her five passengers at Midway. Later, the aviators were taken to Hawaii and Bush hitched a flight to Guam, were he stayed for a few days until he could get back to the *San Jacinto*. For his courage and disregard for his own safety in pressing home his attack, he was later awarded a Distinguished Flying Cross.[3]

On 6 September Task Group 38.4 hit Yap in the western Carolines. Meanwhile, the other three task groups, McCain's Task Group 38.1 with *Hornet, Wasp, Belleau Wood,* and *Cowpens,* Gerry Bogan's Task Group 38.2 with *Intrepid, Bunker Hill, Cabot,* and *Independence,* and Ted Sherman's Task Group 38.3 with *Essex, Lexington, Princeton,* and *Langley,* hit the Palaus 6-8 September. On 9 September, Task Group 38.4 refueled and assumed a supporting role until the 18th, while the others hit Mindanao on the 9th and 10th. The task force encountered almost no enemy resistance and went on to hit the Visayas in the central Philippines 12-13 September, destroying almost 200 enemy aircraft and many ground targets and ships. *Cabot's* VF-25 alone shot down twenty-five enemy aircraft during the strikes over Luzon.[4] Mindanao and the Visayas were hit again on the 14th, and Manila and the Visayas on 21, 22, and 24 September for a total of 893 enemy aircraft destroyed and sixty-seven ships sunk. On the 21st, VF-25 repeated its feat of a few days earlier by downing twenty-five more enemy aircraft during an air battle over Clark Field. Bogan, commander of Task Group 38.2 sent a message to the *Cabot:* "Well done. Your backs must be badly bent carrying the load for this group."[5] Halsey, receiving reports of weak Japanese defenses in the area, recommended that MacArthur's Mindanao landings scheduled for 15 September be canceled in favor of immediate landings on Leyte. His recommendations were passed up the chain.[6]

Return to the Philippines–The Invasion of Leyte

In late July 1944, MacArthur had convinced Roosevelt and Nimitz that the Philippines were a necessary stepping stone to further operations. Once committed to the liberation of the Philippines, the Leyte and later Luzon operations became crucial to the destruction of the Japanese empire. From Leyte, the Americans could deploy ships, aircraft, and amphibious forces to the north and to the west, cutting off Japan from its resources in the East Indies. The Japanese shipping lifeline could be corked at the Luzon bottleneck. In September, MacArthur was to take Morotai and Nimitz Pelelieu. In October Nimitz would take Yap in the Carolines, Ulithi a few days later, then Talaud. In November, MacArthur would occupy Sarangani Bay on Mindanao, and in December, MacArthur and Nimitz would invade Leyte in concert. Decisions regarding further landings, whether on Luzon or Formosa, were left open. Halsey's operations, however, had shown just how weak the Japanese were on Leyte. He recommended canceling the Pelelieu, Morotai, Yap, and Mindanao operations in order to move the invasion of Leyte up by two whole months. Within hours of MacArthur's acceptance of this proposal, the Joint Chiefs of Staff ordered MacArthur and Nimitz to invade Leyte on 20 October, with Vice Admiral Wilkinson's amphibious forces, the III Amphibious Force, joining them after taking Pelelieu. Anguar, a two-mile-long island south of Pelelieu, would be seized and used as a bomber base.[7] Kossol Passage, about sixty miles north of Anguar, became a temporary fleet anchorage and a base for PBM Mariner flying boats. The real prize, however, was Ulithi atoll.

Ulithi

Occupied on 23 September, Ulithi atoll became the major fleet anchorage in the Pacific, but the various task groups went to other anchorages while it was being readied. McCain's Task Group 38.1 anchored in Seadler Harbor at Manus in the Admiralties on 29 September; Bogan's Task Group 38.2 arrived at Saipan 28 September; and Sherman's Task Group 38.3 went to Kossol Passage on 27 September. Davison's Task Group 38.4 stayed off the Palaus until early October. On 1-2 October, Task Group 38.2 and Task Group 38.3 went to Ulithi, which was hit for the next three days by a typhoon.[8] Because the fast carrier force could not even retire to Ulithi when the tempo of operations picked up, an At Sea Logistics Service Group was formed with thirty-four fleet oilers, eleven escort carriers, nineteen destroyers and twenty-six destroyer escorts. Fueling at Ulithi, each replenishment group would sail with a dozen oilers for a rendezvous with the fast carriers. The escort carriers provided air cover for the replenishment group and ferried replacement aircraft and pilots to the fast carriers. Halsey set each refueling rendezvous at the extreme range of Japanese land-based aircraft and the Japanese never succeeded in disrupting replenishment operations. The service group allowed the Third Fleet a strategic mobility unprecedented in naval warfare. It would be needed, for the Third Fleet would face another fleet battle, many weeks of close support operations for ground forces, heavy weather, and a storm of another kind–the kamikazes.

Task Force 38

On 7 October, Task Force 38 rendezvoused 375 miles west of the Marianas to begin a series of pre-landing attacks on Japanese airfields. It was a most formidable force. With eight *Essex*-class carriers, the old *Enterprise*, and seven *Independence*-class light carriers, the fast carrier force carried more than 1,000 aircraft. Halsey's first task was to neutralize Japanese air strength north of the Philippines, primarily at Kyushu, Okinawa, and Formosa, then to shift southward to hit the Luzon and Visayan airfields.[9] Despite poor visibility caused by overcast skies, Task Force 38 successfully attacked Okinawa shipping and airfields on 10 October, sinking nineteen small warships and destroying more than a hundred enemy aircraft, for a loss of twenty-one carrier aircraft. Most of the crews were picked up by the lifeguard submarines. The next day, a less-successful strike was launched against Aparri at the northern end of Luzon. Then Halsey began a series of heavy air attacks on Formosa and northern Luzon.

The Air Battle at Formosa

The carriers of Task Force 38 arrived at their launch positions before dawn on 12 October. At 0544, an hour before sunrise, the first strike, a fighter sweep to clear the air over Formosa and the Pescadores, was launched. In perfect flying weather, no fewer than 1,378 sorties were flown from all four carrier groups on the first day. Over the targets, Japanese air opposition, combined with intense antiaircraft fire, brought down forty-eight carrier aircraft, but at tremendous loss to themselves in aircraft destroyed both in the air and on the ground. After the first sweep, only sixty Japanese fighters were still operational when the second strike arrived, and none when the third struck.

Overly optimistic reports by inexperienced Japanese pilots led Admiral Toyoda to change his air defense plans. Instead of making his last stand in the Philippines, he committed his land-based aircraft to the destruction of the American fleet at this seemingly opportune time and place. Vice Admiral Fukudome's land-based Second Air Fleet, operating primarily from Kyushu, Okinawa, and Formosa, had been committed to the destruction of the American fleet and Admiral Ozawa's 300 under-trained carrier pilots were ordered ashore. It was to be all or nothing at Formosa.

That night, the night flyers of Air Group 41 made their first night interceptions when eight night Hellcats launched from the *Independence*.

Forming into two divisions, one led by Lieutenant Commander Turner Caldwell himself and the other by his executive officer, Lieutenant William E. Henry, they were vectored toward two bogies ten miles away. Bill Henry, a normally reticent veteran of Guadalcanal, began to "chatter like a magpie" as he kept up a running play-by-play account of the interception. Closing within a mile of the enemy, he could make out a shadowy form against the clouds. Moving in behind and slightly below, he lined up a Betty in his sights, but was forced to throttle back when, in his eagerness, he closed too rapidly. As rain pelted his windshield, he more than once thought he had lost his prey, but finally, settling in 700 feet astern and slightly to port , he opened fire. His burst started a small flame along the Betty's port wing stub. Weaving to the other side, he fired another burst. Both engines were now burning as the rest of his division joined in to make firing passes at the enemy. Engulfed in flames, the Betty pulled into a steep glide to port and exploded as it hit the water. Back aboard the *Independence,* everyone who had been hanging on Bill Henry's every word was jumping up and down for joy over the kill–the hard work of the past months had paid off. But that was only the beginning. By the time the night was over, two more Bettys would be shot down and, perhaps most importantly, none got through to attack Task Force 38. It was a good beginning. The four months of night combat ahead would have a significant impact on fast carrier operations.[10]

The next morning, Task Force 38 flew 974 sorties, following the same pattern as the first day, but all strikes were completed before noon. That afternoon, the Japanese struck back. Four torpedoes were aimed at *Franklin,* but all missed. One of her Hellcats, on final approach, noticed another attacking aircraft and took a waveoff to shoot the enemy down. Another enemy aircraft took a direct hit and skidded out of control across the flight deck. The heavy cruiser *Canberra* was hit by aircraft torpedo.

That night, *Independence* got a chance to demonstrate her offensive night capability. At 0345, a night harassing mission with four night Hellcats and four night Avengers was launched to harass airfields in southern Formosa, 140 miles from Task Force 38. Reigaryo and Einansho airfields, and the Toko and Tako seaplane bases were bombed. Three Emily flying boats, probably returning from night patrol missions, were shot down by the night Hellcats.[11]

On the third day the task force launched only 146 sorties, but B-29s from the 20th Air Force's XX Bomber Command based in China took up the slack. Japanese counterattacks crippled the light cruiser *Houston* with a torpedo and she was taken under tow. Halsey later called the three-day air battle a "knock-down, drag-out fight between carrier-based air and shore-based air."[12] The Japanese lost more than 500 aircraft, along with dozens of freighters and smaller craft. Many installations were also destroyed or damaged by the carrier strikes. Toyoda had prematurely sacrificed his air strength for the defense of the Philippines.

Streamlined Bait

The damaged *Canberra* and *Houston*, with cruisers and destroyers as escort and covered by the *Cabot* and *Cowpens*, were assigned to the newly formed Task Group 30.3, which slowly withdrew toward Ulithi on the 15th. Halsey was using the damaged cruisers of "CripDivOne" as bait, hoping to lure the Japanese fleet and both the towing and escorting ships became known as the "streamlined bait." With a speed of only four knots, the towing group was still only about seventy-five miles east of Formosa by the next day.

The 16th would be a memorable day for the *Cabot* and *Cowpens*. At 1325, two large groups of enemy planes from Formosa were picked up by the *Cabot's* radar at about seventy miles. The northern group was on a collision course with the force, while the south-ern group was about fifty miles further south on a similar course. The two divi-sions of VF-29 Hellcats from *Cabot's* combat air patrol were immediately vectored out to meet the incoming attack and all available fighters were launched as soon as possible. At 1335, the fighter direction officer on the *Cabot* told his fighters, "Your target is at 12 o'clock, five miles, look up." A minute later the call came back, "Tally ho. Many, many bogies." Lieutenant Albert J. Fecke, the flight leader, told the leader of the second division, Lieutenant M. G. Barnes, "Okay Max, you and your boys go down and take the twin-engine stuff; we'll take the fighters." The Hellcats tore into the attack group, estimated at sixty to sev-enty-five aircraft of various types, with twin-engine bombers and torpedo planes covered by fighters above, "as

though they were only outnumbered two to one." The Hellcats scattered the attackers, which, much to the relief of the intended victims of the streamlined bait, turned around and headed back to Formosa. The final tally for the *Cabot* was thirty-one enemy aircraft destroyed, most by the original eight Hellcats. Lieutenant Commander Willard E. Eder's VF-29 had started its combat tour off in spectacular fashion. Fecke and his number four man, Ensign Robert Buchanan, had each destroyed five attackers apiece, becoming "aces in a day."

In the meantime, the *Cowpens* took on the southern group, which began to orbit as soon as the northern group was attacked. Twelve Kates were forming to attack the towing group when the Hellcats from VF-22 arrived. They shot down nine, but three broke away to attack the *Houston*, which was torpe-doed again, although antiaircraft fire brought down the three remaining Kates.[14]

Not to be outdone by the fighters in all the excitement, Ensign Robert J. Maghan, a *Cabot* Avenger pilot, was on routine antisubmarine patrol over the force when a Zero being chased by two fighters crossed in front of him. Turning slightly, he lined the Japanese fighter up in his sights, opened fire, and reported, "Splash one Zeke." Later, back aboard, he shrugged his exploit off with the comment, "He got in my way."[15]

In the end, the Japanese did rise to the bait. Based on the exaggerated claims of success against Americans by the inexperienced Japanese fliers, a force of three cruisers under Vice

Admiral Shima had sailed out from Japan to wipe out the "remnants" of Halsey's fleet. As soon as Shima learned that Task Force 38, contrary to claims, was not sinking, he wisely decided to turn around. A few days later, the *Cabot* and *Cowpens* rejoined Task Force 38. Aboard *Cabot,* a message was received from the escort carrier *Hoggatt Bay,* which had been assigned to take over the escorting duties: "Message for captain. Feel just like a WAVE: have released a man to fight."[16]

With Formosa neutralized, Task Force 38 turned its attention to the isolation of the Leyte beachhead. On 15 October, Task Group 38.4 began five days of strikes against Luzon, and was joined by Task Group 38.1 and Task Group 38.2 on the 18th. On 15 October three enemy planes attacked the *Franklin.* One managed to get through her antiaircraft fire and scored a hit on the after outboard corner of the deck edge elevator, killing three men and wounding twenty-two. The next day, the aircraft of the fast carriers paid their first visit to Manila. Suspecting that the Japanese would wait for the Mindoro or Luzon landings before challenging the Americans in a fleet engagement, Halsey made plans to rotate his carrier groups through Ulithi for rest and replenishment. What he did not know was that Toyoda, having lost most of his air strength at Formosa, was forced to revise his plans.

The vanguard of the American invasion forces had been sighted off Suluan on 17 October. That same day,

Ozawa, left with carriers without carrier aircraft, recommended to Toyoda that his force be used as a sacrificial decoy to allow Vice Admiral Kurita's battleship-cruiser force based at Singapore to attack and destroy the landing force off Leyte. Ozawa's carrier decoy force would have just enough aircraft, 116, to launch a shuttle strike to Luzon and convince Halsey that this "northern force" was heading for Leyte. The real blow would come from Kurita's "center force" passing through the central Philippines via the Sibuyan Sea and the San Bernardino Strait to descend upon Leyte Gulf from the north and east of Samar Island. This force would include the super battleships *Yamato* and *Musashi,* two older battleships, six heavy cruisers, a light cruiser, and several destroyers. Two old battleships, one heavy cruiser, and destroyers commanded by Vice Admiral Nishimura, would transit the Sulu and Mindanao Seas and approach the landing area from the south via the Surigao Strait. This "southern force" would be supported by Vice Admiral Shima and his three cruisers from Japan.[17] In every respect, the plan was suicidal. The Japanese navy was laying down its life as a blue-water navy to protect the Philippine lifeline, now part of the interior defenses of Japan itself.

As these plans were put into action, Vice Admiral Onishi, commander of the land-based First Air Fleet in the Philippines, took desperate measures of his own. On 19 October, he activated the Kamikaze Corps of suicide planes.

Chapter 6
Leyte Gulf

American operations in the Philippine Islands fell under the command of General Douglas MacArthur, who relied primarily on Lieutenant General George Kenney's land-based Army air forces for air support. "MacArthur's Navy," the light naval forces of the Seventh Fleet, was commanded by Vice Admiral Thomas C. Kinkaid. As the last non-aviator to command a carrier force in World War II, Kinkaid lost the old *Hornet* in 1942. Since that time, he had little to do with aircraft carriers and would not have been at Leyte if plans had not changed. Under the revised timetable, Halsey was to support the Leyte operation, but remained under the overall command of Admiral Nimitz's Central Pacific theater. This divided command arrangement was the root cause of the problems at Leyte Gulf, especially in communications and coordination between the two fleets. Halsey acted as a free agent as Nimitz's fleet commander, and assumed virtual tactical command of Task Force 38, leaving Mitscher in the lurch. It was not

uncommon to hear Task Force 38 referred to as the Third Fleet, since the Central Pacific amphibious units were under the Southwest Pacific forces for the invasion.

Two divisions of the Sixth Army landed on Leyte Island on 20 October under air cover provided by eighteen escort carriers under the control of Rear Admiral Thomas L. "Tommy" Sprague. The escort carriers operated Hellcats, Wildcats, and Avengers and were organized into three task units known by their call sign "Taffy." "Taffy One" was commanded directly by Tommy Sprague, "Taffy Two" by Rear Admiral Felix B. Stump, and "Taffy Three" by Rear Admiral Clifton A.F. "Ziggy" Sprague. All four of the fast carrier task groups, joined by Fifth Air Force bombers, patrolled or attacked airfields. From the 20th through the 23rd, American aircraft met little resistance in the air and destroyed over a hundred enemy aircraft on the ground. The Sixth Army, moving steadily inland under this cover, hoped to gain as much ground as possible before the

Japanese launched their expected air, naval and ground counterattacks. Meanwhile, equipment and supplies piled up on the beachhead as the transports raced to unload their cargoes and clear the area before the Japanese struck back. For protection, Kinkaid counted on Rear Admiral Jesse B. Oldendorf's battle line of six old battleships, the escort carriers and their aircraft, and the aircraft of the fast carriers, which could range out to 250 miles and still be within striking distance if necessary.

Halsey began to rotate his task groups to Ulithi for rest and replenishment and McCain's Task Group 38.1 was 600 miles to the east when Halsey learned after daybreak on the 24th that two submarines had sighted Kurita's center force west of the Philippines in the Palawan passage.[1] McCain had five carriers with him: *Wasp, Hornet, Hancock, Monterey,* and *Cowpens,* while the *Bunker Hill* had retired to Ulithi on the 23rd for more fighters. This left Halsey with eleven carriers. After carrier search planes had found Kurita's center force and Nishimura's southern force, Halsey ordered his three available task groups to cover the approaches to Leyte Gulf. Sherman's Task Group 38.3 with *Essex, Lexington, Princeton,* and *Langley* would cover the northern approach and was to stay off the Polillo Islands east of Luzon. Bogan's weakened Task Group 38.2 with *Intrepid, Cabot,* and the light carrier *Independence* was off the San Bernardino Strait. Davison's Task Group 38.4 with

Franklin, Enterprise, San Jacinto, and *Belleau Wood* was to the south covering the Surigao Strait. Halsey recalled McCain's Task Group 38.1, arranging an at-sea refueling for the task group for the next morning. Halsey also ordered air strikes to begin, with Sherman and Davison to close on Bogan, who was closest to the enemy. During the morning all three task groups were heavily engaged. To the south, Davison's aircraft made ineffective attacks on Nishimura's southern force, after which Halsey ordered him to assist Bogan, whose planes were attacking Kurita's center force in the Sibuyan Sea. Meanwhile, Sherman's task group came under heavy air attack by Japanese aircraft from Luzon, and he had to break off his air strikes to concentrate on defending his task group.

Aboard the *Princeton,* eight of Lieutenant Commander Fred Bardshar's fighters from VF-27 had been assigned to CAP duty that morning. Following launch in the early morning hours, the two divisions were vectored out to intercept various snooper aircraft, which they promptly shot down. Following these intercepts, they were vectored out to engage a large group of enemy aircraft over Polillo Island in Lamon Bay, off Luzon's east coast. Leading one of the divisions, Lieutenant James A. "Red" Shirley spotted the enemy and radioed back "Talley-ho–Eighty Jap planes," then added thoughtfully, ". . . better send help." Princeton responded that they would send another dozen fighters and call on the *Essex* to help out. After the first pass tore through the enemy formation, Hellcats and various types of Japanese single-engined fighters filled the sky in a swirling mass. The *Princeton's* fighters downed thirty-six bandits, with Ensign Thomas J. Conroy claiming six, while Red Shirley, Lieutenant Carl A. Brown, Jr., and Lieutenant (jg) Eugene P. Townsend got five apiece.[2] Upon their return, some of the victorious pilots were shocked to find their ship in flames. Although more than fifty Japanese aircraft had been shot down or turned away, one got through.

The Loss of the *Princeton*

At 0928, while the *Princeton* was recovering her planes, a lookout spotted a single Japanese plane, identified as a Judy, diving out of the low clouds above the ship. The guns barely had time to open fire before the attacker, making a shallow dive from sharp on the port bow, dropped a 500-pound bomb from about 1,200 feet. It struck forward of the aft elevator just to port of the centerline and crashed through the flight deck, exploding between the hangar and the deck below. *Princeton's* skipper, Captain William H. Buracker, noted that, "from where I stood on the bridge, the hole appeared so small it seemed hardly possible that major damage had been done. I visualized slapping on a patch in a hurry and resuming operations." But the *Princeton* had been hit in her Achilles heel. The bomb had knocked out the aft firefighting system and passed right through the gas tank of a torpedo plane in the hangar. Fire spread to other aircraft as flames shot down the engineering spaces aft and back into the hangar. Smoke was intense from the start, and as it billowed aft, men were forced to jump into the sea. As she slowed and dropped out of formation, the cruiser *Reno* and the destroyers *Cassin Young*, *Gatling* and *Irwin* were ordered to stand by to assist. Destroyers began picking up survivors in the water and prepared to move to assist with fire fighting.

Soon, gasoline and ammunition from aircraft began to go off. At 1001 there was an explosion as torpedoes in the aircraft went off with a roar. The aft elevator had been blown out and the flight deck was burning, with heavy black smoke rolling off the flight and hangar decks. Four minutes later, another explosion buckled the flight deck and left holes in it. Fires raged from aft of the island to the stern and the forward elevator was blown out, with the hot smoke forcing the island to be abandoned. With each explosion there were flying fragments that caused many casualties. Before leaving the bridge, Captain Buracker told the chief engineer to secure below and the word was passed for "all hands topside!" He also turned the ship sixty degrees to the right of the wind, which was blowing at about seventeen knots, to draw the fire and smoke to the aft starboard side and leave the port catwalks clear. The *Princeton* gradually slowed until she was dead in the water. Buracker met Commander Murphy, his executive officer, on the flight deck and asked him to get the men who were not needed to fight fires, control damage, or man the guns, off the ship.

At this point Sherman, seeing the heavy explosions, sent the cruiser *Birmingham* and the destroyer *Morrison* to assist. About 1010, the *Irwin* came alongside to port, the windward side. The seriously wounded were lowered directly to her forecastle, while many men abandoned ship from lines dangling from the *Princeton*. Others jumped and swam to the *Irwin* or to life rafts thrown in the water. A few, caught between the hulls of the two ships, swam under the destroyer to be hauled up on the other side. All told, the Irwin took on between 600 and 700 survivors and also played fire hoses on the fires in the forward part of the hangar deck.

Japanese aircraft were still lurking in the area, and at 1019 *Reno* opened fire on enemy planes approaching at low altitude, shooting down a Judy and a Betty. At 1055 the *Birmingham* came alongside *Princeton* to port, the *Irwin* making way, to provide more fire hoses. Shortly afterward, the *Reno* joined her aft of the *Birmingham* on *Princeton's* port quarter, but could not stay because of the dense smoke and heat. As she drifted astern, she was damaged by the overhang at the aft end of the flight deck. The *Morrison* moved to starboard to provide two more fire hoses, but because of the velocity of the wind and the intensity of the smoke, fire fighting was effective only from the windward side of the carrier. Rolling against the *Princeton,* the *Morrison* suffered severe damage

when her superstructure struck the carrier's projecting stacks and flight deck overhang. The *Birmingham* gradually shifted aft as the fire was forced back.

Around noon the situation seemed to be improving, but enemy aircraft were still in the area and *Reno* pulled off to interpose herself between them and the stricken carrier. At 1300, with many enemy aircraft reported sixty miles away, *Reno* was directed to take charge of all the destroyers not yet occupied with fighting fires or picking up survivors and at 1314 the *Cassin Young* reported a submarine sound contact, which she went to investigate. *Morrison* was wedged between the stacks of the *Princeton* and had lost her foremast, and *Irwin* was couldn't help because one of her engines was out of commission–her condensers were fouled by floating debris. At 1330, with the fires seemingly under control and within a few minutes of being put out, more bogies were reported. The *Birmingham* and the *Morrison*, which finally disentangled herself a few minutes later, left to rejoin the screen. The enemy, a lone Zero, was chased off, but in the meantime the fires built up again.

The *Birmingham* again returned to fight the fires and directed the *Reno* to take the *Princeton* under tow, but the *Reno,* having no tow line, had to set about making one. The seas had picked and the wind increased to twenty knots. At 1524, as the *Birmingham* slowly worked her way into position, the *Princeton's* bomb and torpedo storage went off in a volcanic explosion that blew off the major part of her stern and the aft section of the flight deck, scattering lethal fragments and debris over a wide area. Practically all left aboard were killed or injured. As Captain Buracker remembered, "Captain Hoskins, the prospective commanding officer, was standing with me amidships on the port side. When the blast came, we all started crawling and running forward for protection. Someone noticed that Captain Hoskins couldn't move. Going back, I saw that his right foot was hanging by a shred. He had already applied a tourniquet to his leg, stopping the flow of blood. In the lull which followed the blast, Commander R.O. Sala, our senior medical officer, administered first aid and amputated the captain's foot. Then Captain Hoskins said, "Don't worry about me . . . I hope you save her . . . You deserve to!"

Aboard the *Birmingham* the carnage was incredible. Big chunks of debris and shrapnel had swept her decks, crowded with men preparing to assist the *Princeton*. The *Birmingham* suffered far more casualties than on the *Princeton*–229 dead and 420 injured. Among the injured was her commanding officer, Captain Thomas B. Inglis. The *Reno* was ordered to take over from the ravaged *Birmingham*, which had to back clear after the explosion. With no way of fighting the fires, the order was given to abandon ship. All available boats were sent to pick up survivors. Captain Buracker was the last to leave, at about 1640. As he arrived aboard the *Reno*, a message was received from Sherman: "Destroy *Princeton*. Remaining

ships to rejoin task group." The *Irwin* began firing torpedoes, then opened fire with her five-inch guns, seemingly to little effect. The *Reno* took over, firing two torpedoes at *Princeton*. At 1749, a tremendous explosion lit up the darkening sky. The carrier's forward section was never seen again; the after section, screws up, appeared momentarily in the smoke before it too disappeared. A minute later there was nothing left.[3]

As the drama aboard the *Princeton* was being played out, several of her aircraft still aloft at the time of the attack became orphans. Nine VF-27 Hellcats had to find other carriers to land aboard. Lieutenant Carl Brown had a harrowing experience. As he recalled,

"I don't know how long the fight lasted. It was a long one–my guess is three to five minutes. I finished the fight with four Zekes on my tail arguing about who'd kill me. I used my last ditch maneuver –shove the stick forward as hard as I can with the throttle two-blocked and pitch full low. Nobody can follow that and shoot, so you gain at least a few seconds to think. As soon as I was headed straight down, I put the stick hard to the right for a spiral because the Zero couldn't turn well to the right at high speed. I lost them. *Princeton* was hit and the 'Lex' and *Langley* refused to take me aboard because I had too much damage and might foul their deck. My instrument panel was well shot up, one fuel line in the cockpit was cut, and I had two to four inches of gas in the bottom of the bird. My port elevator hardly existed, and my tailhook was jammed, and I couldn't get it out with my emergency extension. I had two small shrapnel wounds in my left leg, but that was minor. I asked 'Hatchet' (Princeton), who was still on the air although hit and burning, to tell the lead destroyer that I was going to ditch in front of him and to please pick me up. Hatchet said he'd pass the word. At that time Essex came on the air and said, 'Hatchet 31, if you'll land immediately, we'll take you.' You can imagine my relief. I lowered my gear with the emergency bottle–had no hydraulics, so I wouldn't have flaps for landing, nor an airspeed indicator (shot out), cowl flaps or hook. The Essex captain had compassion and guts. I made a 'British' approach from 500 feet. The LSO held a 'roger' on me till I was at the ramp when he gave me a fast , a high dip, and a cut. I had tested my controls and couldn't get the stick all the way back. I took the cut and snapped the stick as far as it would go. My tail hit the ramp hard, knocked the hook out, and I caught the first wire."

Brown, whose Hellcat had 164 holes in it, had flown his final combat mission.[4] After the stray Hellcats from VF-27 had recovered aboard other carriers, their distinctive engine cowl markings, which featured bloodshot eyes and a mouth with large fangs dripping blood, were soon painted over–the Navy took a dim view of such highly individualistic insignia, unlike its sister service, the Army, whose combat aircraft often sported outlandish nose art.

While Sherman continued to beat off fresh attacks, Halsey turned his full attention to the center force, concluding that Kinkaid could deal with the oncoming Japanese southern force, which would be within gun range of Oldendorf's old battleships around midnight. The battle in the Sibuyan Sea lasted from around 1030 to 1400. The striking aircraft met almost no air opposition, since Japanese commanders considered the attack on Sherman's task group to be more important than air cover for Kurita. The 72,000-ton super battleship Musashi, repeatedly hit by bombs and torpedoes, fell behind, sinking. She retired and, later in the early evening, rolled over and sank. Kurita's other ships sustained damage as well, but he still had four battleships, six heavy cruisers, and other escort ships. At around 1400, he turned westward in apparent retreat.

The returning aviators were jubilant and their exaggerated claims led Halsey to believe that the center force no longer represented a serious threat to the Leyte beachhead. Still, Halsey did not discount the possibility that the center force would turn eastward again, and he sent a preparatory battle plan to his task commanders to cover the possibility. Four of his six battleships, two heavy and three light cruisers, and fourteen destroyers would form Task Force 34 under Vice Admiral "Ching" Lee as Commander Battle Line. He later amended the plan by voice radio message to his subordinate commanders: "If the enemy sorties, TF 34 will be formed when directed by me." By accident, Kinkaid had received the first message, but had no way of intercepting the clarification message. He therefore assumed that the Task Force 34 battle line was formed and guarding the San Bernardino Strait. Admiral King in Washington and Nimitz at CincPac headquarters had also received the first message and assumed that Task Force 34 had been formed and was guarding the San Bernardino Strait.

With the Surigao and San Bernardino Straits supposedly covered, the next question on Halsey's mind was the location of the Japanese carriers. Sherman had permission from Mitscher to search to the northeast, and at 1405 launched a search in that direction. Ozawa, for his part, did everything he could think of to get noticed, including sending fake radio messages, sending out air searches, and launching a 76 plane strike against Sherman's task group. The strike was set upon by Sherman's Hellcats and the task group antiaircraft fire, but the Americans thought this was another land-based attack like the one that had bombed the

Princeton. Sherman's searching Helldivers finally located the northern force at 1640, only 190 miles away. After weighing various factors with his advisors, Halsey reasoned that the center force might turn eastward again if he went north to get the Japanese carriers, but felt it unlikely that the center force would enter Leyte Gulf until late in the morning. He could run north to knock off the carriers, then turn south to help drive off Kurita. Besides, Oldendorf should have finished with the southern force by then and be available to assist if needed. Putting his finger on the plot of the northern force, he declared, "We will run north at top speed and put those carriers out for keeps."

The *Independence* launched two night Avengers at 1715 to shadow the Japanese main battle force heading east through the Sibuyan Sea. Relieved by two more Avengers about 1925, the enemy force was covered until about 2215, when the planes were recalled. At the time, the enemy was heading northeast between Burias and Ticao Islands, about sixty miles from San Bernardino Strait. The shadowing planes landed shortly before midnight.

At 1950, Halsey radioed Kinkaid at Leyte: "Central force heavily damaged according to strike reports. Am proceeding north with three groups to attack carrier forces at dawn."Sixteen minutes later, Halsey received a report from an *Independence* night Hellcat that the center force had been sighted in the Sibuyan Sea heading for the San Bernardino Strait at twelve knots. This still did not stop Halsey. After passing on the contact report to Kinkaid,

Halsey ordered Bogan's and Davison's task groups to join Sherman and ordered McCain to stop refueling and return. Kinkaid still thought Task Force 34 was guarding the San Bernardino Strait, but did not question that Halsey was leaving it apparently without air cover. Mitscher, also left in the dark, had assumed that the battle line would be formed when Task Force 38 headed north and did not learn that all the battleships were to accompany the carriers north until midnight, when all the task groups rendezvoused off Luzon. Commodore Burke and Commander Jimmy Flatley, Mitscher's new operations officer, both urged Mitscher to recommend to Halsey that he send the battleships back to the San Bernardino Strait with Bogan's task group to provide air support. Mitscher, still smarting from the rebuff given by Spruance at his suggestions off Saipan, told Flatley: "If he wants my advice he'll ask for it." Ching Lee, Halsey's battleship commander, also told him that the northern force was a decoy, but was ignored. The run north was not really a run. As soon as Bogan and Davison, moving at twenty-five knots, had joined on Sherman, the task force slowed down to sixteen knots. At midnight, Halsey turned over tactical command to Mitscher, who promptly increased the speed to twenty knots.

Halsey ordered a 0100 night search from *Independence*, over Mitscher's protest that it would only alert the Japanese and, about 0100, five Avengers were launched to search

350-mile sectors to the north, for the enemy carrier force reported to be 180-200 miles east of the northern tip of Luzon. These units were found by two of the searching Avengers about 125 miles north of Task Group 38.2 and shadowed until dawn, when they were attacked by all three Task Groups. At 0205, the radar-equipped Hellcats sighted Japanese ships only eighty miles north of the task force. That meant that a night surface action would take place around 0430. Halsey ordered Lee to form the battle line, and more time was lost as Lee slowly and carefully pulled his battleships out of the formation. Halsey again slowed down the task force when he learned that Oldendorf was engaging the southern force in the Surigao Strait. As it turned out, the Japanese ships only eighty miles away were the *Ise* and *Hyuga*, hermaphrodite battleships (old battleships with partial flight decks added to their after superstructures), under the command of Rear Admiral Matsuda.[5] Matsuda's battleships formed the detached van of Ozawa's force, and he was indeed seeking a night surface engagement to attract Halsey north. Ironically, Matsuda, seeing lightning flashes to the south, mistook these for land-based air attacks on Halsey's forces. On the strength of Matsuda's erroneous report, Ozawa ordered the battleships to rejoin the carriers. When no surface battle materialized at 0430, Mitscher assumed incorrectly that the search aircraft had scared the Japanese off. He could only arm his bombers and launch long-range search-strikes at first light.

Meanwhile, Kinkaid was awaiting two night battles. The one in the Surigao Strait began at 2230 on 24 October as PT boats engaged Nishimura's force and reached its peak around 0400 the next day, with the almost complete annihilation of Nishimura's ships by Oldendorf's battle line "capping the T." This was a classic surface engagement maneuver of the type studied by every battleship sailor since Japanese Admiral Togo used it to crush the Imperial Russian Navy at Tsushima Strait in 1905. Shima, following behind Nishimura, took one look at the destruction and wisely turned around, escaping with his force largely intact.

At the recommendation of Captain Dick Whitehead, the air support coordinator assigned to Kinkaid on loan from the Central Pacific forces, the escort carriers prepared two fighter-torpedo strikes for the dawn mop-up. One was for the Surigao Strait, the other for any stray ships that might have slipped past Lee's battle line in the expected second night battle, although Kinkaid had heard nothing further about the northern or center forces. PBY Catalina seaplanes would conduct night searches to the north. As the southern force was being pounded to pieces, Kinkaid held a staff meeting to "check for errors of commission or of omission," but no one could think of anything. After the meeting adjourned around 0400, Kinkaid's operations officer, Captain Richard H. Cruzen, returned and said, "Admiral, I can think of only one other thing. We have never directly asked Halsey if Task Force 34 is guarding San

Bernardino." Kinkaid agreed and at 0412 sent a message to Halsey asking for confirmation of that fact. Halsey received the message at 0648 and replied in the negative at 0705, too late for Kinkaid to do anything about it. After the old battleships had mauled Nishimura's ships, Oldendorf had entered the Surigao Strait looking for cripples. By dawn, Oldendorf's battle force was sixty-five miles from the Leyte beachhead.

At daybreak on 25 October, the battle for Leyte Gulf was about to heat up. The PBY searches had turned up nothing of interest and the search flight for the northern sector was just being launched at 0645, when without any warning, the escort carriers off Samar spotted the center force on the horizon. Within fifteen minutes, 18.1-inch shells from the super battleship *Yamato* were dropping in among the hapless escort carriers of "Ziggy" Sprague's Taffy Three. Taffy Three turned away from the advancing Japanese, laying smoke and calling for help. At 0707, Kinkaid radioed in plain language to Halsey that his ships were under heavy attack by major Japanese surface units. This message, like others in the divided communications setup, took more than an hour to be delivered.

Meanwhile, Mitscher had launched his searches north and then swung them eastward followed by deckload strikes. Ozawa was 190 miles northeast of Task Force 38 and steaming south when his radar picked up Mitscher's search aircraft. He turned away and managed to open the distance by another forty miles before being spotted at 0710. The attack by Task Force 38 began with ten deckload strikes of Mitscher's orbiting planes, which had been waiting for the search aircraft to make contact. First on the scene was Air Group 15 from *Essex* and Commander David McCampbell, the air group commander, became target coordinator.[6] Ozawa launched his last twenty-nine planes. The four Japanese carriers were sitting ducks. Unlike the hurried twilight attack of the Battle of the Philippine Sea, the morning attack was well executed and systematic. The light carrier *Chitose* went down under a heavy bombing attack at 0937. A torpedo struck Ozawa's flagship, *Zuikaku,* forcing him to shift his flag to a cruiser.

After recovery of the first strike, Task Group 38.2, which had steamed 200 miles north during the night, headed south to intercept the main enemy force. A second bombing strike set the *Chiyoda* afire, and she was eventually abandoned. Afternoon strikes by *Lexington's* Air Group 19 and *Langley's* Air Group 44 finished off two of the carriers. The *Zuikaku,* veteran of the Pearl Harbor attack, was repeatedly bombed and torpedoed until she sank at 1414. The light carrier *Zuiho* was continually hit until she sank at 1526. Cruiser fire sank the abandoned *Chiyoda* at 1655. The old hermaphrodite battleships *Ise* and *Hyuga* managed to survive by skillful maneuvering and intense antiaircraft fire.

Meanwhile, the escort carriers battled for their lives and pleaded for help. Although Halsey had received Kinkaid's plea at 0822, he felt that Kinkaid could handle the situation with the forces at his disposal. As he stated later, "I figured that the eighteen little carriers had enough planes to protect themselves until Oldendorf could bring up his heavy ships."[7] The little carriers tried their best. Dick Whitehead recalled the strike planes going after the southern force cripples, and these attacked Kurita, but the other aircraft were armed for combat air patrol, anti-submarine patrol, and ground support operations. Without torpedoes and heavy bombs, these planes could only use what they had and many continued to make dummy runs to divert Japanese fire away from the escort carriers. The destroyers and destroyer escorts valiantly attacked the Japanese with torpedoes and 5-inch gunfire. Oldendorf was still three hours away and the Army bombers over the Visayas could not be contacted. Kinkaid and Ziggy Sprague pleaded by radio with Halsey to send the fast carriers and the fast battleships to save them from the continual pounding.

Halsey had all this information by 0930, but was not deterred. He did, however, order McCain's Task Group 38.1 to the rescue, although McCain's ships were more than 300 miles from Leyte, a long flight for the carrier aircraft. Halsey needed several more hours to finish the northern force with his carriers and battleships. In desperation, Kinkaid called for Lee's Task Force 34 in plain language, but Halsey didn't turn around. Kinkaid realized at last that Task Force 34 was not guarding the San Bernardino Strait, but neither Admiral King in Washington nor Admiral Nimitz at CincPac headquarters knew its whereabouts. Nimitz fired off a coded message to Halsey asking for the location of Task Force 34. Not all of the normal cryptographer's "padding" was removed, and Halsey received the message as: "From CINC-PAC. Where is, rpt, where is TF 34. The world wonders."[8] Kinkaid's communicators correctly removed the padding at both ends of the message, but Halsey's signalman did not, removing only the first phrase. Halsey received this message at 1000 and his first response was immediate. Losing his temper at this obvious criticism from Nimitz, he threw his cap to the deck and began swearing until he could be calmed down by his chief of staff, Rear Admiral Robert B. "Mick" Carney. The Nimitz message prodded Halsey into taking action, but not before another hour had been lost while he thought things over. At 1055, he ordered the entire battle line south. Two battleships under Rear Admiral Oscar Badger and covered by Bogan's Task Group 38.2 were to charge ahead at 28 knots, but Bogan's destroyers needed refueling first. Halsey then informed Nimitz of his decision: "Task Force 34 with me engaging carrier force. Am now proceeding with Task Group 38.2 and all fast BB to reinforce Kinkaid. . ." Halsey wanted all or nothing. He took all the battleships with him, leaving nothing behind to finish off the *Ise* and *Hyuga*. In the end, by not dividing his battleships, Halsey allowed *Ise* and *Hyuga* to escape, and by waiting until 1055 to turn south, he allowed Kurita to escape

as well.

Although Ozawa had succeeded in luring Halsey away, Kurita did not capitalize on the opportunity. The fierce air and destroyer attacks had cost him three heavy cruisers, and at 0911 he ordered his ships to break off their pursuit of the escort carriers, intending to regroup his scattered forces before continuing into Leyte Gulf. He believed he had engaged and sunk several carriers from Task Force 38, although he had sunk one escort carrier, the *Gambier Bay,* and damaged others. After receiving a false contact report that had enemy carriers closing in from the sea, and fearing land-based American air strikes, Kurita decided at 1230 to clear Leyte Gulf.[9] The action off Samar had ended. No American carriers appeared and Kurita, low on fuel, turned for the San Bernardino Strait and home. Just after 1300, as the center force retired, McCain's carriers attacked from far to the east, but did little damage.

At around 2000 that night, Halsey ordered six night Avengers launched from the *Independence.* At 2145, one of these spotted fifteen ships passing along the coast off Samar and into the San Bernardino Strait. This plane and its relief shadowed the Japanese force until 0230 on the 26th, when contact was lost in severe storms. The night carrier men convinced Halsey to let them have a crack at Kurita, and Halsey agreed at 0300, but not before a severe thunderstorm had caused the aircraft shadowing the center force to lose contact. Fifteen minutes after Halsey gave the order, four Avengers with torpedoes and five Hellcats with bombs were launched for a night attack. Equipment failures and poor weather prevented the night Avengers from reaching the target area and the Hellcats, although they had reached the area, could not locate the enemy force because of the limitations of their search radars. McCain and Bogan later launched strikes over the Sibuyan Sea at dawn, with disappointing results – one light cruiser sunk and one heavy cruiser damaged.[10]

The Americans had won the largest naval battle in history. Against American losses of the light carrier *Princeton,* two escort carriers, two destroyers and one destroyer escort, the Japanese lost forty-five percent of all ships engaged, a total of three battleships, one heavy carrier, three light carriers, six heavy cruisers, four light cruisers and nine destroyers. After the battle, Kurita was blamed for his failure to complete the destruction of the American ships in Leyte Gulf, and was banished in December 1944 to the presidency of the Japanese Naval Academy. Ozawa became a hero for successfully completing his part in the battle, and in May 1945 relieved Toyoda as commander of the Combined Fleet, although he was not promoted to full admiral.[11]

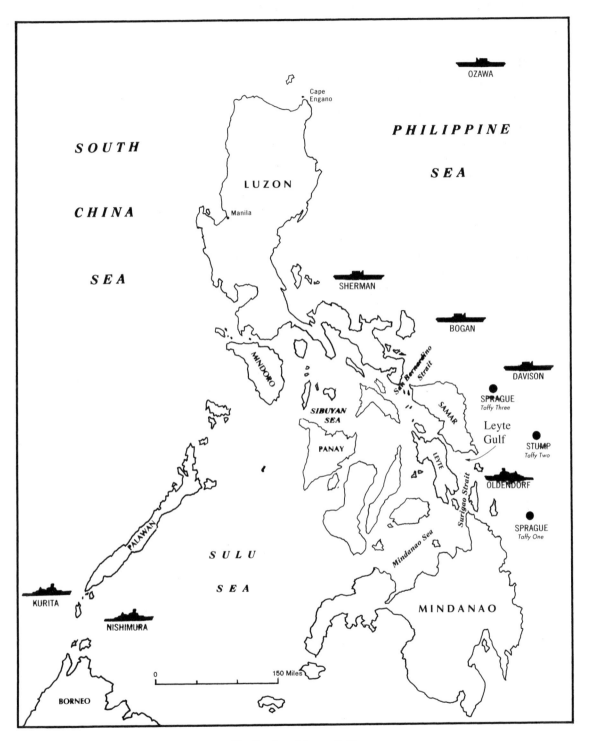

The Battle of Leyte Gulf

Langley *rolling heavily during a Pacific storm. The original photograph was dated 13 January 1945, but has been captioned elsewhere as having been taken during the 18 December 1944 typhoon.*

The Langley *entering Ulithi anchorage with Task Group 38.3, December 1944.*

The Langley *in French service as the* La Fayette, *probably at Toulon, September 1951*

The Bataan *off the Philadelphia Navy Yard, March 1944.*

The Langley enterning Ulithi anchorage with Task Group 38.3, December 1944.

A Japanese Judy passes near the Bataan during an unsuccessful dive-bombing run on Task Force 58, while the task force was operation off Japan on 20 March 1945.

The Bataan at sea in January 1952, with VMF-312 aboard, as she began working up for her second Korean War cruise.

The Cabot *underway, July 1945.*

*The Cabot flies a "homward bound"
pennant as she departs the Western
Pacific for overhaul run in
San Francisco, 13 April 1945.
By tradition, naval ships that have
been away from port for a year or
more make a homeward bound
pennant to fly from the mainmast
when they leave their foreign port.*

*The bridge of the Cabot, showing her "Mohawk"
insignia. Cabot's first commanding officer,
Captain Malcolm F. Schoeffel coined the ship's
slogan: "Up Mohawks, At Em" "Mohawk" was
her radio call sign at the time.*

Cabot-Dedalo *NAH: The* ex-USS Cabot/SNS Dedalo *in what is literally the last ditch in Brownsville, Texas before the shipbreakers began to cut her up for scrap, November 2000. Photo credit: Naval Historical Center / Frank Thompson.*

Arming a TBM wuth a torpedo aboard the San Jacinto, *25 October 1944.*

A TMB gets the take-off signal aboard the San Jacinto, *May 1944.*

Future president George H.W. Bush in the cockpit of his Avenger probably mid-1944. This photograph was part of a montage of VT-51 squadron officers and senior officers of San Jacinto.

San Jacinto *flies her Texas battle flag during the Marianas, "Turkey Shoot," 19 June 1944.*

The San Jacinto *underway off the East Coast, January 1944, with an SNJ Texan training plane parked on her flight deck.*

The Saipan *underway, entering New York Harbor, April 1948.*

The Saipan *was converted to a communications relay ship and renamed the* Arlington.
She is seen underway probably sometime in 1967.

The Wright *underway, May 1947*

The Wright, *as converted to a command and control ship, June 1963*

Chapter 7
Kamikaze

While Kurita pounded the escort carriers on the morning of 25 October 1944, Admiral Onishi, commander of land-based naval aviation in the Philippines, realized what was at stake and ordered his kamikazes to make their first organized attack on the American navy. Several escort carriers were attacked that morning. The first bomb-laden Zero hit the *Kitkun Bay,* causing considerable damage. Two others dived on the *Fanshaw Bay,* but were shot down by antiaircraft fire, while others attacked the *White Plains.* One of the kamikazes damaged by antiaircraft fire turned and crashed into the *St. Lo.* In little more than thirty minutes, the *St. Lo* sank, with the loss of about a hundred men. It was a taste of the future for the fast carriers.

A few days prior to their debut over Leyte Gulf, Onishi proposed to his First Air Fleet staff that suicide attacks, which had occurred on an individual basis before, be organized as an official operation. Kamikaze means "Divine Wind," a reference to the legendary typhoon that saved Japan from a

Mongol invasion in the 13th century. The pilots of the Kamikaze Corps were all volunteers and generally less experienced flyers; the expert aviators served as teachers and escort pilots. Some of the volunteers were motivated by Japanese religious and military traditions of self sacrifice; others were resigned to die in combat anyway and welcomed the opportunity to die gloriously by sinking an enemy warship. The kamikazes proved frighteningly effective. In the Philippines, 424 kamikazes destroyed sixteen ships and damaged eighty others.

Leyte Follow-up Operations

The hectic pace of operations left Task Force 38 at the end of its endurance. By 26 October, the fast carriers were almost out of ammunition and food, which unlike fuel, could not be replenished at sea at this point in the war. Even so, the fast carriers stayed on for a few more days covering Leyte and attacking targets in the Philippines. Pilot fatigue had become chronic. When

Halsey rotated McCain's Task Group 38.1 and Sherman's Task Group 38.3 to Ulithi for replacement air groups, two of the returning air groups had only served five of the required six months in a combat zone. ComAirPac ordered emergency replacement air groups to Manus and Guam, but these would not arrive before December. Naturally, the ships' crews did not get to rotate and remained aboard for the duration.

The *Independence* scored an unusual intercept of a Japanese snooper aircraft on the night of the 27th. These aircraft were often Mavis or Emily flying boats, and had been intercepted on the 15th and 24th, usually relatively near the task force, since the night carrier doctrine at the time prohibited sending interceptors out more than sixty miles. Special permission had been granted this time to vector a night Hellcat out to a distant bogey. By using radar data from the *Intrepid's* SM height-finding radar, the fighter was placed three and a half miles behind a Mavis, at exactly the right altitude, eighty miles from the task force. Closing to within 150 feet, the pilot brought the Mavis down with a three-second burst of fire.[1]

Although control of air operations passed to the Army on 27 October, General Kenney could get only one group of P-38 Lightnings in operation from the rain-soaked airfields on Leyte. These fighters, used for combat air patrol over Leyte, did not provide close air support for the ground troops. Continuing Japanese air raids caused MacArthur to request that both the fast carriers and the escort carriers stay on for a while longer. Bogan's Task Group 38.2 and Davison's Task Group 38.4 were ordered to strike Visayan and Luzon targets, which were hit 28-30

October. After successfully warding off a Japanese submarine attack, these task groups were hit hard by the kamikazes. Task Group 38.2 hit Luzon on the 29th and around mid-day the Japanese were out looking for the task group. The *Intrepid* took a lesser hit when a kamikaze struck one of her portside 20mm gun mounts, killing ten men, but she soon resumed flight operations. Later that afternoon, several small raids began closing the task group, so fighters were kept airborne as a precaution. While landing in a heavy rain squall, one of *Cabot's* fighters crashed into the catwalk on the starboard side and burst into flames. The fire was quickly put out, but one officer on the flight deck died, and the pilot died shortly afterward from severe burns.[2]

The next day was Task Group 38.4's turn. Around noon, enemy aircraft were spotted approaching the task group. The *Franklin* had quickly eliminated two of the five planes attacking her, but the remaining three continued to bore in through the thick antiaircraft fire. One plane missed and splashed near the starboard side, but another crashed into *Franklin's* flight deck, setting the deck afire. A fighter nearby fell through the damaged flight deck to the hangar deck below, starting more fires. The third aircraft slipped to within thirty feet of the *Franklin* before splattering into the aft end of the *Belleau Wood's* flight deck. Aboard *Franklin*, fifty-six died and sixty were wounded, but all fires were under control within two hours.[3] The *Franklin* returned to Ulithi for temporary repairs before sailing for the West Coast. She would not be back in action until March 1945. Meanwhile on the *Belleau Wood* ammunition and depth charges exploded and fires raged, fed by aviation gasoline from smashed aircraft. By the time the fires were under control, ninety-two men had died. *Belleau Wood* limped back to Ulithi, where it was determined that the damage was too severe to repair in the forward area. She went on to Hunters Point Naval Shipyard in San Francisco, where she underwent repairs until January 1945.[4]

Davison's task group was released to head for Ulithi along with the escort carrier groups on 29-30 October. The Fifth Air Force was scheduled to fly in a group of medium bombers a week later, but rain had delayed airfield construction so much that they were delayed until December. At the end of the month only Bogan's three carriers and a handful of Army P-38s and P-61 night fighters were left to cover Leyte.

Back at Ulithi, a bone-tired Mitscher turned command of Task Force 38 over to Vice Admiral McCain. On 31 October Rear Admiral Montgomery took over Task Group 38.1.[5] The slender air defenses over Leyte had invited a Japanese counterattack, which struck 1 November. The attack, combined with decoy reports of the movement Kurita's and Shima's forces, caused American commanders to send Sherman's Task Group 38.3 back to join Bogan's Task Group 38.2 in protecting shipping off Leyte, with Montgomery's Task Group 38.1 soon following suit. The three task groups attacked Japanese airfields on Luzon on 5 and 6 November, taking the Japanese by surprise. The Japanese lost more than 400 planes, most of them on the ground. Halsey lost twenty-five carrier aircraft. The *Lexington* took a kamikaze hit when a group of kamikazes that had avoided the combat air patrols by hiding in cloud cover dived on the carriers. One splashed 1,000 yards off the Lex's starboard beam, but another, although hit repeatedly, crashed into the signal bridge on the island. Within twenty minutes, all fires were under control and flight operations resumed, but forty-seven men were killed and 127 wounded.[6] Vice Admiral McCain turned command of Task Force 38 over to Rear Admiral Sherman, his senior carrier division commander, and shifted his flag from the *Lexington* to the *Wasp*. McCain returned to Ulithi aboard *Wasp* when she retired to change air groups, with Sherman remaining in command until 13 November.

On 11 November, a strike of several hundred carrier planes attacked a convoy carrying 10,000 Japanese troops to Leyte, sinking five transports and four escorting destroyers. Halsey wanted to go after the survivors of the Leyte Gulf battle at Brunei Bay in Borneo or even strike Tokyo, but MacArthur decided that the "support of the fast carriers (was) essential" to the Sixth Army, and Task Force 38 stayed on, attacking Luzon airfields and shipping throughout November. On the 13th and 14th, the fast carriers sank a light cruiser and five destroyers plus seven merchant ships, destroying more than seventy-five planes. Five days later they returned to shoot up more aircraft on the ground.

The *Independence* spent November engaged mainly in providing dusk, night, and dawn combat air patrols for the task force, but did participate in the Luzon strikes. Night harassing strikes were sent out in the early morning hours of 6 and 19 November to enemy airfields. On the 19th, two night

Hellcats sent out to heckle Aparri encountered five Bettys on a reciprocal course about halfway to the target, probably on their way to attack the task force. Two Bettys, and probably a third were shot down, and the night Hellcats were then ordered back to the carrier. As a later operational analysis noted: "The circumstances of this interception must have been quite mystifying to the enemy."[7]

Sherman's Task Group 38.3 eventually returned to Ulithi, where it was joined by Davison's Task Group 38.4 which had tried unsuccessfully to use napalm on bypassed Yap on 22 November. A final strike on Luzon by Montgomery's Task Group 38.1 and Bogan's Task Group 38.2 on 25 November marked the end of fast carrier operations in support of Leyte. The bombing aircraft destroyed several enemy planes and ships, including a heavy cruiser, but the kamikazes struck back.

As the first strike of the afternoon was being launched, enemy aircraft were reported on radar approaching Task Group 38.2. The carriers opened up on a Judy diving for the *Hancock*. The plane released a bomb from low altitude, which exploded as a near miss on her port beam. The attacker exploded only 300 feet from the forward end of the flight deck, showering the *Hancock* with debris that started a fire that was quickly extinguished. At nearly the same time, two Zekes approached at low altitude. One splashed in flames, but the other made a climbing roll and plowed into the *Intrepid* on the port side abeam of the island. Smoke and flame enveloped the *Intrepid*, but the fires were put out in about ten minutes.

At 1254, a Zeke dived on the *Cabot* from astern, aiming for the island. As every gun was brought to bear, pieces of the kamikaze began flying off. As it burst into flame, it became a matter of not if it would hit, but *where.* Passing the island with less than six feet to spare, the Zeke's left wing dropped and sliced into a TBM sitting on the catapult as it was turning up to launch. The Zeke grazed the Avenger's cowling and knocked off its propeller without moving it. The kamikaze hit the flight deck adjacent to the 20mm guns on the port side, where its bomb exploded. The entire 20mm platform was carried away and two 40mm mounts were knocked out. A minute after the first attack, another Zeke was taken under fire from the starboard quarter. Hit hard and hit often, this one spun into the sea. Within moments, another Zeke began its dive, apparently aiming for the same spot that the first had hit. Hit repeatedly and burning, apparently out of control, the third kamikaze did a half-roll to the right as it headed for the water. At the last moment, it swung back to the left and hit the port blister near the waterline. The plane and its bomb exploded, showering the port side from amidships aft with shrapnel and burning debris.

The flight deck and damage control crews worked quickly to put out the fires and patch the flight deck. Flight operations were resumed, although the catapult was out of commission. Four men had been killed instantly, three died shortly afterward as a result of wounds, and two officers and twenty-six men were missing. Many others were injured. The *Cabot* carried on, burying her dead at sea the next morning. She would undergo repairs at Ulithi when the task group returned there.[8]

Over in Task Group 38.3, the *Essex* was damaged when a lone kamikaze made it though the antiaircraft fire, skimmed the flight deck, and crashed into the port side. Fifteen men were killed and forty-four wounded, but less than thirty minutes later, the fires had been put out and the flight deck was operational.

Countering the Kamikaze Threat

The damage done by the kamikazes caused the cancellation of a strike on the Visayas scheduled for 26 November. Task Force 38 returned to Ulithi while the Army air forces assumed responsibility for Leyte's defense.[9] Halsey insisted that the carriers not be exposed in such routine operations as the Philippines support strikes until better defenses could be devised. The immediate need for more fighters aboard the fast carriers led to the Marines being assigned to the *Essex*-class carriers in early December. Vice Admiral McCain, with his operations officer Commander John S. "Jimmy" Thach and the rest of the fast carrier staff, developed defensive tactics to best use these fighters in countering the kamikaze threat.

At the advice of Jocko Clark, who had returned from leave in mid-November, McCain enlarged the task group cruising formations horizontally by stationing radar picket ships, called "Tomcats," sixty miles ahead of the carriers. McCain also started several new combat air patrols: JACKCAP, two to four fighters flying at low altitude in each of the four quadrants; DADCAP, patrols at all altitudes launched at dawn and relieved at dusk by the BAT-CAP of night fighters; RAPCAP radar picket planes; and SCOCAP scouting line planes stationed over the Tomcat radar picket destroyers. Returning air strikes would circle over the Tomcats to be "deloused", and any aircraft not making the identifying turn would be picked off by the defending fighters. Commander Thach also developed the "Three Strike" system, whereby one fighter patrol would remain over an enemy airfield while a second prepared to take off and a third was either on its way to or from the target or was being readied for another strike. The constant patrol would be continued at night by heckling night fighters flying over enemy airfields to discourage the Japanese from launching any night attacks. These measures were part of what McCain called his "Big Blue Blanket" for protecting the carrier task force.

All these techniques were practiced in simulated "Moosetrap" training strikes during maneuvers off Ulithi in late November and early December 1944. The first test of the new tactics would be the landings on Mindoro scheduled for 5 December. Task Force 38, reduced to three day carrier task groups because of the damage done in November by the kamikazes, had departed from Ulithi on 1 December, but was recalled that afternoon when the landings were postponed for ten days. Leyte had been bearing the brunt of Japanese air and kamikaze attacks and Army air forces had not eliminated Japanese air opposition in the central Philippines, a necessary precondition to successful landings. The Luzon landings also changed from 20 December to 9 January 1945.

At the conclusion of the Leyte operations, command changes were made as Montgomery was replaced by Rear Admiral Tommy Sprague, still recovering from the ordeal off Samar, and Halsey's three task groups of four day carriers each were supported by a night carrier task group. The *Enterprise,* which spent December converting to a night carrier, later joined the *Independence* under Rear Admiral Matt Gardner. Operating the night carriers as a separate task group allowed the crews of the day carriers to get some sleep.[10]

Six escort carriers of the newly created Escort Carrier Force Pacific Fleet supported the 15 December Mindoro landings, allowing the fast carriers to strike at strategic targets.[11] Task Force 38 left Ulithi on 10-11 December to strike at targets on Luzon while Army air forces covered all targets south of Manila. To keep the fighters on Luzon grounded, Task Force 38 continuously blanketed Luzon day and night from the 14th through the 16th of December, destroying more than 200 enemy aircraft in the process. Only twenty-seven carrier aircraft were lost, and most of the airmen shot down made contact with friendly Filipinos. Lieutenant (jg) Walter D. Bishop, a five-kill ace from *Cabot's* VF-29, was not so fortunate. On the first day of strikes, he bailed out after surviving a mid-air collision over Subic Bay. He was seen on the ground the next day, but mysteriously disappeared before he could be rescued.[12] Task Force 38 then withdrew to refuel before resuming air strikes in support of the Seventh Fleet landings on Mindoro. While searching for a fueling rendezvous in heavy weather on the night of 17-18 December, the task force blundered into what turned out to be a typhoon.

Halsey's Typhoon

As Halsey maneuvered Task Force 38 in the worsening weather, he did not even consider it to be a typhoon until noon on the 18th when he finally canceled the attempted refueling and strikes planned for Luzon. The task force headed south into a storm blowing east to west. Planes on the carriers broke their lashings and careened around. Others were lost overboard as the carriers plunged wildly into the mountainous waves. Being low on fuel and without enough ballast to keep them steady, the destroyers were in the greatest danger. Three of them capsized and sank with nearly all hands–almost 800 men–lost. In Montgomery's Task Group 38.1, the *Cowpens* and *Monterey* had the worst of it.

As the winds picked up that morning, the *Monterey* began to roll violently. Around nine, five fighters spotted aft on the flight deck broke loose and went over the side. Shortly afterward, another plane on the hangar deck broke loose and was almost immediately enveloped in flames. Within a few minutes burning gasoline had spread the fire to the second and third decks. Worse still, fire penetrated the ventilation intakes to the engineering spaces, the smoke and fumes forcing these spaces to be all but completely abandoned. Skeleton crews with rescue breathing gear kept the pumps and generators going, however, which undoubtedly saved the ship. After Captain Ingersoll turned the ship to a new course to ride out the wind and waves more easily, all engines were stopped and the *Monterey* remained dead in the water until later in the afternoon. When she dropped out of formation, the cruiser *New Orleans* and the destroyers *Twining* and *McCord* were detached to come to her aid if required. Dodging burning aircraft as they slid back and forth, many of the sailors manning the hoses were overcome by the blinding smoke, but as they fell others took their places. One sailor, knocked overboard into the sea, managed to grab a hose thrown out to him by an officer. Clambering back aboard, the drenched sailor said it was "just enough to cool me off after the heat of the damned fire!"[13]

Future president Gerald Ford had joined the *Monterey* as an ensign when she was still fitting out at the shipyard in Camden, New Jersey. Trained as a gunnery officer, he became director of physical training, with additional duties as an assistant navigator. He finished the war as a lieutenant commander. As he recalled later, "During the storm, our carrier caught fire. I was in the sack below at the time general quarters was sounded. I ran up to the flight deck, and the ship was rolling violently, at least twenty-five to thirty degrees. As I stepped out on the flight deck, I lost my footing and slid across the deck like a toboggan. I put my feet out, and fortunately, my heels hit the little rim that surrounds the flight deck–I was heading straight for the ocean. I spun over onto my stomach and luckily dropped over the edge into the catwalk just below."[14]

By half past ten, all fires were out, and all hands turned to the work of pumping and bailing out flooded compartments and cleaning up the ship even as the storm's intensity increased into the early afternoon. The next day, when the weather cleared, memorial services were held for the dead. Three men had been killed in saving the ship and thirty-six injured, ten seriously. Her hangar was gutted, with most of the electrical cables running through it burned out. Below decks, spaces were burned and smashed by explosions and fire and equipment was ruined by salt water.[15]

When the *Monterey* got into trouble, the *Cowpens* was rolling heavily, but nothing had yet gotten loose. However, a roll to starboard soon flooded the radar and radio-transmitter rooms and put the radar and most radio circuits out. This same roll threw a few jeeps and a TBM Avenger over the starboard side of the flight deck, between number two and three stacks, and caused a plane on the hangar deck to break loose and go careening about, with the danger of fire, until it was secured again. Below decks, several 2,000-pound bombs worked loose in the forward bomb magazine. They started banging around with such force that the impact could be felt on the bridge, seven decks above. They were finally lassoed and secured before they battered through the side of the ship. The men who secured these loose bombs were all volunteers, and they all risked their lives in saving the ship.

Virtually blinded by the combination of poor visibility and loss of radar, Captain DeBaun asked for permission from the task group commander to leave the formation and take an easier-riding course. Montgomery assigned two destroyers as guides and escorts, but only the *Halsey Powell* was able to find the blinded *Cowpens*. Guiding her by radio, the *Halsey Powell* served as her "seeing eye" destroyer.

The *Cowpens* was rolling so heavily that, on each roll to starboard, the flight deck edge would hit green water on the starboard side. Captain DeBaun recalled, "On the big rolls one could reach down from the starboard wing of the bridge and touch green water as we rolled to starboard." All hands not on watch were ordered into their bunks for safety reasons as *Cowpens* left the formation.

Finding an easier course, and keeping on it, required steering the ship with her engines. Shortly after 1100, an F6F Hellcat fighter on the after starboard corner of the flight deck broke loose, slid into the catwalk, and caught fire. The wind was on the starboard quarter at that time, so Captain DeBaun had no choice but to turn the ship to port to keep the flames away from the other planes parked around it. During the turn to port the F6F was jettisoned, but before *Cowpens* could come back on course, it took a couple of very heavy rolls to starboard which nearly capsized the ship. A second fire started when a fighter belly tank caught fire from the friction. Because of the wind and seas, fire fighters had to lash themselves to the deck to avoid being washed overboard.

During the struggle to jettison the burning Hellcat, Lieutenant Commander Robert Price, who had escaped death six months before, and who had come back as the ship's air officer after the relief of Air Group 25, went overboard and was lost. Nobody knew he was missing until the detail came in out of the weather. Bob Price was an excellent officer and well-loved by his men.

In spite of the tragedy and tension,

there were humorous moments. Captain DeBaun remembered two young sailors, in their teens, who came up in the middle of things to relieve the lookouts, "I heard one of them say to the lookout he was relieving, 'it's a stinker, ain't it' just enjoying it and not the least bit fearful."[16]

In Bogan's Task Group 38.2, the *Cabot* was well buttoned up and all her planes were secure, except for one which had its rudder torn off. At one particularly bad point, as she rolled heavily, Captain Michael said to his helmsman, "Watch it, son, or we'll go into a snap roll."[17]

Over in Sherman's Task Group 38.3, the *San Jacinto* suffered severe damage from the excessive rolls as a plane on her hangar deck broke loose and smashed into other parked aircraft, loosening them in turn. Soon the hangar deck was a mass of sliding planes, engines, tractors and other heavy equipment that smashed into the sides of the hangar, carrying away ventilation ducts and air intakes. Small fires were put out by repair parties and volunteers, and the hangar deck was secured by that afternoon. Although able to operate aircraft, her hangar deck was a mess and her crew began the work of repairing the damage on the way back to Ulithi.[18]

The next day the weather was balmy and clear, and later on, the *Cowpens, Monterey,* and *San Jacinto,* along with three destroyers, were formed into a task group under Captain Ingersoll of the *Monterey* for the trip back to Ulithi. *Cabot* was shifted from Task Group 38.2 to Task Group 38.3 for the time being.[19] *Cowpens* and *San Jacinto* were repaired at Ulithi and rejoined the fast carrier task force when it sailed on 30 December.[20] That same day, the more seriously damaged *Monterey* departed for Pearl Harbor by way of Eniwetok. From there she went on to Bremerton. Arriving 22 January 1945, she spent the next two months in overhaul and repair. Improvements included a second catapult on the starboard side, replacement of the nineteen single 20mm gun mounts with eight new twin mounts (which saved topside weight), and various gunfire control upgrades.[21]

Although the damage caused by the storm kept the fast carriers out action for several days, the Army air forces on Leyte were now strong enough to cover Mindoro. Task Force 38 returned to Ulithi on 24 December and Nimitz arrived to spend Christmas Day with Halsey aboard the battleship *New Jersey*.[22] Rear Admiral Radford relieved Montgomery as commander of Task Group 38.1 a month early when Montgomery was injured in a boat accident.[23] Fast carrier operations resumed on 30 December to support MacArthur's landings at Lingayen Gulf on Luzon.

Starting on 3 January, Task Force 38 spent six days hitting Japanese airfields on Luzon, Formosa, the Pescadores Islands, the Sakishima Gunto, and Okinawa. Heavy weather allowed Japanese aircraft to penetrate the air defenses over the landing area and several ships were damaged or sunk by kamikazes off Lingayen, while an escort carrier was sunk by a kamikaze near Mindoro.

On 5 January, Rear Admiral Matt Gardner arrived with the *Enterprise* to form Night Task Group 38.5 along with the *Independence*. During the day, the night carriers would still operate with Task Group 38.2, but for night operations, the *Enterprise, Independence,* and six destroyers would operate as a separate task group.

More than 150 Japanese aircraft were destroyed and when the landings took place on 9 January, there was no effective enemy air opposition. Other enemy aircraft were grounded because of strikes on Formosa and the Ryukyus. Losses, however, had been unusually high. Eighty-six carrier aircraft were lost, forty of them operationally. Many operational accidents involved the inexperienced Marine pilots, who had little carrier landing practice.[24]

Halsey still wanted to track down the surviving Japanese surface fleet and Nimitz released Task Force 38 from its support role on the morning of the landings. Naval intelligence had placed the *Ise* and *Hyuga* at Camranh Bay in French Indochina and Halsey hoped to surprise them before they could run south to Singapore. Task Force 38 passed through the Luzon Strait into the South China Sea on the night of 9-10 January and refueled on the 11th. Halsey ignored a reported convoy of more than a hundred Japanese merchant ships off the Chinese coast and headed for the Formosa Straits in order to surprise the ships that had eluded him at Leyte Gulf. When Halsey struck, they had already gone. But other targets in Indochina were plentiful. On 12 January alone, Task Force 38 sank forty-four enemy ships and destroyed more than a hundred planes for a loss of twenty-three carrier planes, with most of the crews being rescued by natives and smuggled into China.

Heavy weather made refueling difficult, but Halsey ran north for a series of strikes against Formosa and the nearby China coast on 15 January. Hong Kong, Hainan, Canton, Swatow, and Macao were hit the next day with minimal results. Twenty-two aircraft were lost to Japanese antiaircraft fire.[25] Heavy monsoon weather forced Task Force 38 south, and Halsey wanted to exit the South China Sea through the Surigao Strait. This would take the fast carriers out of the war for a week and expose them to land-based air attack in confined waters. Nimitz rejected the idea and told Halsey to wait until the weather cleared before passing over the top of Luzon.

Steaming northward after the weather lifted, the three task groups spent 21 January bombing Formosa, the Pescadores, and the Sakishimas. As the carriers came under fierce kamikaze attack, Lieutenant Clement M. Craig, acting commanding officer of VF-22, led his division into a formation of kamikazes off Formosa. When he returned to the Cowpens, he had five Tojos to his credit and had become the first ace of the new year.[26]

Around noon, a group of enemy aircraft approached the task force from up sun. Fighters tried to break up the attack, but some got through as the antiaircraft guns opened up. A Zeke dived on the Langley, releasing two bombs from 500 feet before it crashed into the sea close aboard. One bomb fell into the water just off the port beam, the other struck her flight deck just forward of the forward elevator, blasting a hole fourteen feet long and ten feet wide, and starting fires on the gallery deck and the next deck below. Minutes later, a second Zeke plunged into the new Ticonderoga, which had joined Task Force 38 at the end of October. It struck the Big T's flight deck abreast the

number two twin 5-inch mount, more than a hundred men were killed or wounded when the plane's bomb went off just above the hangar deck, starting many fires.

As the Langley fought her fires, the smoke rising from the Ticonderoga's more spectacular fires made her an easy target–three more kamikazes were shot down before another crashed into the island. All fires were under control within two hours and the Ticonderoga limped back to Ulithi.[27] Another kamikaze hit a radar picket destroyer, while that same day, an operational accident on the Hancock took fifty-two lives when a stray bomb from a landing Avenger exploded and started a fire.

The Langley was lucky that the bomb that hit her was small–it hit near the bomb stowage locker and the aviation gasoline storage tanks. If it had been a bigger bomb, she might have suffered the fate of her sister ship, the Princeton, a few months before. She was able to repair her flight deck in time to participate in strikes the next day.[28]

That night, seven Avengers sank a tanker off Formosa, and the next day the fast carriers hit the Sakishimas and Ryukyus, photographing the islands, especially Okinawa, in anticipation of future landings. These strikes were the last fast carrier operations in support of the Philippines landings, and Task Force 38 headed for Ulithi, arriving on 25 January. Halsey hauled down his flag the next day to begin planning the next series of operations under the Pacific "two platoon" system.

This respite also marked the end of the Independence's night career. Air Group 41's tour had been eventful –twenty major Japanese ships destroyed or damaged and fifty-five

aircraft destroyed, plus seven probables
and nineteen damaged. Of the enemy
aircraft destroyed, forty-five were in
the air and twenty-five of these were at
night – the night flyers generally
regarded one night kill as being worth
a dozen day kills. Lieutenant Bill Henry
became the ace of night flyers with ten
kills. Ensign John Berkheimer, who had
been lost over Manila, was the runner
up with eight.[29] It was realized by the
higher-ups that *Independence* was too
small for effective night operations. Her
place would be taken by the larger
Saratoga, and plans for *Bataan* to operate as a night carrier were canceled.
The fact that the *Independence* and her
air group were so successful is a great
tribute the skill and effort of her flyers
and crew. As Turner Caldwell noted
afterward, "All I can say is that we got
away with it!"[30] On 30 January,
Independence departed Ulithi for Pearl
Harbor to convert back to a day carrier.

Meanwhile, the Sixth Army had
moved inland at Lingayen. General
Kenney flew his aircraft into newly
seized airfields and relieved the
Seventh Fleet from covering the beach

head on the 17th. The Fifth Air Force
supported the drive on Manila, picking
up close air support tricks from the
Marines, who brought seven squadrons
of old SBD Dauntless dive bombers
from the Solomons at MacArthur's
request.

The Allies entered Manila on 3
February and organized resistance on
Luzon ended on 14 April 1945.
Operations in the southern Philippines
continued into the summer. By early
February, Army air forces were operating from Luzon and the Navy was
using Manila. A major base and
anchorage was being built at Leyte-
Samar, which would eventually be
used by the fast carriers. With the
Philippines largely in American hands,
the Luzon bottleneck was corked.
Japanese ships going from the East
Indies to the Japanese home islands
had to run a gauntlet of Philippine-
based aircraft, submarines, and mine
fields laid by B-29 bombers. In losing
the Philippines, Japan had not only lost
her lifeline to the oil, rubber, and gasoline in the Dutch East Indies but ultimately, the war.[31]

Chapter 8
Okinawa

On 26 January 1945, the Third Fleet again became the Fifth Fleet as Spruance resumed command of the Central Pacific Forces. The Allies, having decided to secure bases from which to launch the final assault on Japan, shifted their focus to Okinawa and Iwo Jima. By this time in the war, the carrier pilots facing the Japanese were the best. All air group commanders were veterans, and all pilots averaged 525 hours of flying time in training before being assigned to combat. By stark contrast, the average Japanese pilot had only 275 hours of training by December 1944, and by July 1945, this number was down to a meager hundred hours. All the fast carrier task group commanders were also veterans: Jocko Clark had returned to become Mitscher's right-hand man as commander of Task Group 58.1; Dave Davison took command of Task Group 58.2; Ted Sherman had his leave postponed to command Task Group 58.3; and Arthur Radford continued to command Task Group 58.4 at sea. With the realization that the *Independence* was too small to operate

as a night carrier, Matt Gardner would lead the night carrier group Task Group 58.5 with the old *Enterprise* and *Saratoga*. Four new *Essex*-class carriers would also join Task Force 58: *Bennington, Randolph, Shangri-La,* and *Bon Homme Richard.*[1] Although carrier doctrine and tactics had not changed from the previous months, Task Force 58 faced two equally demanding roles: softening up the beaches and supporting the troops, as well as defending against air attack.

Iwo Jima
The islands of Formosa and Saipan form the base of a strategic triangle, with legs 1,500 miles long, pointed at Tokyo. The eastern leg, Saipan to Tokyo, was the route flown by B-29s on their way to targets in Japan. A halfway point was needed, both to recover damaged B-29s unable to make it back to the Marianas, and as a base for fighter escorts. Only Iwo Jima met these requirements. The original date for the landings was set at 20 January 1945, but

prolonged resistance on Leyte and Luzon pushed the target date back to 19 February.[2] Tragically for the Marines who later assaulted it, this gave the Japanese another month to turn the island into a nearly impregnable fortress.

Fifth Fleet was to conduct carrier strikes in the Tokyo area to reduce the possibility of Japanese interference with the Iwo Jima landings. Task Force 58 sailed from Ulithi on 10 February. Aboard the *Cabot* to observe life on a carrier, was the famous war correspondent Ernie Pyle. He had come to the Pacific in January to tell the American public about war from a personal viewpoint, as he had done so well in covering the ground war in Europe, making him the friend of thousands of ordinary soldiers. Pyle found that "It's easy to get acquainted aboard a naval vessel. The sailors are just as friendly as the soldiers I'd known on the other side. Furthermore, they're so delighted to see a stranger and have somebody new to talk to that they aren't a bit standoffish. They're all sick to death of the isolation and monotony of the vast Pacific. I believe they talk more about wanting to go home than even the soldiers in Europe."[3]

On the 12th, Pyle got to witness firsthand the hazards of flying off a carrier. One of the pilots he had become acquainted with, Lieutenant James B. Van Fleet, was scheduled to fly the morning patrol. Watching the launch, as he later wrote in his column,

"We knew the very moment he started that Jimmy was in trouble. His plane veered sharply to the right, and a big puff of white smoke spurted from his right brake band. Then slowly the plane turned and angled to the left as it gained speed. The air officer in the 'island' sensed catastrophe, and put his hand on the warning squawker. All the sailors standing on the catwalk, with their heads sticking up over the edge of the flight deck, quickly ducked down. Yet such is the rigidity of excitement, I never even heard the squawker. It was obvious Jimmy couldn't stop his plane from going to the left. He had his right wheel locked, and the tire was leaving burned rubber on the deck, yet it wouldn't turn the plane. And it was too late for him to stop now. It had to happen. About midway of the flight deck, exactly opposite from where I was standing, he went over the side at full tilt, with his engine roaring. His wheels raked the anti-aircraft guns as he went over, his propeller missed men's heads by inches, his left wing dropped, and in a flash he disappeared over the side. It had all happened in probably no more than six seconds. I had stood frozen while it went on, unable to move or make a sound, eyes just glued to the inevitable. We all thought it was the end for Jimmy. But it wasn't. We got him back three days later."

Van Fleet had managed to free himself from his wrecked fighter as it sank and made it to the surface, where he was picked up by the destroyer *Franks*.[4] Pyle left the *Cabot* on the 23rd and was killed on the island of Ie Shima off Okinawa that April. His shipmates aboard the *Cabot* would be among the many who would mourn his death.

After hitting the Bonins on 15

February, the fast carriers launched a series of strikes against airfields and aircraft plants in and around the Tokyo area on 16 and 17 February. This marked the first time aircraft from carriers had attacked the Japanese capital since Mitscher launched the Doolittle raid from the old *Hornet* in April 1942. The first strikes were launched at dawn on the 16th while sixty miles off the coast of Japan and 120 miles from Tokyo. The weather over Honshu was overcast and cold. Although warned not to be drawn off by the Japanese, many inexperienced aviators could not resist breaking formation to dogfight with Japanese fighters. Although the Japanese lost more than 300 aircraft to the fighter sweep, Task Force 58 lost sixty carrier aircraft. One of *Cabot's* Hellcats participating in a strike on the Tachikawa engine plant developed trouble, and Ensign Robert L. Buchanan was forced to land in the water north of the small island of O Shima, which guards the entrance to Sagami Bay, just outside Yokohama. Members of his flight, led by Lieutenant Fecke, ace of the "streamlined bait" operation back in October, stayed over him for an hour and a half. Since visibility was low, the only way Buchanan could maintain visual contact was by using his emergency reflector mirror. The submarine *Pomfret* was contacted and proceeded to pick up the downed pilot, at one point coming within three miles of O Shima without drawing hostile fire. As the members of his flight ran low on fuel, Lieutenant Fecke sent them home one by one, but he stayed on. When the rescue was finally made and the pilot picked up unharmed, Fecke, dangerously low on fuel, headed for home, leaving the *Pomfret* to withdraw with

out air cover.[5]

Among the air groups from the light carriers, many of whom had to be content with providing CAP over the task force, *San Jacinto's* VF-45 made and impressive showing. Led by their skipper Commander Gordon Schechter, who shot down three Zekes and shared two kills in the morning, followed by an Oscar in the afternoon, and Ensign Robert R. Kidwell, who also shot down five in two missions, the squadron knocked down twenty-eight Japanese aircraft.[6] Matt Gardner's night-flying Avengers kept the Japanese night fighters grounded around Tokyo, but they failed to turn up any shipping targets. Foul weather the next day allowed only one strike to be made.

After heading south, Task Force 58 shifted to close support of Iwo Jima. Radford's Task Group 58.4 bombed Chichi Jima 18 February, while two of the battleships and three of the cruisers joined the bombardment forces working over Iwo. After dawn on 19 February, planes from Task Group 58.2 and Task Group 58.3 swept over the beaches to bomb and strafe just as the Marines landed. The Marines appreciated the support, but neither the carrier strikes, nor the pre-landing bombardment seriously affected the dug-in Japanese defenders; Iwo would be taken yard by yard at terrible cost. Although the distance from other Japanese air bases reduced the threat of kamikazes, the old *Saratoga,* detached by Mitscher to provide night cover for the landings and operating with the escort carriers, was hit by three bombs and two kamikazes northwest of Iwo on the afternoon of 21 February. Later that evening, Sara took another bomb hit, and the escort carrier *Bismark Sea* was lost to a lone kamikaze in the same attack.[7] Task Force 58 continued to support the Iwo landing, sharing close air support duties with the escort carriers until departing late on 22 February. The fast carriers turned to strike Japan again, but bad weather forced the cancellation of strikes against Tokyo, scheduled for the 25th, and Nagoya, scheduled for the next day. Instead, Task Force 58 hit targets on Honshu and the Nansei Shoto, the southwestern islands of Japan which include the Ryukyus and Amami Oshima. Task Force 58 paused to refuel and Mitscher detached Radford's Task Group 58.4 to Ulithi while the rest of Task Force 58 hit Okinawa again on 1 March. Turning south, the rest of Task Force 58 anchored at Ulithi 4 March.

The escort carriers continued their support until 11 March, when they withdrew to begin preparations for Okinawa. The *Enterprise* stayed behind to provide night cover for the landing force, keeping planes aloft for 174 consecutive hours over Iwo Jima between 23 February and 2 March. By the time the escort carriers departed, Seventh Air Force P-51 Mustangs were providing close air support. Even before the island was secured, the first crippled B-29 had landed there. Major resistance ended on 26 March and in April, the Mustangs began flying escort missions to Japan.

Okinawa–Operation Iceberg

The massive preparations for the Okinawa landings called for the neutralization of Japanese land-based air power on Okinawa, Formosa, the China coast, and Japan itself. Extensive minesweeping, underwater demolition, and naval bombardment operations would be carried out under the protection of Task Force 58. The British Pacific Fleet now joined in the Okinawa operation and, although designated Task Force 57, the British carrier force was more comparable to a U.S. task group. The British lacked the at-sea replenishment capabilities of the American navy and could not keep at sea for extended periods. Nevertheless, their contribution to the operation was significant.

While at Ulithi, Mitscher reshuffled his task groups in preparation for the Okinawa landings. At a conference with his carrier admirals aboard his flagship, *Bunker Hill,* he admitted that he no idea what the Japanese might do next. For all he knew, he said, they might even use poison gas. The Japanese, it turned out, still had a few tricks to play. The night following Mitscher's conference, 11 March, a long-range, twin-engined Frances kamikaze aircraft flew all the way to Ulithi and crashed into the after flight deck of the new *Randolph* as she was lighted while loading ammunition. Like other carriers anchored at Ulithi, members of the *Randolph's* crew were enjoying a movie on the hangar deck. The crash killed twenty-five men and wounded 106 others and the *Randolph* was out of action for nearly three weeks.[8] The *Lexington* and *Cowpens* went home for overhaul and many air groups rotated out. The overhauled *Franklin, Intrepid,* and *Bataan* rejoined the fleet. Mitscher recalled Gerry Bogan to be a standby carrier division commander and Bogan hoisted his flag aboard the *Franklin* in Task Group 58.2. Tommy Sprague, scheduled to relieve Jocko Clark in the middle of the upcoming operation, was aboard *Wasp*. Matt Gardner, aboard the Enterprise, was attached to Radford's Task Group 58.4. The new *Bon Homme Richard*, still in the U.S., would replace the *Saratoga* in the night carrier role, but a two-carrier night task group would not be possible until later that year.

Task Force 58 left Ulithi on 14 March, replenishing at sea on the 16th. The next day, Japanese search aircraft located Task Force 58 while it was 160-175 miles from Kyushu. Admiral Ugaki, commander of the Fifth Air Fleet, which controlled most of the aircraft in the Kyushu area, had time to disperse his aircraft to other locations. Task Force 58 struck airfields in the Kyushu area the next day. After bombing hangars and barracks with few Japanese aircraft getting caught on the ground, Mitscher sent his crews farther inland looking for targets. At Kobe and Kure several fleet units were spotted, including the super battleship *Yamato* and the aircraft carrier *Amagi*. That same day, the Japanese counterattacked–fifty Japanese aircraft hit Radford's Task Group 58.4 75 miles south of Shikoku. Early that morning, the *Enterprise* had a lucky escape when a bomb dropped on her failed to explode. The *Intrepid* was damaged by a near miss which spread fires, killing two and wounding forty-three of her crew. Three Judy dive bombers attacked the *Yorktown* around 1300, hitting the signal bridge with a bomb that went through to the next deck before exploding, leaving two gaping holes in her side. Five sailors died and twenty-six were wounded.

The next day Task Force 58 again sent out strikes to the Inland Sea looking for shipping and naval units at Kobe and Kure. Antiaircraft fire was particularly intense around the naval installations and, although seventeen ships, including the *Yamato* and *Amagi*, were hit, no serious damage was done. The Japanese counterattacked again in the early morning, hitting Davison's Task Group 58.2 hard. The *Wasp* was hit by an undetected aircraft and suffered heavy casualties since the bomb penetrated down to the mess decks, where breakfast was being served, before exploding. Fires on five decks, ruptured avgas tanks, and broken water mains added to the *Wasp's* troubles, but excellent fire fighting and damage control allowed her to recover her aircraft within an hour. Casualties on the *Wasp* were high: 101 killed and 269 wounded.

The *Franklin's* Ordeal

That same morning, the *Franklin*, Davison's flagship, was launching her second strike against Kure while a third was getting ready on the hangar deck below. A few minutes after seven, a lone Japanese aircraft appeared over the bow out of nowhere and dropped two 550-pound bombs on her flight deck. The first went through the flight deck near the forward elevator and exploded on the hangar deck; the second exploded on the flight deck amid aircraft warming up to launch. Both bombs started huge fires fed by the high-octane avgas in the plane's tanks. A series of explosions rocked the ship as bombs burst in their racks. Some of the aircraft in the *Franklin's* air group carried the large 11.75-inch Tiny Tim rockets, and as the flames grew hotter, these began to go off. Hundreds were killed in the first blasts. The entire after end of "Big Ben" was a mass of flame as explosions tossed aircraft and crewmen into the air. Other men were trapped in spaces below.

A destroyer came alongside to take Davison and his staff off, and later the light cruiser *Santa Fe* came alongside to pick up survivors, help fight the fires, and take off the wounded. Only a skeleton crew remained and the rest went into the water to be picked up. Dead in the water, listing thirteen degrees and still ablaze, the fires were under control by noon and her list stabilized. The heavy cruiser *Pittsburgh* moved in to take her in tow, working her around to a southerly course as crewmen aboard the *Franklin* worked to free her rudder, which was jammed hard left, and relight the boilers. Early the next morning, the *Franklin* had regained power and could make seven knots. At noon the next day, the tow was cast off. *Franklin* became the most heavily damaged aircraft carrier to survive the war, although at the cost of 724 killed and 260 wounded.

The Japanese aircraft did not get away unscathed, however. When *Franklin* was first hit, the *Bataan*, which had to turn to avoid a collision with the stricken carrier, had just launched a strike against Kobe. One of her fighters from the strike pursued the lone attacker and, after a twenty-mile chase, shot it down.[9]

After the 19 March attacks on the *Wasp* and *Franklin*, Task Force 58 slowly retired. Mitscher sent fighter sweeps over the Kyushu airfields to keep Japanese aircraft grounded, but in the afternoon of 20 March, Task Group 58.2, still protecting the crippled *Franklin*, again came under attack. This time, flaming debris from a downed Zero kamikaze crashed into the

destroyer *Halsey Powell* while she was alongside the *Hancock* refueling. The hit jammed her steering gear and almost caused the destroyer to ram the *Hancock*.

Late that afternoon, fifteen to twenty Japanese aircraft closed in on the *Enterprise*. Their bombs missed, but friendly antiaircraft fire caused a flight deck fire, severely hampering her ability to conduct night flying operations. Japanese aircraft continued to shadow the task force throughout the night and around 1400 the following day, a large Japanese force was detected to the northwest. About 150 aircraft intercepted a group of forty-eight enemy aircraft sixty miles from the task force.

Eighteen of the Japanese aircraft were Bettys carrying the new Ohka one-man piloted suicide bomb. Capable of speeds up to 600 miles per hour, the Ohka, later dubbed "baka" ("fool" in Japanese) by the Americans, was almost impossible to shoot down once launched. Carrying the Ohka bombs made the Bettys difficult to maneuver, however, and they became easy prey for the defending fighters. No Japanese aircraft got through the fighter screen to the task force.

On 22 March, Task Force 58 replenished and was reorganized into three task groups, leaving Davison's Task Group 58.2 as a "cripple" task group to escort the damaged *Franklin*, *Enterprise*, and *Wasp* back to Ulithi. Clark's Task Group 58.1 now included *Hornet*, *Belleau Wood*, *San Jacinto*, and *Bennington*. Sprague had shifted his flag to the *Bennington* after the *Wasp* had been hit. Sherman's Task Group 58.3 now comprised five carriers: *Essex*, *Bunker Hill*, *Hancock*, *Bataan*, and *Cabot* while Radford's Task Group 58.4 had *Yorktown*, *Intrepid*, *Langley*, and the newly arrived *Independence*.

That same day there was a serious operational accident aboard the *Cabot*. While recovering aircraft, a fighter pilot came in too low and hit the ramp, shearing off his arrestor hook. Bouncing over the barriers, he crashed into the aircraft that had landed before him, which had just been pulled forward from the landing area. The pilot sitting in this plane was killed in the crash, but the pilot who had crashed into it was uninjured. Six fighters were so badly damaged that they had to be pushed over the side.[10]

In all, Task Force 58 pilots had claimed 528 aircraft destroyed on the ground and in the air.[11] These losses delayed a major Japanese response to the Okinawa landings until 6 April. The carrier task groups settled in to a routine of fueling and striking in rotation in the week before the 1 April landings, maintaining constant alert to air attack. Visual aircraft detection was necessary as the Japanese had discovered that U.S. radar could detect neither single aircraft coming in low, nor small groups at very high altitude.

While the fighters protected the fleet, the bombers worked over Okinawa.[12] In addition, Clark's Task Group 58.1 sank a convoy of eight ships north of Okinawa on 24 March. With the air strikes, Okinawa got seven days of shelling by the bombardment ships. Beginning 24 March, and for the next three months, escort carriers also provided support. With three fast carriers taken out of the war in one month, *Saratoga, Franklin,* and *Wasp*, the arrival of four British carriers on 25 March was most welcome. Task Force 57 took on the responsibility of neutralizing the Sakishima Gunto, the islands southwest of Okinawa used as a staging base for Japanese aircraft shuttling between Kyushu and Formosa.[13]

Aircraft from the escort carriers and the fast carriers also covered the operations in the Kerama Retto. The Kerama Retto islets, close to the southwestern tip of Okinawa, were seized before the main landings to provide a sheltered anchorage for a fleet base and for flying boats. Keise Island, between the Kerama Retto and Okinawa was also seized to provide an artillery base to support the landings on southern Okinawa. About eighty enemy aircraft were destroyed and many other targets, such as bridges, small craft and some submarine pens were attacked. Army Air Force B-29s struck Kyushu on 27 and 31 March to further isolate Okinawa from Japanese aerial attack and in the last seven days of March, Task Force 58 flew 3,095 sorties. But the Japanese still managed to launch fifty or so raids against the American ships off Okinawa during the period 26-31 March, damaging ten, including the battleship *Nevada* and the cruisers *Biloxi* and *Indianapolis*. Eight of the ten were hit by kamikazes. The Japanese, however, lost around 1,100 aircraft.

Vice Admiral Richmond "Kelly" Turner, commander of the amphibious phase of the operation, had set up a series of protective screens around the vast armada of ships lying off Okinawa. He placed destroyers around the transport area, as well as anti-submarine screens, anti-suicide boat screens, and surface forces positioned to intercept any surface attacks by Japanese naval units. Beyond these were the radar picket destroyers. Task Force 57, the British carrier force, was positioned to the southwest, between Okinawa and Formosa, while Task

Force 58 was between Okinawa and Kyushu. The landings on 1 April went well – too well. The Japanese had decided not to oppose the landings on the beaches, choosing instead to prolong the struggle and take as many American lives as possible.

Two Avenger pilots from *Cabot's* VT-29 each had their own bizarre "April Fool's Day" experiences that day. Lieutenant (jg) Howard H. Skidmore was taking off for a close air support mission, when the ship rolled to port, causing his plane to leave the port edge of the flight deck about fifty feet short. He fought for control as his right wing rubbed across the deck while his left wing and wheels were in the air. Struggling to stay airborne, Skidmore managed to land his damaged aircraft aboard the *Essex* and returned the next day. In *Cabot's* first strike over Okinawa, Ensign Lyle A. Zemanek's engine began cutting in and out, forcing him to land wheels up in a rice paddy about a mile and a half from the western coast. As a division of fighters circled protectively overhead, Zemanek calmly told them that he and his crew would take their rubber raft and walk to the beach if they could make it. Zemanek led the way, his .38 revolver drawn. An Okinawan farmer spotted them, but was not hostile–he was scared and ran away. Crossing the main highway the crew walked into the water, inflated their boat and paddled out to sea, where they were picked up by PBM rescue plane.[14]

The pre-landing strikes had delayed a major Japanese counter stroke, although a limited number of small-scale, but determined air attacks, including kamikazes, and suicide boat attacks had been made against ships off Okinawa. The breather did not last long. The Japanese planned to launch the first of their massed "kikisui" (floating chrysanthemum) kamikaze attacks, which were intended to destroy the American fleet.[15] For Task Force 58, tied to Okinawa to protect the invasion, the trial by kamikaze was only beginning.

At the same time the kikisui attacks were launched, the Japanese sent the remains of their once proud surface fleet on a suicide mission of its own. The super battleship *Yamato,* the cruiser *Yahagi* and seven destroyers were to proceed at top speed to Okinawa. The *Yamato* had only enough fuel for a one-way trip, and it was hoped that she could beach herself and sink as many of the American ships with her 18.1-inch guns as possible before being destroyed. The force left Kure on 6 April but was spotted by the submarines *Threadfin* and *Hackleback* around 2000 that evening. Alerted by the submarine contact reports, Mitscher prepared to deal with this new threat.

Meanwhile, the first of the kikisui attacks had been launched during the afternoon of 6 April, with the outer radar picket destroyers being the first to suffer. Before the end of the day, almost 900 planes had attacked the American fleet, and at least 355 of these were kamikazes. Mitscher stowed his bombers below and scrambled all his fighters. By nightfall the Americans had lost three destroyers, two ammunition ships, and one LST. At least eight destroyers, a destroyer escort and a minelayer suffered major damage. Clark's Task Group 58.1 and Sherman's Task Group 58.3 were under constant attack as the many fighters and excellent gunnery took their toll.

In Task Group 58.1, a single suicider dived on the *Bennington* shortly after noon and missed. About an hour later, four more attacked the formation, two of them heading for the *San Jacinto.* The gunners on the San Jock knocked the wing off one, and it plunged into the sea off her starboard quarter. The second dove in from astern. Hit repeatedly, it burst into flames about a hundred yards away and crashed into the ship's wake. One dove on the *Belleau Wood,* which suffered a near miss and the last was shot down before picking out a target. A few minutes later, another kamikaze broke out of the low clouds less than four thousand yards from the *San Jacinto.* Her gunners concentrated their fire on the attacker. It was hit repeatedly but kept coming, finally crashing into the sea only fifty feet off the starboard bow. The resulting explosion spattered the flight deck and island with debris – pieces of plane, pilot, shrapnel, oil, and water. One officer and four men were wounded, one fatally, but damage to the ship was slight.[16]

The *Belleau Wood's* fighters from VF-30 had shot down forty-seven of the incoming Japanese planes that day with three ensigns claiming 16.5 kills between them–Carl C. Foster got six, Kenneth J. Dahms got five and a half, and Johnnie G. Miller bagged five. *Belleau Wood's* skipper, Captain William G. "Red" Tomlinson, signaled to his task group commander, Jocko Clark: "Does this exceed the bag limit?" Clark replied: "Negative. There is no limit. This is open season. Well done."[17] Task Force 58 claimed to have downed 249 incoming planes and, of the 182 that had arrived over the fleet, 108 were shot down. Attacks continued the next day, although with reduced intensity.

The battleship *Maryland,* a destroyer, and a destroyer escort were all rammed by kamikazes.

In Task Group 58.3, around noon, a Judy managed to get past the intercepting CAP and dove on the *Cabot,* which took it under fire. On the way down, the Judy dropped a bomb, which fell short on the starboard quarter. A split second later the Judy burst into flames and one wing fell off. Passing closely up the starboard side, it crashed into the sea off the bow. An hour later two more aircraft were spotted on radar about 30 miles out. As they closed, the *North Carolina* shot down one and the other picked *Cabot* as its target, aiming for the middle of her flight deck. Every gun that could be brought to bear opened up as the Zeke made a long shallow run. Passing over the flight deck with only a few feet to spare, the Zeke's wing hit the radar antenna before it crashed into the water close to the starboard side, showering the deck with shrapnel and chunks of metal. Steering, as well as all power in the after part of the ship, was temporarily lost, but power was quickly restored and repairs by the next morning.[18] Also that afternoon, the *Hancock* was attacked by a single kamikaze, which cartwheeled across her deck and into aircraft spotted on her forward flight deck, the enemy's bomb exploding on the port catapult. She managed to recover her aircraft at 1630, but had lost seventy-two killed and over eighty injured.The losses were not all one sided, however. That same day, Task Force 58 destroyed the world's largest battleship.

The Death of the *Yamato*

Mitscher had ordered his task groups to take up position northeast of Okinawa and launched search-strikes, arming the Helldivers with 1,000- and 250-pound bombs, the fighters with 500-pound bombs, and the Avengers with torpedoes. Task Force 58 search aircraft spotted the *Yamato* force at 0823 on 7 April and Mitscher signaled a warning to the gunfire and bombardment force off Okinawa.[19] Two seaplanes trailed the *Yamato* force for five hours and guided the carrier aircraft in on the Japanese. The first attack started just after noon as Task Group 58.1 and Task Group 58.3 launched 280 planes, including ninety-eight torpedo bombers, at the Japanese ships. Clark's Avengers hit *Yamato* with four torpedoes and she began listing. More strikes followed from Task Group 58.4, and the Japanese faced air attacks throughout the remaining daylight hours. By 1300, the cruiser *Yahagi* was dead in the water, the destroyer *Hamakaze* sunk, and the *Yamato* had already received two bomb hits and a torpedo hit. Within the next hour, she received another five torpedo hits. Listing heavily, with her steering impaired and losing speed, the *Yamato* was helpless against the onslaught of carrier aircraft and at 1423 rolled over, exploded, and sank. The *Yahagi* took another dozen bomb hits and nine torpedoes before going down. Of the seven destroyers, only three made it back to port. Task Force 58 lost ten planes and twelve men.

Mitscher reshuffled his task groups again. Clark's Task Group 58.1 and Sherman's Task Group 58.3 remained the same, but *Independence* moved from Radford's Task Group 58.4 to Davison's reformed Task Group 58.2 joining *Randolph* and *Enterprise,* which had returned during the night of 7-8 April. The kamikazes, mostly coming from Kyushu, continued their relentless assault. The *Enterprise* was hit on 11 April, and the *Intrepid* on 16 April. The unlucky *Intrepid* received her fourth kamikaze hit, which killed eight crewmen. The kamikaze hit the flight deck in a vertical attitude with such force that the imprint of its wings was smashed into the deck. The plane's bomb exploded on the hangar deck, but the *Intrepid's* experienced fire fighters soon had the fires out.[20]

The radar picket destroyers also continued to suffer. Mitscher reshuffled his task force again on 17 April, dissolving Task Group 58.2 and sending Davison back to Ulithi with the damaged *Hancock* and *Enterprise,* the task force again losing its night carrier. With the detachment of the *Cabot* for overhaul, there were no reorganizations from 17 to 28 May, although Clark's Task Group 58.1 returned to Ulithi on 28 April for 10 days of rest. Tommy Sprague was to relieve Clark, but Mitscher wanted his right-hand man to stay until the Okinawa operation was over.

News arrived that the Commander in Chief, President Roosevelt, had died on 12 April 1945. On first hearing of his death, many troops ashore thought it might be a Japanese propaganda trick, but they soon learned it was not. No one had time to mourn, since Japanese attacks continued unabated. During the interceptions on 12 April, one VF-31 pilot , Ensign Michele Mazzocco, learned just how tough the F6F Hellcat really was. Although he had scored hits on a Tojo, its pilot, apparently an experienced aviator, continued to fight.

After chasing each other down from 18,000 feet, the two opponents came at each other head on. Both fired, and each scoring hits on the other, but Mazzocco realized "he wasn't going to veer off, and a collision was not only inevitable, but planned by him. I waited until the last possible moment, my heart in my throat, then pulled up hard and to the right. His left wing came through the bottom arc of my prop and debris flew all over the sky. The concussion was tremendous, and jarred me to the bone, and I lost control of my plane for a moment that seemed an eternity. When I recovered, I could see him spinning slowly down toward the sea. My wingman checked my plane and told me my belly tank had taken most of the punishment in the collision." He managed to jettison the belly tank and make an emergency landing aboard the *Belleau Wood*. As he recalled later, "Mr. Grumman surely built a tough one when he built that Hellcat. God bless him."[21]

By mid-month, everyone aboard the ships off Okinawa was dead tired; the repeated attacks wore down Mitscher's pilots and crews, and sleep was a precious commodity. The general sentiment was expressed in a message sent to "Jocko" Clark by his task group's antiaircraft screen commander: "See Hebrews 13, verse 8." Clark chuckled as the read the passage in the Bible: "Jesus Christ, the same yesterday, and today and forever." Clark circulated the message to his ships, adding, "No irreverence intended."[22]

As Army and Marine troops struggled to clear the Japanese from the southern end of Okinawa, the fast carriers provided close air support. Land-based Marine Corsairs occupied two airstrips on Okinawa, but these aircraft were needed to counter increasing kamikaze attacks. One of the airstrips was rained out, then shelled by the Japanese, leaving the Marines only one operational airfield through April. As long as there were not enough Marine aircraft for both roles, the fast carriers had to stay on. On 19 April, a strike of more than 650 aircraft, 300 of them from Task Force 58, hit Shuri Castle, the center of Japanese defenses. The strikes could not penetrate the caves sheltering the fanatical Japanese defenders, and Shuri held. The nearby island of Ie Shima was seized for its airfield, with Army P-47s arriving in May. Rain halted all airfield construction and repairs until June, but by 1 July, when the first Okinawa-based strike on Kyushu was launched, more than 750 aircraft were available. In the meantime, the carriers held off kamikaze attacks while striking Japan, Okinawa, and the Sakishima Gunto. Despite heavy commitments, Mitscher rotated his task groups into Ulithi for rest. Task Group 58.4 detached when Task Group 58.1 returned on 12 May, and when Task Group 58.4 returned at the end of May, Task Group 58.3 left for the new base at Leyte.

The *Bunker Hill*

On the morning of 11 May, *Bunker Hill*, Mitscher's flagship, was seventy-six miles east of Okinawa. Shortly after 1000, while some of her aircraft were flying strikes against Okinawa, others were ready on her flight deck, and still more were fueling and arming on her hangar deck. Emerging from low cloud cover on the starboard beam, a Zero headed for the flight deck, dropped a bomb aft of the number three elevator and then crashed into parked aircraft. The bomb penetrated the flight deck, exploding on the gallery deck. About the same time, a second aircraft screamed down in a vertical dive and smashed into the flight deck near the base of the island, spreading fires throughout its passageways. The two kamikaze hits turned the *Bunker Hill* into a blazing inferno. As other ships tried to screen her from further attack, three destroyers and the cruiser *Wilkes-Barre* trained hoses on the fires. The attack killed more than 350 men, including thirteen of the admiral's staff and most of her fighter pilots, who were asphyxiated in their ready room. Only the *Franklin* had suffered more. *Bunker Hill* limped home and would not return to the war.[23]

After passing command to Ted Sherman, Mitscher shifted his flag from the *Bunker Hill* to the *Enterprise,* which had rejoined the task force on 6 May. Mitscher went north to attack Kyushu. The *Enterprise* got off a successful night heckler mission with sixteen night Avengers on the night of 12-13 May, followed by day strikes by the task force. On the 14th, however, a kamikaze found the *Enterprise* and hit her. Good damage control saved her, but she was out of the war for months. Mitscher, who was bald, remarked to Jimmy Flatley, his operations officer: "Jimmy, tell my task group commanders that if the Japs keep this up they're going to grow hair on my head yet."

The next day, Mitscher shifted his flag to *Randolph,* where Gerry Bogan loaned him some of his staff officers. On 18 May, Mitscher requested that Task Force 58 be detached from the sixty-mile square operating area, which

was less than 350 miles from Kyushu, where it had been for two months. Spruance, however, had no choice but to keep them on station because they were still needed. The worst was over, however, and no more serious kamikaze attacks threatened the carriers.

The British had also suffered from the kamikaze attacks, and although their armored flight decks helped protect them from major structural damage, their aircraft and radars were vulnerable. After replenishing at Leyte in late April, the British carriers rejoined the operation. On 4 May, kamikazes hit the *Formidable* and *Indomitable.* On 9 May, two more kamikazes hit *Formidable* again and *Victorious.*[24] Task Force 57 flew its last strikes against the Sakishima airfields on 25 May and withdrew to Sydney to refit and prepare for the final operations against Japan. Task Force 57's performance had earned it a prominent place in the war in the Pacific. Spruance recommended that the British Pacific Fleet be integrated into the U.S. Fast Carrier Task Force, and Nimitz agreed.

Halsey Returns

With the job of taking Okinawa largely done, Nimitz made the last "two-platoon" shift of the war. He had wanted the change to take place on 1 May to allow Spruance to begin planning for the scheduled landings in Japan, but the situation on Okinawa had not permitted that. On 27 May, while at sea, Halsey relieved Spruance, who immediately headed for Nimitz's advance headquarters on Guam. Fifth Fleet once again became Third Fleet and Task Force 58 became Task Force

38. The next day Mitscher turned command of the fast carriers over to Slew McCain, who hoisted his flag in the new *Shangri-La*, which had been in combat for one month. Mitscher, tired and ill, reported back to Washington to become Deputy Chief of Naval Operations (Air).[25] The task group commanders remained the same until the scheduled return to Leyte in June, except for Dave Davison, who was relieved as commander of Task Group 38.2 by Rear Admiral Clifton A.F. "Ziggy" Sprague.[26] Ziggy Sprague had hoisted his flag aboard the repaired *Ticonderoga* which had rejoined the fast carrier force after a practice strike on the bypassed island of Maloelap on 17 May. Tommy Sprague remained aboard *Bennington* and Gerry Bogan aboard *Randolph*.[27]

Another Typhoon

As Halsey resumed command of the fast carriers, he was not faced with being tied down to defending the beach at Okinawa. He detached Sherman's Task Group 38.3 for a rest period and ran north with the other three task groups to hit Japan. Unfortunately, Halsey's bad luck with weather plagued him again, as Task Force 38 ran into heavy seas. After getting off strikes against airfields on Kyushu on 2-3 June, the task force encountered yet another typhoon. The storm, which was small and tight like the one met the previous December, was discovered on the morning of 3 June. By early the next evening it was heading north and the task force was heading east away from it. Based on the advice of his aerologist, Commander Kosko, who had been involved in the previous fiasco in December, Halsey turned the task force westward to cross in front of and ahead of the storm. Halsey did not consider the affect on Clark's task group, which was refueling from Servron 6.

In the early hours of 5 June, Halsey ordered the task force back into the path of the typhoon. The replenishment force commander, realizing what was happening, signaled McCain that the new course would take them back into the storm. McCain ordered a turn to the north, which did not effect Radford's Task Group 38.4, but Clark, sixteen miles away, needed time and sea room to come to the new course. By the time Clark gave up trying to maintain course and ordered his ships to maneuver independently, he was in the eye of the storm. By the afternoon Clark's task group was clear of the storm. No ships were lost, but the bow of the cruiser *Pittsburgh* was broken off, and the flight deck overhangs on the *Hornet* and *Bennington* collapsed.

Refueling and heading south–the *Hornet* and *Bennington* conducting flight operations by backing down–the task force launched support strikes to Okinawa on 6 June. Also reporting to Task Group 38.1 that day was the *Bon Homme Richard* as the new night carrier. The following day, the task force ran north to bomb the Kanoya airfield on Kyushu on 8 June. Clark detached *Bennington* to return to Leyte for repairs, and on 9 June the rest of the carriers dropped napalm on enemy emplacements on Okino Daito Shima. The fast battleships bombarded Minami Daito Shima on 10 June.[29] When Task Force 38 arrived at Leyte on 13 June, they were greeted by the sight of the damaged *Randolph*. Her flight deck had been damaged by the crash of a stunt-flying Army P-38.[30]

Chapter 9
Target Japan

When Task Force 38, now organized in three task groups, sortied from Leyte on 1 July, it was the beginning of the final operations against Japan.[1] The target would be the Tokyo area. Fueling east of Iwo Jima on 8 July, Halsey launched his strikes on 10 July. Although prepared for counterattack, only two snooper aircraft approached the task force, and these were promptly shot down. Although the antiaircraft fire was stiff, the attacking carrier aircraft met little opposition over Tokyo as the Japanese had dispersed their aircraft to revetments away from the airfields. The Japanese had apparently given up on trying to destroy the American fleet and were conserving their strength for the final battle for the home islands. Despite this, the fighter-bomber sweeps destroyed more than a hundred enemy aircraft on the ground. Moving north, Task Force 38 was to hit targets in northern Honshu and Hokkaido, but Halsey, who seemed to attract typhoons like a magnet, had to delay the strikes until 15 July. Again, the Japanese did not respond and the

dispersed aircraft were difficult to find, although the carrier aircraft did sink more than 50,000 tons of coastal shipping and light naval craft. A battleship-cruiser force also bombarded the Kamaishi and Muroran iron factories.

As the Third Fleet refueled on 16 July, the British carrier force, which had departed Sydney on 28 June, joined the American fleet as Task Force 37, marking the first time British carriers became part of an American tactical carrier formation. After inconclusive air strikes and shelling in the Tokyo area 17-18 July, refueling, and intermittent heavy weather, the fast carriers launched the last strikes of the war against the immobile Mobile Fleet on 24 and 25 July. Strikes by Army B-24s and the carrier aircraft severely damaged several warships at Kure naval base, some of which sank, settling on the shallow bottom. The ships included the elusive hermaphrodite battleships *Ise* and *Hyuga,* and the battleship *Haruna.* The carriers *Amagi* and *Katsuragi* and the light carrier *Ryuho* were also severely damaged. The incomplete carriers

Kasagi, Aso and *Ibuki* were also hit. Night attacks kept up the pressure. Task Force 38 paid a high price, however–133 aircraft and 102 airmen. The British were diverted to other targets, as Halsey wanted the U.S. Navy alone to have the satisfaction of destroying the Japanese surface fleet. Aerial combat occurred on only six days during July and most of the enemy aircraft were shot down – fifty-six of the fifty-nine kills claimed – during the strikes at Kure, Kobe and elsewhere in the Inland Sea on the 24th, 25th and 28th.

On the 25th, *Belleau Wood's* VF-31 claimed eight kills over Yokaichi airfield–four of these were Franks brought down by Lieutenant (jg) Cornelius N. "Connie" Nooy. Despite the fact that it would be the only aerial combat of his second cruise, it raised his wartime total to nineteen kills, making him the leading ace from the light carriers. VF-27 had also returned to combat after a turn around of only seven months, this time aboard the *Independence*. Their skipper, Lieutenant Commander Fred A. Bardshar, was impressed with the scale and organization of the strikes: "During July and August 1945, we hit Kure, Niigata, Muroan, Yokosuka and Utsunomiya, among others. Kure's defenses were, I think, the strongest and certainly the most spectacular. They used colored bursts for air spotting as we did with surface naval rifles. Concern with flak at Kure was somewhat tempered by concern with mid-air collisions. The raids were large, rather well coordinated and concentrated, and the density of U.S. aircraft over the targets was high."[2]

The month ended with heavy weather. Honshu was shelled on 29 July and air strikes hit Kobe and Nagoya the next day. Typhoons in the area delayed refueling, and Nimitz ordered Task Force 38 to withdraw from southern Japan. Unknown to most of the commanders in the Pacific, the atomic bomb was going to be dropped on Hiroshima on 6 August. Nimitz wanted the fleet to be far away from the then unknown effects of this revolutionary new weapon. The second atomic bomb would be dropped on Nagasaki on 9 August. Meanwhile, MacArthur had requested carrier strikes on Misawa air base in northern Honshu, where intelligence had reported a large air fleet and airborne troop unit being assembled for what was thought to be a large-scale suicide landing on Okinawa.[3]

After his battleships shelled the Kamaishi factory on 8 August, Task Force 38 aircraft hit Misawa the next day, destroying more than 200 aircraft in revetments and breaking up the attack. More strikes were flown over Honshu on 10 August, and the battleships continued shelling targets. The Soviet Union had declared war on Japan the day before, and Halsey reasoned that the raids on northern Japan would help the Russian effort by preventing long-range Japanese strikes against the Russians. For the first time since June, the Japanese counterattacked, sending about twenty aircraft at the fleet. Although most were shot down, one crashed a radar picket destroyer, causing heavy casualties. Until this point, all operations were according to the plan for Operation Olympic, the landings on Kyushu in southern Japan, scheduled for 1 November 1945. But now, with signs that surrender was near, Task Force 38 stayed on, refueling on 11 August.[4]

The next day a typhoon caused Halsey to stand clear of his proposed operating area off Tokyo. On the 13th and again on the 15th, with a refueling in between, the last air operations of the Fast Carrier Task Force against Japan took place. On 13 August, full deckload strikes claimed more than 250 aircraft destroyed on the ground, while the combat air patrol shot down eighteen more. A smaller strike of 103 planes hit Tokyo after dawn on 15 August, shooting down thirty to forty enemy aircraft. Another small strike of seventy-three carrier aircraft was on its way when Halsey received word from Nimitz to suspend all further air attack operations. Air Group 47 from the *Bataan* was on its way to strike Tokyo when word was received that hostilities had ceased. Radio silence was broken as the pilots began singing, "Oh, What A Beautiful Morning."[5] Other air groups were not so fortunate. *Belleau Wood's* VF-31 tangled with Zekes offshore, splashing six, and *San Jacinto's* VF-31 claimed seven more off Mito. *Hancock's* VF-6 shot three down over Sagami Bay, just before the imperial announcement. Although *Yorktown's* VF-88 was jumped over Atsugi, the outnumbered Hellcats fought back, shooting down nine and losing four. No Japanese aircraft got through to the task force.[6] The CAP was reinforced and, as Japanese pilots, either uninformed of the surrender or unwilling to accept defeat, continued to attack the fleet, Halsey ordered them to be shot down "in a friendly fashion." A few more intruders were shot down, and around 1400 Ensign Clarence A. Moore of VF-31 beat the other elements of his division within gun range of a Judy to score his first victory. It was the last aerial victory of the day, and of the war.

Although the war was now over, the Third Fleet continued to maintain constant vigilance as preparations for the actual surrender were worked out. Halsey ordered Task Force 38 to an area 100 to 200 miles southwest of Tokyo known as "Area McCain." The three task groups maintained their normal wartime patrols through 23 August. On the 16th and 17th, the task force steamed in unusually tight formations while commemorative aerial photographs were taken. On 21 August the *San Jacinto* swapped her Air Group 49 for the *Bataan's* Air Group 47, just in time to participate, on the 22nd and 23rd, in massing overhead for photographs.[7]

Early in August, Admiral Montgomery, now ComAirPac, finally ordered all the light carrier air groups to have thirty-six F6Fs and no torpedo bombers, but the only light carrier available at Eniwetok to make the change was the *Cabot*. On 18 August, VT-32 was decommissioned and more F6Fs flew aboard the next day. As such, *Cabot* became the first and only light carrier to have an all-fighter air group.[8] Later that month, the *Langley*, having returned to Hawaii on her way to the forward area, would operate F4U Corsairs for a day off Pearl Harbor. Mitscher, now Deputy Chief of Naval Operations (Air), felt that Hellcats should be taken off the light carriers altogether, since they were too slow to intercept high-flying snooper aircraft, and had recommended that they be replaced with Corsairs pending the availability of the new F8F Bearcat. The Bearcat used the same R-2800 engine as the Hellcat and Corsair, but was smaller and lighter, with a high rate of climb.

A light carrier could carry forty-eight of these new fighters, but the end of the war led to a cancellation of these plans.[9]

Late on 23 August, Halsey assigned the carriers new operating areas. While some carrier aircraft flew surveillance over Japanese airfields, others dropped food and supplies to prisoners of war. Halsey had planned to take many of his surface ships into Tokyo's outer bay, Sagami Wan, but two typhoons appeared on the day before. Unfortunately, one of these storms made an unexpected turn and hit Bogan's Task Group 38.3 off Shikoku.[10] On 27 August, the day after the typhoon, ships of the Third Fleet entered Sagami Wan, with the light carrier *Cowpens* the sole representative of the fast carriers. Ted Sherman, recently promoted to commander of the fast carriers, protested that the carriers had earned the right to be in on the surrender ceremony, but Halsey, who feared the Japanese might commit some act of treachery, wanted his carriers where they would have the sea room to launch aircraft, if needed, and sent Sherman a sharp rebuke to mind his own business. (Later, the *Bataan* would also enter Tokyo Bay four days after the surrender ceremony.)[11]

Not to be outdone by MacArthur's forces, a fighter pilot from *Yorktown's* VF-88 landed at Atsugi airfield on 27 August and ordered the Japanese to put up a banner for the Army paratroopers arriving the next day. It read:

"Welcome to the U.S. Army from the Third Fleet." On 28 August, staff officers landed at Atsugi to begin preparatory talks with the Japanese for the ceremony arrangements. VF(N)-91 from the *Bon Homme Richard* flew the last night combat air patrol on the night of 27-28 August and the next night, the entire fleet lighted ship.

On 30 August, the ships in Sagami Wan entered Tokyo Bay and Halsey shifted his flag ashore from the *Missouri* to the Yokosuka naval base. The surrender ceremony took place on the deck of the *Missouri* on 2 September. MacArthur signed on behalf of the Allies and Nimitz on behalf of the United States. Just as the ceremony ended, 450 carrier planes roared overhead in massed formation at low altitude. Above the carrier planes droned formations of B-29s. The war had ended. A few days after the second atomic bomb had been dropped on Nagasaki, Mitscher, back in Washington, D.C., issued a press release in his new capacity as the head of naval aviation. While careful to acknowledge the indispensable contributions made by the rest of the Navy, Army troops, Marines, and land-based air forces, he left no doubt that the starring role had been played by the aircraft carriers. "Japan is beaten," he asserted, "and carrier supremacy defeated her." The light carriers, a wartime expedient, had done their part and more.

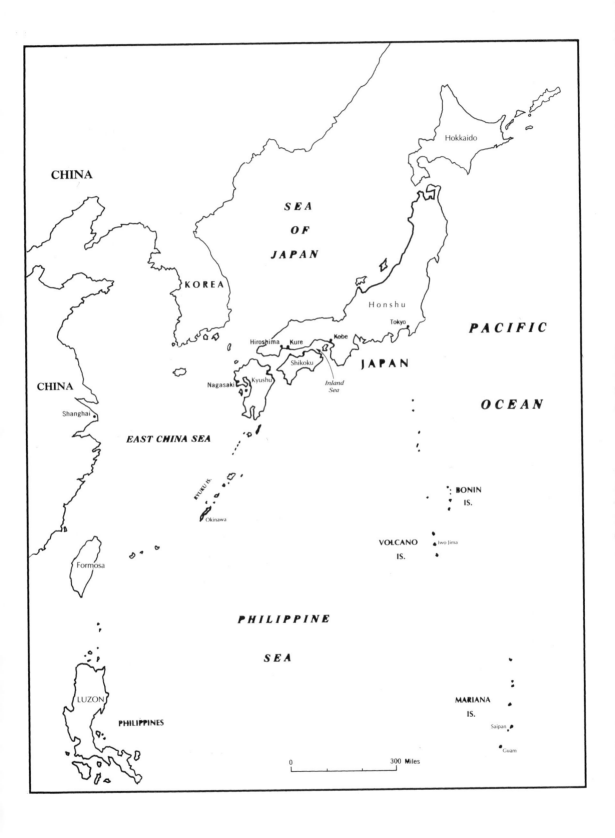

CHINA

CHINA

KOREA

SEA

OF

JAPAN

Hokkaido

Honshu

Tokyo

PACIFIC

Hiroshima Kure   Kobe

Shikoku

JAPAN

Nagasaki Kyushu

Inland
Sea

OCEAN

Shanghai

EAST CHINA SEA

RYUKYU IS.

Okinawa

BONIN

IS.

VOLCANO

Iwo Jima

IS.

Formosa

PHILIPPINE

SEA

LUZON

MARIANA

IS.

PHILIPPINES

Saipan

Guam

0   300 Miles

Chapter 10
Aftermath

With the victory won, America immediately began dismantling its military and naval forces and demobilizing personnel. While some forces remained on occupation duty immediately after the war, the only thing that mattered to most Americans overseas was "getting home" as quickly as possible. As the postwar era unfolded, the Navy struggled to adapt to the growing demands of the Cold War while justifying its continued existence in an age dominated by atomic weapons and jet-propelled aircraft. The *Independence*-class light carriers would be too small to have a role in the new era of fast carrier operations. Of the eight ships that survived the war, one, the *Independence* herself, would soon be expended in tests to determine whether the Navy could survive in the new atomic age. The remaining seven would all be laid up in reserve by early 1947. Some of the surviving ships would later be reactivated for other roles, such as training or antisubmarine warfare (ASW), and a few served in foreign navies, but for the most part their careers were over.

Magic Carpet

Between October 1945 and May 1946 more than one million men were transported home from Europe and the Pacific in what the Navy called Operation Magic Carpet.[1] Aircraft carriers were pressed into service transporting troops home as quickly as possible. As the carriers arrived in the U.S., many were modified to be able to carry more passengers on succeeding trips. Crew complements were reduced, and extra galley facilities and three to five tiers of bunks were installed on the hangar decks to accommodate the returning troops. All of the surviving *Independence* class carriers participated. The *Independence* departed Tokyo Bay on 22 September 1945 for San Francisco, arriving 31 October. She departed on the first of several Magic Carpet trips to the Pacific area, the last completed at San Francisco on 28 January 1946. The *Belleau Wood* completed three trips in the Pacific and the *Cowpens* two to Pearl Harbor, Guam, and Okinawa before the end of January 1946. The *Monterey* transferred to the

103

Atlantic and participated in the 17 October 1945 Navy Day celebration in the New York Navy Yard before participating in several trips to Naples, Italy.

The *Langley* was on her way back to the forward area when the surrender came. She operated as a training carrier out of Pearl Harbor for a while and completed two Magic Carpet trips to San Francisco before leaving for the Navy Day celebration at the Philadelphia Navy Yard. She departed 15 November on the first of two trips to Europe. *Cabot* became part of Task Force 72, which left Okinawa on 1 September to support occupation landings in China and Korea until mid-September. She continued to operate in the Yellow Sea until mid-October, when she was ordered to Guam for Magic Carpet duty to the West Coast by way of Pearl Harbor.

The *Bataan* left Okinawa on 10 September with passengers for Pearl Harbor. Leaving Pearl for the New York Naval Shipyard on 25 September, she was among the first carriers to transit the Panama Canal after the war and was featured in *Life* magazine's "Picture of the Week" which showed her as she entered the Mira Flores locks. After some time in the Panama Canal area, she proceeded on to New York and then to Providence, Rhode Island, for Navy Day celebrations. After alterations in the Boston Navy Yard, she completed two trips to Italy, repatriating Italian prisoners of war and returning with American troops. The *San Jacinto* left Tokyo Bay in mid-September for San Francisco. After alterations, she departed on 25 November for a Magic Carpet trip to Guam. Her second trip was to Manila and Subic Bay in the Philippines.[2]

Operation Crossroads

In the postwar world of atomic weapons, the Navy had to learn how survivable ships would be in any future nuclear combat. Accordingly, Joint Task Force One was assembled at Bikini Atoll in the Marshall Islands in the summer of 1946 under Vice Admiral William H.P. "Spike" Blandy. A force of 42,000 men, 242 ships and 10,000 instruments would participate in the tests, code named Operation Crossroads by Blandy because, as he said, "It was apparent that warfare, perhaps civilization itself, had been brought to a turning point by this revolutionary weapon."[3] The lessons learned would have a profound impact on the Navy's future. A group of more than ninety vessels of various kinds were assembled as targets. Many of the ships, including former German and Japanese warships, had fought in crucial battles of the recently ended war. Five battleships included the *Arkansas,* a veteran of both World Wars, the *Nevada,* survivor of Pearl Harbor, and the *Nagato,* Yamamoto's flagship. The cruisers included the German *Prinz Eugen,* which had sailed with the *Bismark* and *Scharnhorst* (both of which had been sunk in the Atlantic) before surrendering. Aircraft carriers were represented by the proud old *Saratoga* and the *Independence.*

The first test, named Test Able, was an air burst. On 1 July, a B-29 dropped a 23-kiloton atomic bomb, which burst 520 feet over the target fleet. Five ships, two destroyers, two transports and the Japanese heavy cruiser *Sakawa* – were sunk as a result of the test, and many others damaged. The operation went smoothly except that the test weapon was dropped some what off target. The radioactivity creat-ed by the burst had only a transient effect, and within a day nearly all the surviving target ships had been safely reboarded. The ship inspections, instru-ment recoveries, and remooring neces-sary for the next test proceeded on schedule. The *Independence,* positioned 560 yards from surface zero, sustained considerable damage from the air blast, including buckling of the flight deck and loss of the superstructure. Several fires were extinguished by attending salvage vessels. Radiation was slightly above tolerance levels, so she could not be boarded immediately, but a few days later, an initial boarding team inspected her and pronounced her safe for reboarding. Some members of her crew worked aboard, preparing for the next test, for periods up to seven hours a day before returning to the *Rockwall,* a transport ship assigned as one of the support vessels for the tests.

In Test Baker, the weapon was sus-pended ninety feet beneath an auxiliary craft anchored in the midst of the target fleet. On 23 July, the *Independence* was positioned 1,390 yards from surface zero when s second 23-kiloton weapon was detonated. Eight vessels were sunk, including the battleships *Arkansas* and *Nagato.* The *Saratoga,* staggering under a force of two million tons of water and sediment that had been hurled more than a mile upward, was blown 800 yards away atop a forty-three-foot wave. With her distinctive funnel blown over and the aft portion of her flight deck crushed as if under the heel of a giant, she sank seven and a half hours later. As a *New York Times* correspondent noted, "She died like a queen–proudly."

The *Independence* sustained no

severe physical damage from Test Baker, but a more insidious danger soon became apparent as salvage efforts began. The surviving ships seethed with radiation from the radioactive mist that had swept over them. Rear Admiral William S. Parsons, who as a captain had participated in the first atomic bombing at Hiroshima, was the deputy commander of Joint Task Force One. He described the foggy outsurge of Test Baker as "a wet caress, a kiss of death."[5] Scrubbing, painting, foaming and other efforts to decontami-nate the ships had little effect. In frus-tration, the Navy decided to tow the surviving vessels 200 miles to Kwajalein to try other countermea-sures.

The *Independence* was not boarded until 18 August, and then only for a period of less than five hours. She was boarded again by a limited number of crew members over the next three days for periods of four hours or less. She was towed to Kwajalein on 25 August by the fleet tug *Munsee,* arriving two days later. She was deactivated at Kwajalein on 28 August. After being transferred to Pearl Harbor, she was subsequently taken to San Francisco for further tests and was finally sunk in weapons tests off the California coast on 29 January 1951.

Mothballs

As the postwar drawdown got into full swing, the deactivation of the *Independence* in August 1946 was soon followed by the decommissioning of the *Belleau Wood* and *Cowpens* on 13 January 1947. The *Monterey, Langley, Cabot,* and *Bataan* followed on 11 February, and the *San Jacinto,* the last ship of the class to be decommissioned, followed the others on 1 March.

Unlike previous methods of preserving inactive ships, when all movable, corrodible, or valuable equipment was removed and the empty hulls left to weather the elements, the Navy devised new methods to preserve the postwar "mothball" fleet. All exposed surfaces were protectively insulated and plastic paint was used to cover corrodible parts below decks. Topside gear, such as binnacles and direction finders "looked like gray ghosts" under strippable plastic hoods, sprayed on in several coats. Gun mounts were covered by metal "igloos" that were sealed at the base. All openings were sealed and deck spaces were dehumidified.

In theory, a ship preserved this way could last indefinitely, but there was only one way to find out for certain. For two years, while the *Cabot* swung lazily at her moorings in the Philadelphia Naval Shipyard, a team of six men of the Reserve Fleet had made regular inspection rounds of the *Cabot*, running through a thirty-six-page checklist each week. Below decks, dehumidifying machines kept air at a steady thirty percent relative humidity. Pipes of the ship's fire-fighting system sucked air into the machines, where it was dried and sent out again. In different spaces, sensing stations sent impulses to "recorder controllers" that graphed a record of temperature and humidity throughout the ship.

In 1948 the *Cabot*, the first carrier to undergo the modern method of preservation in the 16th Fleet, was due for a regular three-month overhaul as part of the ongoing maintenance allotted ships in the Reserve Fleet. Since some protective covering would have to be removed to allow workmen in anyway, the commander of the Atlantic Reserve Fleet ordered her activation to find out how long it would take to to make her operational again. First, a hundred hull experts, ordnancemen, machinists, and electricians of the Reserve Fleet came aboard to begin the process of "unzipping" the *Cabot*. A few days later a new crew reported aboard, to work under the supervision of the experts. All the required actions filled seven books°the volume for the engineering department alone was 1,000 pages and six inches thick.

Arresting cables, which had been stowed in dehumidified spaces, had to be cleaned and reassembled. Whaleboats had to be filled with water to swell out dried seams. More than a thousand engines had to be cleaned, checked and put in working condition. The brown protective compound that coated all rustable parts worked well and, if necessary, equipment could be operated without removing it. Likewise, in an emergency, the flight deck could be used without removing its protective composition covering.

Some problems had been anticipated, but there were surprises – some of them pleasant ones. An old chief bos'n of the activation team noted that there was "No live stock on board." As he explained, "In the old days, when you went to open a hatch on a secured ship, you'd hear tapping on the other side. It was the cockroaches and rats, knocking to come out. Had to open it quick and stand aside or they'd shove you over in the rush. Nothing like that here. This ship was real lonesome when we opened her up."

Another pleasant surprise was that there wasn't a speck of dust in any of the dehumidified spaces. But using the fire system to dehumidify the air had its drawbacks, as the activation crew found out when water was reintroduced into the pipes. Water sprayed everywhere–the gaskets in the fire main had shriveled–and there were a few damp moments until the gaskets could soak up water and swell tight again.[6] Overall, the reactivation of the *Cabot* exceeded expectations and she was recommissioned on 27 October 1948. Many of her former crew members, including Admiral Schoeffel, one of her former captains, were on hand for the ceremonies.

Antisubmarine Modernization

The *Cabot* was assigned to the Naval Air Reserve training program and operated out of Pensacola, then Quonset Point, on cruises to the Caribbean and had one tour of duty in European waters from January to March 1952. The *Bataan* was also recommissioned in May 1950 as a training and antisubmarine carrier, only to be replaced in that role by the *Monterey* after the outbreak of the Korean War. Both ships received modest modernizations as part of their ASW upgrades after recommissioning, the most noticeable features being the combination of four funnels into two and a new island design with a two-level bridge. Other provisions included stronger flight decks and elevators (the aft elevator was strengthened to take a 22,000-pound aircraft), torpedo detection sonar (both active and passive), provisions for new ASW weapons (500 sonobouys and thirty-six aerial homing torpedoes), and new radars.

On the port side, an H-4B catapult

(similar to those installed in the *Essex* class) replaced one of the H-2-1 catapults and blisters provided weight and stability compensation.[7] These modernizations took place under SCB 54 in Fiscal Years 1949 and 1951. *Cabot* had her modernization during a nine-month overhaul at the Philadelphia Naval Shipyard between late 1950 and early 1951.[8] The *Bataan* had her overhaul at the Puget Sound Naval Shipyard in Bremerton, Washington, from July to November 1951, between her first and second Korean War cruises. These changes allowed the operation of the new Grumman Guardian, in its day, the largest single-engine aircraft to operate from a carrier. Working in hunter-killer pairs, the primary mission of the AF-2S was to attack submarines located by its companion, the AF-2W search version, which was equipped with radar and electronic countermeasures search equipment. Laying down a pattern of sonobouys to determine the exact location of the submarine, the AF-2S could attack with acoustic homing torpedoes, rockets, or depth charges.

The *Saipan* Class

During the war, Admiral King, Chief of Naval Operations, felt that a light carrier should be "brigaded" with a pair of larger carriers in each task group to provide local air cover, freeing the larger ships to conduct offensive strikes. Since it was anticipated that eighteen large carriers would be in commission by the end of 1945, and assuming two light carriers would be lost through normal attrition, two new light carriers were ordered in July 1943 to bring the number of light carriers back up to the original nine.

Even before the first *Independence*-class light carrier had really entered service, the Bureau of Aeronautics (BuAer) was dissatisfied with the design. In connection with the design of the *Saipan* class, BuAer commented that "perhaps the most general adverse comment regarding aircraft operation in the CVL-22s is the narrow hangar . . . due to the multitude of vent ducts and uptakes which pierce the hangar deck inboard of its outer boundary and to the fact that the flight deck supporting bents were not landed outboard of the hangar deck proper, i.e., on the blister. It is strongly recommended, therefore, that the maximum possible hangar width be achieved on this new class. . ."[9] The Bureau of Ships (BuShips) had already started designing a follow-on to the *Independence* class based on the *Baltimore*-class heavy cruisers. Although based on the *Baltimore* class, the *Saipan* class was given a new hull form that eliminated the need for blistering. The design also featured better protection than the earlier design, with more protected magazine space, and two H-2-1 catapults were included from the beginning. These "conversions" were built as carriers from the keel up. The *Saipan* (CVL-48) was laid down at the New York Shipbuilding Corporation at Camden, New Jersey on 10 July 1944, followed by the *Wright* (CVL-49) on 21 August 1944. Both were completed after the war; the *Saipan* was commissioned in July 1946, and the *Wright* in February 1947.

Although there were plans for modernizing *Saipan* and *Wright* as fleet, antisubmarine or training carriers, these were later canceled and they received only minimal ASW upgrades. Since their machinery was still

quite modern, however, they were converted to other roles. In 1962, the *Wright* began conversion to a national emergency command post afloat (NECPA) as the *Wright* (CC-2) and the *Saipan* began a similar conversion the following year. The *Saipan* eventually became a major communications relay ship and was renamed *Arlington* (AGMR-2). Both former CVLs were decommissioned in 1970.[10]

The Korean War

Although she was recommissioned in May 1950 to serve as an antisubmarine and training carrier, the *Bataan* was soon called to service in the Korean War following the invasion of South Korea by North Korea on 25 June. Arriving in San Diego near the end of July, she spent three months qualifying pilots before being ordered to the war zone. On 16 November 1950, she left San Diego with a load of Air Force personnel, machinery and equipment, and a deckload of F-84 Thunderjets.

Off-loading in Yokosuka, Japan, she sailed for Kobe where she took aboard VMF-212, a Marine F4U Corsair squadron. After a brief stop at Sasebo for fuel, ammunition and provisions, she joined Task Force 77 off the east coast of Korea. On 15 December she launched her first air support missions, covering the evacuation of Hungnam. She left Task Force 77 on New Year's Day, 1951, to join Task Group 96.8 on the west coast of Korea and continued to provide combat air patrols, reconnaissance, and close air support missions over Korea until 9 January. After replenishment in Sasebo, she set out on 15 January for the west coast of Korea to relieve the British light carrier

Theseus. For the next five months, through the winter and into late spring, *Bataan* alternated on station in the Yellow Sea with the *Theseus* and another British light carrier, HMS *Glory*, providing air support for United Nations forces. In March, the VMF-312 Checkerboards replaced VMF-212, and near the end of April, pilots from this squadron scored the first Marine victories of the war against enemy propeller-driven aircraft.[11]

On April 21, two Corsairs on an armed reconnaissance near Chinnamp'o were bounced by four Yaks. The Yaks surprised the section leader, Captain Philip DeLong, a South Pacific ace with eleven kills, and scored hits on his plane, though none were serious. DeLong's wingman, Lieutenant Harold Daigh, slipped behind the Yaks and opened up on one of them, blowing away its wing and sending it down.

Recovering from his initial surprise, DeLong rolled into a split-S, dove to pick up speed, pulled up into a high-speed climb and, still climbing, shot down a Yak while in a turn. He saw Daigh heading east, pursuing the Yak leader, but tailed by another Yak. DeLong quickly radioed a warning and Daigh broke hard, turning under the trailing Yak and opening fire on it as it overran him. The Yak, streaming a thick banner of smoke, was credited only as "damaged" at the time, although it was later confirmed as a kill. Meanwhile, DeLong caught up with the Yak leader and after a short, intense dogfight, DeLong riddled the Yak, whose pilot bailed out. Both Corsairs returned safely to the *Bataan*.[12]

In early June, *Bataan* off-loaded VMF-312 in Pusan and headed for San Diego, arriving on the first anniversary of the start of the Korean War, 25 June 1951. In July, she sailed up the coast to Bremerton, Washington, for a four month yard overhaul in the Puget Sound Naval Shipyard, where she received modifications similar to those done on the *Cabot*. In November, she returned to San Diego for underway training operations off the coast of southern California.

On 27 January 1952, she departed from San Diego to begin her second Korean War cruise, again transporting aircraft (this time, Marine F9F Panthers), vehicles, and equipment to be off-loaded in Yokosuka, where she arrived on 11 February. On Valentine's Day, she departed for Okinawa, dropping anchor in Buckner Bay two days later. She was soon operating a squadron of Grumman Guardian anti-submarine aircraft from VS-25 as the flagship of a "hunter-killer" group. For the next two months, between February and April 1952, she conducted ASW exercises, in company with destroyers and escorts, between Okinawa and Japan. After a stay in Yokosuka, *Bataan* returned to the war, stopping at Kobe to embark the Checkerboards, now redesignated as an attack squadron, VMA-312, and disembark VS-25. In late April, *Bataan* loaded ammunition and supplies in Sasebo and resumed operations off the west coast of Korea, launching her first strike on 30 April.

In ten days of operations, she launched more than 400 sorties, enforcing the United Nations blockade, defending friendly islands off the coast, spotting for naval gunfire, and providing combat air patrols. During this period one of her aircraft was shot down near Sukch'on while on armed reconnaissance. The downed pilot's squadronmates protected him from enemy ground troops while they directed an Air Force helicopter to the scene. Despite heavy fire, the pilot was returned to the *Bataan* unharmed.

Also during this period, a rocket exploded on her flight deck, tearing a three-foot hole in the flight deck and injuring three men. *Bataan* returned to Sasebo on 11 May and made her way back to Yokosuka for repairs, arriving on 28 May. When repairs were completed, she was underway on 5 June for the forward area. On 9 June one of her aircraft was shot down over enemy territory; the pilot suffered facial burns, but was picked up by helicopter. *Bataan* completed two more line periods off the west coast of Korea, interspersed with trips to Sasebo. On 15 July, two days into her final line period, *Bataan* suffered her first pilot loss of her second war cruise when one of her aircraft that had been forced down by enemy fire onto a desolate airstrip known as "K-6" crashed on takeoff. On 21 July she launched her last mission and flew off VMA-312 to Inchon. She pulled into Inchon Harbor the next day to disembark the rest of the Marines aboard. After stops in Sasebo, Kobe, and Yokosuka, the carrier departed in mid-August for Pearl Harbor and then on to San Diego, arriving there on 26 August.

After brief stays in San Diego and Long Beach, *Bataan* departed from San Diego on 28 October 1952 with VS-871 aboard to begin a third cruise to the Far East. After a brief two-day stay at Pearl Harbor in early November, *Bataan* proceeded to Okinawa and again conducted ASW exercises, alternating between Buckner Bay in Okinawa and Yokosuka, until 9 February 1953, when VS-871 was disembarked in Yokosuka,

and VMA-312 embarked. *Bataan* completed five patrols off the west coast of Korea, alternating with the HMS *Glory* in the familiar pattern of combat air patrol, armed reconnaissance, strike, and naval gunfire spotting operations in the Yellow Sea, interspersed with trips to Sasebo.

On 8 May 1953, VMA-312 was detached and, after two days of liberty in Yokosuka, *Bataan* headed home. Stopping briefly in Pearl Harbor, she proceeded to San Diego, where she arrived on 26 May. In June and July the ground fighting in Korea had reached a crescendo as both sides struggled to gain advances that would give them a better bargaining position in the peace talks. The pace of air operations also intensified as Task Force 77 provided close support to United Nations forces. Unable to prevail, the Communists agreed to a ceasefire on 27 July 1953. The Korean War was over. The *Bataan* remained in the San Diego area until the end of July, then headed for Hawaii, Japan, and back to Pearl Harbor, completing various training exercises. Upon arrival at Pearl Harbor, the inactivation process began and, in early 1954, *Bataan* was decommissioned and placed in the Pacific Reserve Fleet.

The *Langley* and *Belleau Wood* in French Service

The State Department decided to transfer the *Langley*, after four years in mothballs, to France as part of the Mutual Defense Assistance Program. Work to refurbish and rearm the carrier began in January 1951 and on 2 June the French flag was raised as she was rechristened *La Fayette* (R-96).

Departing the East Coast on 1 September, she arrived in France at the port of Toulon ten days later. There she embarked the 12th flotille (12F) equipped with Hellcats and the 4th flotille (4F) equipped with Avengers. Participating in various exercises, *La Fayette* operated off Provence and Corsica and later, in 1952, off Bizerte, Casablanca, and Agadir.

In November 1952, *La Fayette* returned to the U.S. to load aircraft for transfer to France. An exceptionally heavy storm encountered during the Atlantic crossing caused extensive damage. After a period of recovery at Norfolk, some Corsairs were taken aboard and *La Fayette* later participated in another exercise before sailing for the Far East.

Arriving at Tonkin, she took aboard the 2nd and 12th flotilles and carried out such missions as supporting the withdrawal of the garrison at Sam-Neua, defense of the Plain of Jars, attacking road traffic and the Phu-Dien-Chau battery at Xien-Kouang, and interdiction of the route between Sam-Neua and Maichau. At the conclusion of these operations *La Fayette* was ordered back to Toulon.

Modernized between February 1953 and September 1954, the carrier again participated in several inter-allied exercises before returning to the Far East in the spring of 1955 for a second tour, which lasted from mid-April to mid-July. Before departing the Far East, the 14th flotille from the *Bois Belleau* replaced the 12th flotille and La Fayette returned to Toulon. Again participating in exercises along the Mediterranean coast, *La Fayette* departed in January 1956 with the 15th flotille for a third Far East cruise, which lasted into June.

After participating in exercises with the British carriers *Albion* and *Centaur*, she returned to France.

In July 1956, *La Fayette* went back to Norfolk to ferry helicopters and light planes to Algeria, where French forces had been fighting Algerian insurgents since 1954. After quickly being refurbished that summer, she sailed at the end of October with the 15th flotille and half of the 14th flotille to another hot spot. Operating off Damiett for a month, the carrier supported the French campaign during the Suez crisis.

In July 1956, Gamal Abdal-Nasser, president of the Egyptian republic, had announced the nationalization of the Suez Canal, mainly in retaliation for American unwillingness to finance the Aswan dam project. In the midst of international negotiations over the future of the Suez Canal, France, Britain, and Israel acted unilaterally against Egypt. Israel attacked Egypt on 29 October 1956 and achieved immediate, stunning military success. The next day, a joint Anglo-French ultimatum called for the immediate withdrawal of both sides from the area of the Suez Canal. Since Israel had no forces in that area, it accepted the ultimatum, while Egypt rejected it. The British and French then launched air attacks on Egyptian airfields and other targets, and landed forces near Port Said on 5 November, in defiance of a United Nations resolution. Under pressure, Britain agreed to a withdrawal. British and French forces were gone by December, but much of the canal area was in a shambles. British and French influence in Egypt vanished and the Soviet Union gained influence as it quickly moved to rearm Egypt.

Israel was also forced to pull back from the territory it had conquered.

After a few landings on the coasts of Tunisia and Provence, *La Fayette* returned to Toulon in mid-December. Much of 1957 was spent participating in major allied exercises and in the spring of 1958, the carrier was ordered to patrol off Tunisia in support of the French army. In July, after participating in the Toulon Naval Review sponsored by General Charles de Gaulle, *La Fayette* began an extensive shipyard period at Toulon, which lasted into September 1959. (In 1958, during the political crisis created by the civil war in Algeria, De Gaulle became premier with the power to rule by decree for six months. A new French constitution, with strengthened presidential powers, was drawn up and, in 1959, De Gaulle became president of the new Fifth Republic.)

In 1960 *La Fayette* participated in most of the exercises and French fleet movements off the coast of Africa, joining in the rescue efforts for the Moroccan city of Agadyr, which was destroyed by an earthquake in March 1960, and visiting the French-speaking countries of West Africa, receiving a particularly warm welcome in Abidjan. The following spring the carrier took part in a second African cruise, with port calls at LaLuz, Port-Etienne, Dakar, and Libreville.

In 1962, *La Fayette* participated in both antisubmarine warfare exercises with heavy helicopters and anti-air exercises with Corsairs. With Corsairs aboard, her participation in Exercise Big Game marked the first time the entire French fleet operated with the U.S. Sixth Fleet. Afterwards, as flagship, she had port calls in Naples and Palma de Majorca. Joining the Light Squadron, *La Fayette* later called at Barcelona. With events in Algeria coming to a climax, she repatriated the first refugees to France following the signing of the armistice. (In 1962, DeGaulle reached a settlement with the insurgents which led to Algerian independence.)

In March 1963 *La Fayette* was returned to the U.S., having sailed more than 340,000 nautical miles under the French flag. She had 19,805 aircraft landings on her flight deck and had participated in the Indo-Chinese, Suez, and Algerian campaigns. Struck from the Naval Vessel Register, she was scrapped in Baltimore the following year.[13]

In September 1953, in San Francisco, the *Belleau Wood* followed the *Langley* into French service. Under the name *Bois Belleau* (R-97) she sailed from Norfolk to Bizerte on 11 December 1953. Early in 1954, after participating in numerous exercises in the Mediterranean, aircraft were loaded in Toulon for transport to Indochina. *Bois Belleau* arrived at Tonkin Bay in early May and in July, after having a boiler repaired in Hong Kong, the carrier launched air strikes against northern and central Vietnam. She also aided in the evacuation of refugees and troops from North Vietnam. The *Bois Belleau* left Indochina the year after, on 5 October 1955, and arrived in Toulon on 16 December. After a long overhaul of approximately one year, she participated in several training sorties and national and NATO fleet exercises.

Between 18 May and 22 July 1957, during the traditional spring cruise, *Bois Belleau* conducted port calls in Fort de France, New York, and Norfolk, where she took part in a naval review.

The first half of 1958 was dedicated to fleet training. In 1959 she was designated a flagship when she embarked Rear Admiral Lahaye, Commander Naval Aviation Mediterranean. As such, she participated in the spring cruise, with port calls at Naples, Athens, and Istanbul. She was also present at the grand naval review held at Mers-el-Kebir in June 1959. From October 1959 until July 1960 she carried out, on behalf of the French Air Force, six transatlantic crossings, ferrying airplanes between Norfolk and Brest and Saint-Nazaire. In that ten-month period she sailed a total of 46,000 miles. The aircraft carrier left Toulon on 23 August for Norfolk, and arrived in Philadelphia on 2 September, where she was officially returned to the U.S. Navy on 12 September. In the seven years that *Bois Belleau* was loaned to France she steamed more than 180,000 nautical miles. She was struck on 1 October 1960 and scrapped at Chester, Pennsylvania, in 1962.[14]

The *Cabot* in Spanish Service

The *Cabot* had been decommissioned and placed in the reserve fleet in January 1955, and in 1959 had been redesignated as an auxiliary aircraft transport (AVT-3). Between 1965 and 1967, she was overhauled at the Philadelphia Navy Yard in preparation for transfer to Spain as part of an agreement in which the U.S. activated, repaired, altered, and outfitted the ship before leasing it to Spain for five years. Commissioned as *SNS Dedalo* (PH-01) on 30 August 1967 at Philadelphia, she became flagship of the Spanish navy and for the next decade, *Dedalo* served as the mainstay for the training of helicopter pilots and crewmen and the development of Spanish naval air doctrine.[15] In 1972 she was stricken from the Naval Vessel Register and Spain purchased the vessel outright in 1973.

After being equipped with AV-8A Harriers in 1976, *Dedalo* was redesignated R-01, following the NATO standard designation for aircraft carriers. A year later, she became the flagship of the newly formed Fleet Naval Air Group, Spain's combat task force. The next twelve years were characterized by *Dedalo's* participation in regularly scheduled exercises with NATO naval forces. Replaced by the new *Principe De Asturias* in 1988, Spain agreed to donate the ship to a U.S. preservation group because of her historical significance.[16] On 13 July 1989 *Dedalo* departed Rota, Spain on her final ocean voyage bound for the country of her birth. Almost forty-six years had passed since the date of her original commissioning in 1943. In her twenty-two years under Spanish colors, more than 39,000 officers and men served on *Dedalo*. She was decommissioned on 5 August 1989 at New Orleans for preservation by the *Cabot/Dedalo* Foundation, an umbrella organization of several veterans groups and other organizations.

Attempts to Save the *Cabot/Dedalo*

Despite being in excellent condition and essentially unaltered from her World War II configuration, she sat at a pier in New Orleans as attempts were made to preserve her. Funds set aside for restoration and preservation were spent for other purposes, and in time, the preservation group fell into debt and various organizations involved sued the group over financial mismanagement.

In 1995, she was put up for sale to pay off debts and was bought by a Singapore ship breaker for $1.4 million. However, since she was on the National Historical Register, she could not be exported and could not be economically scrapped in the U.S. because of all the hazardous materials, such as asbestos insulation, that make the scrapping process long and costly. (The process is cheaper overseas because of cheap labor and lack of environmental concern.) Thus, she was still the property of the association.

In August 1995, the American Academy of Industry began a fundraising campaign to save her, but efforts fell short. To add to the complexity, the owners filed for bankruptcy in July 1996. Since their assets, including the ship, were now in the custody of the Federal Court, she was either to be sold at auction or turned over to the scrapper to satisfy their debts. She had been docked for seven years in the Port of New Orleans, where she ran up substantial wharfage fees, and was damaged from sideswipes by other vessels.

In July 1997, the Coast Guard intervened and made emergency repairs, cleaning up hazardous liquids and moving her to the Violet Dock, downriver from New Orleans. Before the Coast Guard's contract to dock the ship at Violet expired, the USS *Cabot/Dedalo* Foundation, Inc., moved her to Port Isabel, Texas. The *Cabot/Dedalo* was moved to a ship breaking berth in Brownsville, Texas in August 1998, where initial scrapping activities occurred, in an effort to offset the debts run up by the ship. In 1999, the Department of Justice, acting for the Coast Guard, seized the *Cabot* so

that it could be auctioned to satisfy the debts incurred by the Coast Guard in performing emergency repairs.[17]

In the meantime, on 31 August 1999, preservation of the vessel was designated an "Official Project" by Save America's Treasures–a public and private partnership between the White House Millennium Council and the National Trust for Historic Preservation. This did not provide direct funding, but it was the first step in becoming eligible for future grants and provided national recognition. In the end, however, it did not matter. On 9 September 1999 Sabe Marine Salvage, part of the Global Maritime Group, was the high bidder for the *Cabot/Dedalo*, beating out ECOSAT (Education Council for Space Age Technology), a Miami-based group trying to save her as a museum. The federal government had contributed $2 million toward saving the *Cabot/Dedalo*, but in the end, lack of private funds scuttled plans to save her. As Bill Anderson, past president of the USS *Cabot* Association was quoted in the press: "When you get an obsolete ship, as far as your navy is concerned, you scrap it." . . . "We've done that with airplanes and ships to the point that we have very few historic ones (left)."[18] Those trying to save the *Cabot/Dedalo* were unable to raise enough money to purchase the ship from Sabe and ensure her future as a museum ship.

The Verdict of History

The official assessment of the *Independence* class could be summed up in an excerpt from a 1945 Pacific Fleet Board review of lessons learned in ships' characteristics. The board had recommended that there should be no further construction of light carriers in view of the fact that:

"the CVL-22 type's lack of air group strength and lack of flight deck and hangar deck flexibility of operation (due, primarily to a lack of beam) . . . Their presence in a force containing large carriers provides CAP and other air details without compromising the readiness, launching or landing of complete strikes from the larger ships, but this advantage is not sufficient to warrant diversion of such tonnage as may be available for this purpose. Ton for ton, CVLs can launch and land airplanes more rapidly than can CVs because airplanes must be launched or landed in succession regardless of ship size, but the overhead in screen vessels and ship's organizations, and complications of communications, maneuvering and aircraft rendezvous modify this advantage.

"It appears now, that conversion of the nine cruiser hulls to CVLs was expedient in that these vessels, completed as carriers, inflicted more damage on the enemy than they would have inflicted, probably, had they been completed as cruisers, but their lack of air strength, vulnerability, uncomfortable living conditions, lack of capacity for reserve airplanes, inadequate ship control and signal accommodations, catapult limitations, and suitability for night flying operations . . . are believed inherent in high speed carriers of this tonnage."[19]

The review went on to say that

motion in a seaway, which had been feared might prevent operations at times, was more hazardous than in larger ships, but "this hazard is almost always accepted and the pilots and crew, by superior skill developed through necessity, make the operations successful."[20] There could be no more fitting tribute to the men who served in the light carriers.

By the mid 1950s there were no longer any roles on active service for the light carriers – they could not operate modern jets or the latest ASW aircraft, the twin-engine Grumman S2F Tracker. As the new *Forrestal*-class "super carriers" were commissioned, the larger and more modernized *Essex*-class carriers took over the antisubmarine and training duties. On 15 May 1959, all of the inactive ships were reclassified as "auxiliary aircraft transports," AVT, although none of them actually served as such. Most of these were soon stricken from the register of Naval vessels and scrapped. Only the *Cabot/Dedalo* remains and her ultimate fate is now sealed.

Perhaps a more appropriate assessment of the *Independence* class comes from Ernie Pyle. Writing of the *Cabot* in 1945, his words are, perhaps, representative of the contributions to victory made by all the light carriers:

"My carrier is a proud one. She's small, and you've never heard of her unless you have a son or husband on her, but still she's proud, and deservedly so. She has been at sea, without returning home, longer than any other carrier in the Pacific, with one exception. She left home in November 1943. She is a little thing, yet her planes have shot two hundred thirty-eight of the enemy out of the sky in air battles, and her guns have knocked down five Jap planes in defending herself. She is too proud to keep track of little ships she destroys, but she has sent to the bottom twenty-nine big Japanese ships. Her bombs and aerial torpedoes have smashed into everything from the greatest Jap battleships to the tiniest coastal schooners.

"She is known in the fleet as 'The Iron Woman,' because she has fought in every battle in the Pacific in the years 1944 and 1945. Her battle record sounds like a train-caller on the Lackawanna Railroad. Listen –Kwajalein, Eniwetok, Truk, Palau, Hollandia, Saipan, Chichi Jima, Mindanao, Luzon, Formosa, Nansei Shoto [Ryukyu Islands], Hong Kong, Iwo Jima, Tokyo . . . and many others.

"She has been hit twice by Jap bombs. She has had mass burials at sea . . . with her dry-eyed crew sewing 40-mm shells to the corpses of their friends, as weights to take them to the bottom of the sea. Yet she has never even returned to Pearl Harbor to patch her wounds. She slaps on some patches on the run, and is ready for the next battle. The crew in semi-jocularity cuss

her chief engineer for keeping her in such good shape they have no excuse to go back to Honolulu or America for overhaul. She has been out so long that her men put their ship above their captain. They have seen captains come and captains go, but they and the ship stay on forever. They aren't romantic about their long stay out here. They hate it, and their gripes are long and loud. They yearn pathetically to go home. But down beneath, they are proud–proud of their ship and proud of themselves. And you would be too."[21]

Yes, this one ship stood for all her sisters and for all the crews and aircrews that have served in them. For those who have never been to sea in a warship, it is difficult for those who have to express how it really feels. It is important to a free society to remember the sacrifices of those who have defended it. History teaches us many lessons, but in a world of "virtual" experiences, there is still nothing like experiencing the real thing. Future generations needed to walk her decks, to feel history underfoot, to imagine the sights, sounds and smells. As of this writing, the cutters torches are dismantling her, even as various groups try to salvage at least some portions of her for posterity. The destruction of such a ship is a national shame.

Appendix A
Technical Data

Length (overall):   622'6"
Length (waterline):   600'
Beam (extreme):   109'2"
Beam (waterline):   71'6"
Flight Deck: 552' x 73'
Hangar Deck: 285' x 55' (17'4" clear height)
Elevators: 2 42' x 44' (capacity 28,000 lbs.)
Catapults: 1 H 2-1 hydraulic catapult (second added 1944-45;
     1 H 4B in ASW conversions postwar)
Arresting Gear: Mk 4 ?
Design Standard Displacement: 11,000 tons
Design Displacement: 14,220 tons
Design Full Load: 15,100 tons
Draft: 26'
Machinery: 4-shaft geared turbines; 4 Babcock & Wilcox
     boilers (565 psi, 850 F.)
     4 600kW ships service turbine generators
     2 250kW diesel generators
Shaft Horsepower: 100,000 (design); 106,001 (trial) (CVL-28 Cabot)
Fuel Capacity: 2,632.6 tons
Speed: 31.6 knots (design)
Endurance: 8,325 nm at 15 knots
Tactical Diameter:
Armament: 24 40mm (2 x 4, 8 x 2) guns
     16 20mm guns
Fire Control System: 10 Mk 51 fire control directors for 40mm mounts

Protection: Flight deck - none
            Protective deck - 2″
            Armor belt - 5″ tapered to 3.25″
            (none in CVL-22 and CVL-23)
            Bulkheads - 5″ and 3.75″
            Conning tower - none; 15 lb. STS on bridge
            Steering gear - 5″ bulkheads, 2.25″ above,
            .75″ below
Aircraft: 12 fighters, 9 bombers, 9 torpedo bombers,
            1 utility (see remarks)
Aviation Ordnance: 331.4 tons
Aviation Gasoline: 122,243 gals.
Complement (ship & air group):140 officer/1,321 enlisted (see remarks)

Remarks: The first two ships, *Independence* (CVL-22) and *Princeton* (CVL-23) were completed without the 5″ armor belt. The original design called for single 5″/38 guns fore and aft, but these were only fitted to the *Independence* and *Princeton* and were replaced with 40mm quad mounts after only six weeks. As completed in April 1943, *Independence* had 14 20mm single mounts. Armament was later increased to 2 quad 40mm, 9 dual 40mm, and 16 single 20mm mounts (20mm mounts increased to 22 on some ships). Later, the single 20mm mounts were replaced with 5 20mm twin mounts (6 in *Monterey*). Original complement increased to total of 1,569.

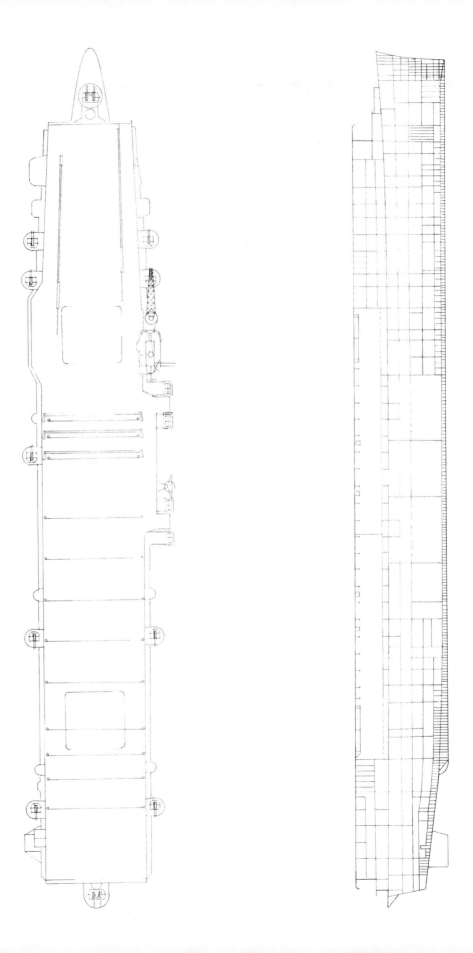

Appendix B
Individual Ships

CVL-22 *Independence* **class**
Builder: New York Shipbuilding Corporation, Camden, NJ
CVL-22 *Independence*
Keel laid 1 May 1941 as *Amsterdam* (CL-59); reclassified as CV-22 10 January 1942; launched 22 August 1942; commissioned 14 January 1943; redesignated CVL-22 15 July 1943; atomic test target ship July 1946; decommissioned 28 August 1946; sunk as target 29 January 1951.

World War II: Pacific Raids 1943: Marcus Island Raid, 31 August 1943; Wake Island Raid, 5-6 October 1943. Treasury-Bougainville Operation Rabaul Strike, 11 November 1943. Gilbert Islands Operation 19–20 November 1943. Western Carolina Islands Operation Capture and Occupation of Southern Palau Islands, 6 September–14 October 1943. Leyte Operation 3rd Fleet Supporting Operations Okinawa Attack, 10 October 1944. Northern Luzon and Formosa Attacks,13–14 October 1944; Visayas Attacks, 21 October 1944; Luzon Attacks, 5 October 1944, 17–19 October

1944, 5–6 November 1944, 19–25 November 1944, 14–16 December 1944; Battle of Surigao Strait, 24–28 October 1944. Luzon Operation: Formosa Attacks, 3–4 January 1945, 9 January 1945, 15 January 1945, 21 January 1945; China Coast Attacks, 12 January 1945, 16 January 1945, Nansei Shoto Attack, 22 January 1945. Okinawa Gunto Operation: 5th and 3rd Fleet Raids in Support of Okinawa Gunto Operation, 17 March–11 June 1945. Third Fleet Operations against Japan, 10 July–15 August 1945.

Eight battle stars. Severely damaged by aerial torpedo 20 November 1943.

Air Groups: CVLG- 22–September–November 1943; CVLG-41(N)–September 1944 January 1945; CVLG-46–February–June 1945; CVLG-27–July–August 1945.

Post World War II: "Magic Carpet" 15 November 1945–28 January 1946; Bikini atomic test target July 1946, subsequently towed to Kwajalein and decommissioned; returned to Pearl

Harbor and then San Francisco for radiation tests; sunk off coast of California in weapons tests.

Remarks: Known as "Evil I" at one point; nickname later attributed to the *Intrepid* (CV-11). Name continued by CVA-62.

CVL-23 *Princeton*
Keel laid 2 June 1941 as *Tallahassee* (CL-61); reclassified as CV-23 14 February 1942; launched 18 October 1942; commissioned 14 January 1943; redesignated CVL-23 15 July 1943; sunk 24 October 1944.

World War II: Pacific Raids 1943: Tarawa Island Raid, 18 September 1943. Treasury-Bougainville Operation Buka-Bonis Strike, 1–2 November 1943; Rabaul Strike, 5 November 1943; Rabaul Strike, 11 November 1943. Gilbert Islands Operation:10–20 November 1943. Marshall Islands Operation Occupation of Kwajalein and Majuro Atolls, 29 January–8 February 1944; Occupation of Eniwetok Atoll, 17 February–2 March 1944. Asiatic-Pacific Raids 1944: Palau, Yap, Ulithi, Woleai Raid, 30 March–1 April 1944; Truk, Satawan, Ponape Raid, 29 April–1 May 1944. Hollandia Operation (Aitape-Humboldt Bay-Tanahmerah Bay), 21–24 April 1944. Marianas Operation Capture and Occupation of Saipan, 11–24 June 1944; Battle of the Philippine Sea, 19–20 June 1944; Capture and Occupation of Guam, 12 July–15 August 1944. Western Caroline Islands Operation Capture and Occupation of Southern Palau Islands, 6 September–14 October 1944; Assaults on the Philippine Islands, 9–24 September 1944. Leyte Operation 3rd Fleet Supporting Operations Okinawa Attack, 10 October 1944; Northern Luzon and Formosa Attacks, 11–14 October 1944; Luzon Attacks, 15 October 1944, 17–19 October 1944; Battle of Surigao Strait, 24 October 1944.

Nine battle stars. Sunk 24 October 1944.

Air Groups: CVLG-23–September 1943–April 1944; CVLG-27–June–October 1944.

Remarks: Known as "Peerless P." Name continued by CV-37 and CG-59.

CVL-24 *Belleau Wood*
Keel laid 11 August 1941 as *New Haven* (CL-76); reclassified as CV-24 14 February 1942; launched 6 December 1942; commissioned 31 March 1943; redesignated CVL-24 15 July 1943; decommissioned 13 January 1947; loaned to France 5 September 1953; renamed *Bois Belleau* (R-97) 9 September 1953; returned September 1960; struck 1 October 1960; scrapped at Chester, PA 1962.

World War II: Pacific Raids 1943: Tarawa Island Raid, 18 September 1943; Wake Island Raid, 5–6 October 1943. Gilbert Islands Operation 19 November–4 December 1944. Marshall Islands Operation Occupation of Kwajalein and Majuro Atolls, 29 January–8 February 1944. Asiatic-Pacific Raids 1944: Truk Attack, 16–17 February 1944; Marianas Attack, 21–22 February 1944; Truk, Satawan, Ponape Raid, 29 April–1 May 1944. Hollandia Operation (Aitape-Humboldt Bay-Tanahmerah Bay) 21–24 April 1944. Marianas Operation Capture and Occupation of Saipan, 11–24 June 1944; First Bonins Raid, 15–16 June 1944; Battle of the Philippine Sea, 19–20 June

1944; Second Bonins Raid, 24 June 1944; Capture and Occupation of Guam, 12 July–15 August 1944. Western Caroline Islands Operation Capture and Occupation of Southern Palau Islands, 6 September–14 October 1944; Assaults on the Philippine Islands, 9–24 September 1944. Western New Guinea Operations Morotai Landings, 15 September 1944. Leyte Operations 3rd Fleet Supporting Operations Okinawa Attack, 10 October 1944; Northern Luzon and Formosa Attacks, 11–14 October 1944; Luzon Attacks, 15 October 1944, 17–19 October 1944; Battle of Surigao Strait, 24–28 October 1944. Iwo Jima Operation 5th Fleet Raids against Honshu and the Nansei Shoto, 15–16 February 1945, 25 February 1945, 1 March 1945; Assault and Occupation of Iwo Iima, 15 February–4 March 1945. Third Fleet Operations against Japan, 10 July–15 August 1945.

Presidential Unit Citation. Twelve battle stars. Severely damaged by Kamikaze 30 October 1944.

Air Groups: CVLG-24–September 1943–June 1944; CVLG-21–July–November 1944; CVLG-30–February–June 1945; CVLG-31 –July–August 1945; CVLG-28–September–October 1945.

Post World War II: "Magic Carpet" 28 October 1945 – 31 January 1946; in reserve until transferred to France under Mutual Defense Assistance Program, 5 September 1953. Name changed to *Bois Belleau.* Returned to US September 1960; stricken and sold for scrap.

Remarks: Equipped with the SP and DRBV-22 (French) radars in 1955-1957. Name continued by LHA-3.

CVL-25 *Cowpens*

Keel laid 17 November 1941 as *Huntington* (CL-77); reclassified as CV-25 27 March 1942; launched 17 January 1943; commissioned 28 May 1943; decommissioned 13 January 1947; redesignated AVT-1 15 May 1959; struck 1 November 1959; scrapped at Portland, OR 1962.

World War II: Pacific Raids 1943: Wake Island Raid, 5–6 October 1943. Gilbert Islands Operation 19 November–4 December 1944. Marshall Islands Operation Occupation of Kwajalein and Majuro Atolls, 31 January–5 February 1945. Asiatic-Pacific Raids 1944: Truk Attack, 16–17 February 1944; Marianas Attacks, 21-22 February 1944; Palau, Yap, Ulithi, Woleai Raid, 30 March–1 April 1944. Western New Guinea Operation Morotai Landings, 15 September 1944. Marianas Operation Capture and Occupation of Saipan, 11–24 June 1944; First Bonins Raid, 15–16 June 1944; Battle of the Philippine Sea, 19–20 June 1944. Western Caroline Islands Operation Capture and Occupation of Southern Palau Islands, 6 September–14 October 1944; Assaults on the Philippine Islands, 9–24 September 1944. Leyte Operation 3rd Fleet Supporting Operations Okinawa Attack, 10 October 1944; Northern Luzon and Formosa Attacks, 11–14 October 1944; Luzon Attacks, 15 October 1944, 17–19 October 1944, 5–6 November 1944, 13–14 November 1944, 19–25 November 1944, 14–16 December 1944. Luzon Operation Luzon Attacks, 6–7 January 1945; Formosa Attacks, 3–4 January 1945, 9 January 1945, 15 January 1945, 21 January 1945; China Coast Attacks, 12 January 1945, 16

January 1945; Nansei Shoto Attack, 22 January 1945. Iwo Jima Operations 5th Fleet Raids against Honshu and the Nansei Shoto, 15–16 February 1945, 25 February 1945, 1 March 1945; Assault and Occupation of Iwo Jima, 15 February–4 March 1945. Third Fleet Operations against Japan, 10 July–15 August 1945.

Navy Unit Commendation. Twelve battle stars.

Air Groups: CVLG-25–October 1943–June 1944; CVLG-22–September 1944–January 1945; CVLG-46–February–June 1945; CVLG-50–June–August 1945.

Post World War II: "Magic Carpet" 8 November 1945 – 28 January 1946.

Remarks: Known as "Mighty Moo." Name continued by CG-63.

CVL-26 *Monterey*

Keel laid 29 December 1941 as *Dayton* (CL-78); reclassified as CV-26 27 March 1942; launched 28 February 1943; commissioned 17 June 1943; decommissioned 11 February 1947; recommissioned 15 September 1950; redesignated; decommissioned 16 January 56; redesignated AVT-2 15 May 59; struck 1 June 70; scrapped.

World War II: Gilbert Islands Operation 19 November–8 December 1943. Bismarck-Archipelago Operation Kavieng Strike, 25 December 1943, 1 January 1944. Asiatic-Pacific Raids 1944: Truk Attack, 15–17 February 1944, Marianas Attack, 21–22 February 1944, Palau, Yap, Woleai, Ulithi Raid, 30 March–1 April 1944; Truk, Satawan, Ponape Raid, 29 April–1 May 1944. Marshall Islands Operation Occupation of Kwajalein and Majuro Atolls, 29 January–8 February 1944. Hollandia

Operation (Aitape-Humboldt Bay-Tanahmerah Bay), 21–24 April 1944. Marianas Operation Capture and Occupation of Saipan, 11–24 June 1944; Battle of the Philippine Sea, 19–20 June 1944; Third Bonins Raid, 3–4 July 1944. Western New Guinea Operation Morotai Landings, 15 September 1944. Western Caroline Islands Operation Capture and Occupation of Southern Palau Islands, 6 September–14 October 1944; Assaults on the Philippine Islands, 9–24 September 1944. Leyte Operation Third Fleet Supporting Operations Okinawa Attack, 10 October 1944; Northern Luzon and Formosa Attacks, 11–14 October 1944; Luzon Attacks, 15 October 1944, 17–19 October 1944, 24–26 October 1944, 13–17 November 1944, 19 November 1944, 14–16 December 1944. Okinawa Gunto Operation 5th and 3rd Fleet Raids in Support of Okinawa Gunto Operation, 9–30 May 1945. Third Fleet Operations against Japan 10 July–15 August 1945.

Eleven battle stars.

Air Groups: CVLG-30–November 1943–April 1944; CVLG-28–June–December 1944; CVLG-34–April 1945. Post World War II: "Magic Carpet" October 1945 – ? (Atlantic); reactivated as training carrier during Korean War.

Remarks: Known as "Monty." Name continued by CG-61.

CVL-27 *Langley*

Keel laid 11 April 1942 ordered as *Fargo* (CL-85), reclassified as *Crown Point* (CV-27) 27 March 42; renamed *Langley* 13 November 1942; launched 22 May 1943; redesignated CVL-27 15 July 1943 ; commissioned 31 August 1943; decommissioned 11 February 1947; loaned to France 8 January 1951;

renamed *La Fayette* (R-96) 2 June 1951; returned 20 March 1963; struck 1963; scrapped at Baltimore, MD 1964.

World War II: Marshall Islands Operation Occupation of Kwajalein and Majuro Atolls, 29 January–8 February 1944; Occupation of Eniwetok Atoll, 17 February–2 March 1944. Hollandia Operation (Aitape-Humboldt Bay-Tanahmerah Bay), 21–24 April 1944. Asiatic Pacific Raids 1944: Palau, Yap, Ulithi, Woleai Raid, 30 March–1 April 1944; Truk, Satawan, Ponape Raid, 29 April–1 May 1944. Marianas Operation Capture and Occupation of Saipan, 11–24 June 1944; First Bonins Raid, 15–16 June 1944; Battle of the Philippine Sea, 19–20 June 1944; Capture and Occupation of Guam, 12 July–15 August 1944. Western Carolines Islands Operation Capture and Occupation of Southern Palau Islands, 6 September–14 October 1944; Assaults on the Philippine Islands, 9–24 September 1944. Leyte Operation 3rd Fleet Supporting Operations Okinawa Attack, 10 October 1944; Northern Luzon and Formosa Attacks, 11–14 October 1944; Luzon Attacks, 15 October 1944, 17–19 October 1944, 5–6 November 1944, 13–14 November 1944, 19–25 November 1944, 14–15 December 1944; Visayas Attacks, 21 October 1944; Battle of Surigao Strait, 24–26 October 1944. Luzon Operation Formosa Attacks, 3–4 January 1945, 9 January 1945, 15 January 1945, 21 January 1945; Luzon Attacks, 6–7 January 1945; China Coast Attacks, 12 January 1945, 16 January 1945; Nansei Shoto Attack, 22 January 1945. Iwo Jima Operation Assault and Occupation of Iwo Jima 15 February–1 March 1945; 5th Fleet Raids against Honshu and the Nansei Shoto, 15–16 February 1945, 25 February 1945. Okinawa Gunto Operation 5th and 3rd Fleet Raids in Support of Okinawa Gunto Operation, 17 March–24 May 1945.

Nine battle stars. Damaged by bomb 21 January 1945.

Air Groups: CVLG-32–January–September 1944; CVLG-44–October 1944–January 1945; CVLG-23–February–April 1945.

Post World War II: "Magic Carpet" November 1945 – January 1946 (Atlantic); in reserve until transfer to France under Mutual Defense Assistance Program.

Remarks: Equipped with SK-2 and SP radars in French service, and SPS-6 and SP radars from 1956.

CVL-28 *Cabot*

Keel laid 16 March 1942 as *Wilmington* (CL-79); reclassified as CV-28 2 June 1942; launched 4 April 1943; redesignated CVL-28 15 July 1943; commissioned 24 July 1943; decommissioned 11 February 1947; recommissioned 27 October 1948; decommissioned 21 January 1955; redesignated AVT-3 15 May 1959; loaned to Spain 5 December 1967; renamed *Dedalo* (PH-01); struck 1 August 1972; sold to Spain 5 December 1972; decommissioned 5 August 1989.

World War II: Marshall Islands Operation Occupation of Kwajalein and Majuro Atolls, 29 January–8 February 1944. Asiatic Pacific Raids 1944: Truk Attack, 19–17 February 1944; Palau, Yap, Ulithi, Woleai Raid, 30 March–1 April 1944; Truk, Satawan, Ponape Raid, 29 April–1 May 1944. Hollandia Operation (Aitape–Humboldt Bay-Tanahmerah Bay), 21–24 April 1944. Marianas Operation Battle of the

Philippine Sea, 19–20 June 1944; Third Bonins Raid, 3–4 July 1945; Capture and Occupation of Saipan, 11–24 July 1944; Capture and Occupation of Guam, 12 July–15 August 1944; Palau, Yap, Ulithi Raid, 25–27 July 1944; Fourth Bonins Raid, 4–5 August 1944. Western Caroline Islands Operation Capture and Occupation of Southern Palau Islands, 6 September–14 October 1944; Assaults on the Philippine Islands, 9–24 September 1944. Leyte Operation 3rd Fleet Supporting Operations Okinawa Attack, 10 October 1944; Northern Luzon and Formosa Attacks, 13–14 October 1944; Luzon Attacks, 15 October 1944, 5–6 November 1944, 19–25 November 1944; Visayas Attack, 21 October 1944; Battle of Surigao Strait, 24–26 October 1944. Luzon Operation Formosa Attacks, 3–4 January 1945, 9 January 1945, 15 January 1945, 21 January 1945; Luzon Attacks, 6–7 January 1945; China Coast Attacks, 12 January 1945, 16 January 1945; Nansei Shoto Attacks, 22 January 1945. Iwo Jima Operation 5th Fleet Raids against the Nansei Shoto and Honshu, 15–20 February 1945, 25 February 1945, 1 March 1945; Assault and Occupation of Iwo Jima, 15 February–1 March 1945. Okinawa Gunto Operation 5th and 3rd Fleet Raids in Support of Okinawa Gunto Operation, 17 March–9 April 1945.

Presidential Unit Citation. Nine battle stars. Damaged by Kamikaze off Luzon 25 November 1944.

Air Groups: CVLG-31–January– September 1944; CVLG-29–October 1944–April 1945; CVLG-32–August– October 1945.

Post World War II: Occupation landing support September–October 1945; recommissioned to support Naval Air Reserve training October 1948 – January 1955; overhauled at Philadelphia Navy Yard before transfer to Spain under Mutual Defense Assistance Program where she served as the flagship of the Spanish Fleet.

Remarks: Equipped with SPS-6 and SP radars 1951-1954; SPS-40, SPS-6, and SPS-8A radars from 1967; SPS-40, SPS-52. and SPS-6 radars from 1978. Known as the "Iron Woman."

CVL-29 *Bataan*

Ordered as *Buffalo* (CL-99), reclassi- fied as CV-29 2 June 42; keel laid 31 August 1942; redesignated CVL-29 15 July 1943; launched 1 August 1943; commissioned 17 November 1943; decommissioned 11 February 1947; recommissioned 13 May 1950; decom- missioned 9 April 1954; redesignated AVT-4 15 May 59; struck 1 September 59; scrapped.

World War II: Hollandia Operation (Aitape-Humbolt Bay-Tanahmerah Bay) 21–24 April 1944. Asiatic-Pacific Raids 1944: Truk, Satawan, Ponape Raid, 29 April–1 May 1944. Marianas Operation Capture and Occupation of Saipan, 11–24 June 1944; First Bonins Raid, 15–16 June 1944; Battle of the Philippine Sea, 19–20 June 1944; Second Bonins Raid, 24 June 1944. Okinawa Gunto Operation 5th and 3rd Fleet Raids in Support of Okinawa Gunto Operation, 17 March–30 May 1945. Third Fleet Operations against Japan, 10 July–15 August 1945.

Six battle stars.

Air Groups: CVLG-50–April–July 1944; CVLG-42 (N)–October 1944–?; CVLG-47–March–August 1945.

Notes: *Bataan* was to operate as a night carrier and trained off Hawaii with CVLG-42 (N). Reverted to a day carrier with CVLG-47. In August 1945, *Bataan* swapped air groups with *San Jacinto,* which was returning to the U.S. CVLG-49 operated with *Bataan* in early post war operations while CVLG-47 returned with *San Jacinto.*

Post World War II: "Magic Carpet" October 1945 _ January 1946 (Atlantic); in reserve until reactivation for Korean War.

Korean War: Three deployments December 1950 – June 1951; May 1952 – August 1952; October 1952 – May 1953. **Seven battle stars.**

Air Groups: 16 November 1950–25 June 1951 VMF-212 (aboard 11 December 1950–5 March 1951); VMF-312 (aboard 5 March–6 June 1951); HU-1 Det 8. 27 January–26 August 1952 VMA-312 (aboard 21 April–21 July 1952); VS-25; HU-1 Det. 28 October 1952–26 May 1953 VMA-312 (aboard 9 February–8 May 1953); VS-871; VS-21; HU-1 Det.

Remarks: Name continued by LHD-5.

CVL-30 *San Jacinto*

Keel laid 26 October 1942 as Newark (CL-100); reclassified as *Reprisal* CV-30 2 June 1942; renamed *San Jacinto* 30 January 1943; redesignated CVL-30 15 July 1943; launched 29 September 1943; commissioned 15 December 1943; decommissioned 1 March 1947; redesignated AVT-5 15 May 59; struck 1 June 79; scrapped.

World War II: Marianas Operation Capture and Occupation of Saipan, 11–24 June 1944; Battle of the Philippine Sea, 19–20 June 1944; Capture and Occupation of Guam, 12

July–15 August 1944; Palau, Yap, Ulithi, Raids, 25–27 July 1944; Fourth Bonins Raid, 4–5 August 1944. Western Caroline Islands Operation Raids on Volcano-Bonin Islands and Yap Islands, 31 August–8 September 1944; Capture and Occupation of Southern Palau Islands, 6 September–14 October 1944; Assaults on the Philippine Islands, 9–24 September 1944. Leyte Operation 3rd Fleet Supporting Operations Okinawa Attack, 10 October 1944; Northern Luzon and Formosa Attacks, 11–14 October 1944; Luzon Attacks, 15 October 1944, 17–19 October 1944, 13–14 November 1944, 19 November 1944, 14–16 December 1944; Battle of Surigao Strait, 24–26 October 1944. Luzon Operation Formosa Attacks, 3–4 January 1945, 9 January 1945, 15 January 1945, 21 January 1945; Luzon Attacks, 6–7 January 1945; China Coast Attacks, 12 January 1945, 16 January 1945. Iwo Jima Operation Assault and Occupation of Iwo Jima, 15 February–4 March 1945; 5th Fleet Raids against Honshu and the Nansei Shoto, 25 February 1945, 1 March 1945. Okinawa Gunto Operation 5th and 3rd Fleet Raids in Support of Okinawa Gunto Operation, 17 March–11 June 1945. Third Fleet Operations against Japan, 10 July–15 August 1945.

Presidential Unit Citation. Five battle stars. Minor damage by kamikaze 6 April 1945.

Air Groups: CVLG-51–May–November 1944; CVLG-45–November 1944–April 1945; CVLG-49–May–August 1945; CVLG-47 –August 1945

Post World War II: "Magic Carpet" November 1945 – ?

Remarks: Known as "San Jock." Name continued by CG-56.

Air Group Notes

Beginning in 1942, carrier air groups were assigned numbers, the first being Carrier Air Group NINE (short title CAG-9), commissioned in March 1942. Later, on 29 June 1944, air group letter designations were changed to reflect the complements of different classes of carriers, i.e. CVBG for large carriers of the *Midway* class, CVG for fleet carriers, mainly of the *Essex* class, CVLG for light carriers, and CVEG for escort carriers of the *Sangamon* class. (Other CVE classes were assigned composite squadrons, VC, although they were listed as air groups during the war.) For simplicity, air groups are listed above as "CVLG" regardless of the date assigned.

Originally, the air group complement for the *Independence* class was established at 24 Wildcat fighters, 12 Dauntless dive bombers, and 9 Avenger torpedo bombers, with the fighters assigned to a VF squadron and the dive and torpedo bombers to a VC squadron. When the new, larger, Hellcat replaced the Wildcat, fewer fighters could be carried. In October 1943, the authorized complement for CVL air groups was officially established at 12 fighter (VF), 9 dive bomber (VB) and 9 torpedo bomber (VT), but the dive bombers were eventually eliminated and the light carrier air group complement was revised in November 1943 to 24 VF and 9 VT and remained at that level through the war, despite recommendations from the fleet for the light carriers to have all-fighter air groups. In August 1943, in the forward area of the Pacific, the *Independence, Princeton,* and *Belleau Wood* had their Dauntlesses detached and 12 plane Hellcat detachments from VF-6 added until the official organization was changed. The remaining torpedo bombers retained their VC designations until later.

The first five light carrier air groups were commissioned between May and December 1942, eleven more were added in 1943, ten in 1944 (four of these were night groups, but only Air Group 41 made a combat tour), and only two in 1945. Of the total (28), all but seven made combat tours (Air Group 38 was land based) and eight (Air Groups 22, 23, 25, 27, 30, 31, 32 and 50) had two tours. The *Cowpens, Independence* and *Belleau Wood* all deployed four air groups, but *Cowpens* was the most active, spending more time engaged in operations than her sisters. Of the 24 months from her first operation in September 1943 until V-J Day, the "Mighty Moo" spent 18 months (except for a brief overhaul on the west coast in early 1945) in combat in the Central and Western Pacific. *Belleau Wood* was close behind with 17 months and all the others except *Bataan* spent a year or more operating combat air groups.

Among the light carrier Hellcat squadrons, two squadrons were credited with 160 aerial kills in two tours – VF-30 with tours on *Belleau Wood* and VF-31 aboard *Cabot* and *Belleau Wood.* Third was VF-27, which avenged the loss of the *Princeton* when it returned to combat aboard the *Independence* late in the war to bring its total to 137. The top CVL ace was Lieutenant Cornelius "Conny" Nooy, who scored 19 victories in two tours with VF-31.

Camouflage

In January 1941, the Navy issued new camouflage instructions calling for different systems or "measures" to be used for various ships operating under different conditions. These measures were revised in September 1941 and again in June 1942. The June 1942 instructions and later supplements remained in effect during the rest of World War II and were not officially revised until 1953, although the use of camouflage was discontinued after the war ended. The "dazzle" patterns so popular during much of the war were intended to confuse the enemy as to a ship's true course and speed and reflected concern for attack by submarines. Several different designs were drawn up for aircraft carriers; some designs were on more than one ship, but others were unique to a particular ship. Later in the war, as kamikazes became a threat, solid color schemes designed to reduce observation from the air became more predominant. It was not unusual for a given ship to be painted in several different schemes over the course of the war, and photo-

graphs can often be dated by changes in camouflage patterns.

The colors used on the *Independence*-class carriers, from the lightest to the darkest, included Pale Gray (5-P), Light Gray (5-L), Haze Gray (5-H), Ocean Gray (5-O), and Navy Blue (5-N). These colors were made by adding various amounts of a dark blue-black tinting material (5-TM) to white paint (5-U) and all had a purplish-blue cast. Dull Black (BK) was also used in some camouflage patterns. Deck Blue (20-B), as its name implies, was only used on horizontal surfaces. For use on carrier flight decks a special "blue flight deck stain (No. 21)" was issued in 1942. The relative brightness of these colors is given by their reflectance: black has a reflectance of about 2% while pure white has a reflectance of about 85%. Measure 13, overall Haze Gray (5-H) with Deck Blue (20-B) horizontal surfaces, was not used on the wartime *Independence-class* carriers, but is still in use as the most effective camouflage measure under most operating conditions. The reflectances of the camouflage colors are given below:

Pale Gray (5-P)   55%
Light Gray (5-L)   35%
Haze Gray (5-H)   27%
Ocean Gray (5-O)   18%
Navy Blue (5-N)   9%
Deck Blue (20-B)   5%

Each camouflage pattern had an identifying number, such as 33/7A, that included both the measure, which indicated the color range, and the design number. The letter following the design number indicated the type of vessel the design was prepared for: A for aircraft carrier, D for destroyer, C for cruiser, etc. Designs with the same number but different letters had no relation to each other. A design could be used for more than one measure and for different types of ships. The pattern used on the *Independence,* for example, was originally drawn up for destroyers.

In all the camouflage measures used on aircraft carriers, horizontal surfaces were solid Deck Blue (20-B). The actual color of the blue flight deck stain varied because of weathering and other factors. A darker version of this stain, matching Deck Blue (20-B) came into use in 1944. In 1943 shipyards were issued a light gray for flight deck striping, while yellow was used in the Pacific. Both were later replaced with white dashed lines. Flight-deck numerals were usually dark, either black or Deck Blue (20-B) and were sometimes either outlined in a light color or painted a solid light color, such as white or yellow. The standard marking for aircraft elevators was an "X" across the elevators. Individual ships occasionally deviated from the "standard"markings.

Camouflage Measures

Measure 12

Measure 12 was a "graded system" that provided moderately low visibility to aerial and surface observers in all types of weather. The measure used on carriers in 1945 was a "new" version of the original three-color measure. All vertical surfaces, from the boot topping to a line parallel to the waterline at the level of the hangar deck, were painted Navy Blue or Navy Gray (5-N). In 1945, with blue pigment in short supply, many ships were painted in Navy Gray (5-N), which had the same reflectance and designation as Navy Blue (5-N). Above this band, the rest of the vertical surfaces were painted Ocean Gray (5-O).

Measure 13

Measure 13 was a "solid" measure; all vertical surfaces were painted Haze Gray (5-H). It offered lowest visibility to surface observers in hazy and foggy weather, but high visibility to surface observers when lighted by sun or moon and to aerial observers when lighted by searchlight. This is the standard scheme for post-World War II Navy ships.

Measure 14

Measure 14 was another "solid" measure; all vertical surfaces were painted Ocean Gray (5-O). It offered the lowest visibility to surface observers in bright sunny weather and moonlit nights, but increased visibility to aerial observers. Most of the early *Independence*-class carriers appear to have been commissioned in this scheme.

Measure 21

Measure 21 was another "solid" measure; all vertical surfaces were painted Navy Blue (5-N). It offered the lowest visibility to aerial observers, day and night. Most early *Essex* carriers were completed in Measure 21, and many later carriers converted to it in 1945.

Measure 22

Measure 22 was another graded system intended for use in areas of predominantly bright weather and fair visibility. All vertical surfaces from the boot topping to the level of the hangar deck were Navy Blue (5-N) with the rest of the ship Haze Gray (5-H).

Measure 32

Measure 32 was a "medium pattern system" considered to be the best all-around antisubmarine measure. The colors used were supposed to resolve to a medium shade with a reflectance of 20-40%. To produce the greatest deception, bold contrast between the colors was considered necessary.

Measure 33

Measure 33 was a "light pattern system" similar to Measure 32, except that the overall reflectance was approximately 40-50%. The light colors used in this measure made it highly visible to high angle aircraft observation and it was discontinued in 1945.

Camouflage Designs

Design 3D

This design, as the letter "D" indicates, was originally drawn up for destroyers. It was used on the *Belleau Wood* and *Monterey* with Measure 33, which called for Pale Gray (5-P), Haze Gray (5-H), and Navy Blue (5-N).

Design 7A

Design 7A was designated to use Measure 33, which used Pale Gray (5-P), Haze Gray (5-H), and Navy Blue (5-N). It was used on the *Princeton*,

Cowpens, and *San Jacinto.*

Design 8A

This was an "open" measure design that only specified one color (White 5-U) on the undersides of some sections of the overhangs. The design was originally prepared as Ms 32/8A, but Measure 33 may have been used. Both the *Independence* and *Bataan* used this pattern.

Individual Ship Camouflage

Independence (CVL-22): April 1943-Ms 14; early 1944–Ms3_/8A.

Princeton (CVL-23): Ms 14? 21? 31?; early 1944–Ms 33/7A.

Belleau Wood (CVL-24): Ms 13; July 1944–Ms 33/3D; January 1945–Ms 21.

Cowpens (CVL-25): Ms 21; August 1944–Ms 33/7A; March 1945–Ms 12.

Monterey (CVL-26): Ms 22; July 1944–Ms 33/3D; January 1945–Ms 21.

Langley (CVL-27): Unknown–Langley never carried a "dazzle" pattern.

Cabot (CVL-28): Unknown–Cabot never carried a "dazzle" pattern.

Bataan (CVL-29): 1943 unknown; fall 1944–Ms 3_/8A.

San Jacinto (CVL-30): Ms 33/7A.

Some camouflage patterns were drawn up without specifying which "measures" should be used. For example, Ms 3_/8A used on the *Bataan* could be painted in either Measure 32 or Measure 33. Such "open measures" were indicated by an underline for the second number of the measure. Since the apparent shades of paint vary with weathering, lighting, and difference in photographic quality, it is not always possible to definitely identify colors for some ships.

This design was originally prepared as Ms 32/8A, but the designator was removed to make it an "open" measure design. The single 5" open mounts on the bow and stern represent the INDEPENDENCE class as originally designed. They were included on all the master camouflage design sheets.

DECKS AND OTHER HORIZONTAL SURFACES ARE DECK BLUE (20-B)
FLIGHT DECK IS BLUE FLIGHT DECK STAIN NO. 21

PAINT ALL THIN SUPERSTRUCTURE
CONSTRUCTIONS WITH 5-P

COUNTERSHADING INSTRUCTION —

PAINT WHITE (5-U) — UNDERSIDES OF
ALL OVERHANGING HORIZONTAL SURFACES
AND ALL VISIBLE VERTICAL SURFACES IN
DEEP RECESS

CHECKED BY EVERETT WARNER, DECEMBER 9, 1943

CVL-22 class

measure 3_

camouflage design **8A**

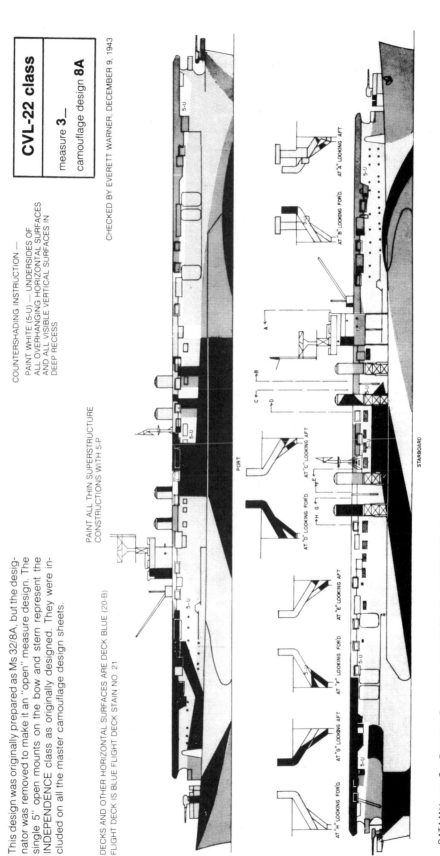

PORT

STARBOARD

AT "A" LOOKING AFT

AT "B" LOOKING FOR'D

AT "A" LOOKING FOR'D

AT "B" LOOKING AFT

AT "C" LOOKING AFT

AT "D" LOOKING FOR'D

AT "E" LOOKING AFT

AT "F" LOOKING FOR'D

AT "G" LOOKING AFT

AT "H" LOOKING FOR'D

5-U

BATAAN leaves San Francisco Bay on her way to the Pacific, April 19, 1945. Like most carriers returning to duty, she's ferrying aircraft. This is another poor picture and again, the navy blue appears to be dull black. It is seven months later, perhaps the paint has been changed. There is cause for doubt. Note that BATAAN's forward numerals are set back about 30 feet

3_ /8A

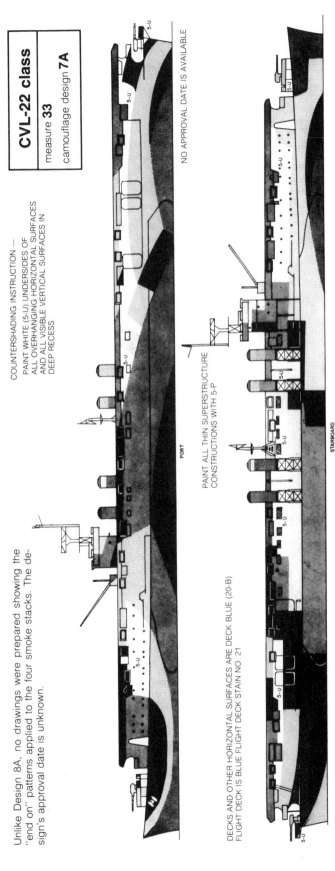

CVL-22 class

measure **33**

camouflage design **7A**

Unlike Design 8A, no drawings were prepared showing the "end on" patterns applied to the four smoke stacks. The design's approval date is unknown.

COUNTERSHADING INSTRUCTION —
PAINT WHITE (5-U) UNDERSIDES OF
ALL OVERHANGING HORIZONTAL SURFACES
AND ALL VISIBLE VERTICAL SURFACES IN
DEEP RECESS

NO APPROVAL DATE IS AVAILABLE

PAINT ALL THIN SUPERSTRUCTURE
CONSTRUCTIONS WITH 5-P

PORT

DECKS AND OTHER HORIZONTAL SURFACES ARE DECK BLUE (20-B)
FLIGHT DECK IS BLUE FLIGHT DECK STAIN NO. 21

STARBOARD

SAN JACINTO off Philadelphia on January 17, 1944. Note the color change between the port and starboard overhangs (steel covered) next to the wooden flight deck. The forward black numeral has been painted on top of the dash lines, about 30 feet short of the deck edge. Three thin dashes start on the fantail, but only the centerline runs the entire length of the flight deck.

Camouflage drawings reprinted courtesy of The Floating Drydock, P.O. Box 250, Kresgeville, PA 18333. The Internet address for information on plans, parts, photographs, etc. is: http://www.floatingdrydock.com. A catalog is also available.

MURDERERS' ROW, Ulithi, during December '44. The major combat ships are (from left to right): WASHINGTON (Ms22), an INDEPENDENCE class CVL in design 7A, LEXINGTON (Ms21), IOWA (design 1B) is nearly invisible (just above the CVL in Ms21) as are SOUTH *DAKOTA (Ms21) and NEW JERSEY (Ms21). The ESSEX class CVs in the row are (front to back): WASP (design 10A), YORKTOWN (design 10A), HORNET (design 3A), HANCOCK (design 3A, using black) and TICONDEROGA (design 10A).*

Besides the INDEPENDENCE class, Design 3D can be seen on: ten destroyer and escort classes, the OMAHA and CLEVELAND class light cruisers, CASABLANCA class CVEs and NEW

MEXICO class battleships. It was also drawn up for the battleship PENNSYLVANIA, but we have no proof that it was ever applied.

DECKS AND OTHER HORIZONTAL SURFACES ARE DECK BLUE (20-B)

FLIGHT DECK IS BLUE FLIGHT DECK STAIN NO. 21

CVL-22 class

measure **33**
camouflage design **3D**

- □ pale gray (5-P)
- ▨ haze gray (5-H)
- ■ navy blue (5-N)

CHECKED BY EVERETT WARNER, JANUARY 26, 1944

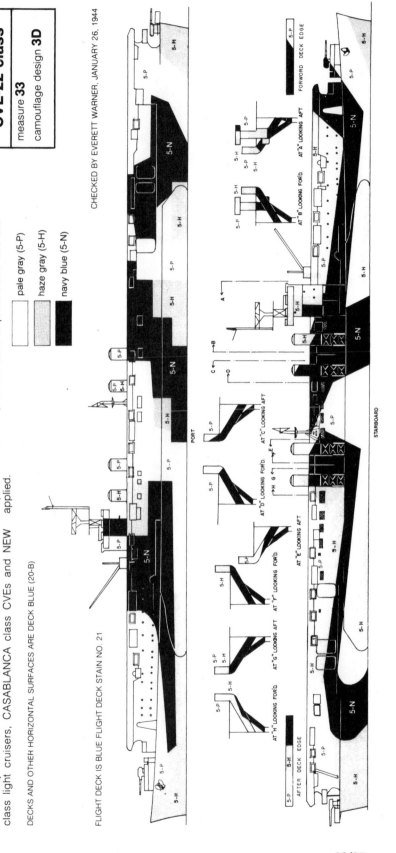

33/3D

Saipan Class Technical Data

Length (overall):   683'6"
Length (waterline):   664'
Beam (extreme):   108'
Beam (waterline):   76'9"
Flight Deck: 611' x 80'
Hangar Deck: 284' x 68' (17'8" clear height)
Elevators: 2 48' x 44' (capacity 30,000 lbs.)
Catapults: 2 H 2-1 (1 H 4B and 1 H 2-1 postwar)
Arresting Gear: Mark 5-0
Design Standard Displacement: 14,500 tons
Design Displacement: 17,820 tons
Design Full Load: 18,750 tons
Draft: 25'
Machinery: 4-shaft geared turbines; 4 Babcock & Wilcox
     boilers (600 psi, 850 F.)
     4 740kW ships service turbine generators
     2 500kW and 2 60kW diesel generators
Shaft Horsepower: 120,000 (design); 119,247/117,568 (trial)
Fuel Capacity: 2,550 (design)
Speed: 33 knots (design)
Endurance: 11,000 nm at 15 knots
Tactical Diameter:
Armament: 42 40mm (5 x 4, 11 x 2) guns
     32 20mm (16 x 2) guns
Fire Control System: Mk 51

Protection: Flight deck - none
               Protective deck(s) - 2.5"
               Armor belt - 4" tapered to 2.5" plus 2" lower
               belt forward
               Bulkheads - 4" and 1.5"
               Conning tower - none
               Steering gear - 4" bulkheads, 2.5" above,
               .75" below
Aircraft: 18 fighters (F6F-3), 12 bombers (SB2C-2),
               12 torpedo bombers (TBF-1C)
Aviation Ordnance: 331.4 tons
Aviation Gasoline: 122,243 gals.
Complement: 78 officer/1,339 enlisted (ship); 48 officer/212
               enlisted (air group)

CVL-48 *Saipan*

Builder: New York Shipbuilding Corporation, Camden, NJ.

Keel laid 10 July 1944; launched 8 July 1945; commissioned 14 July 1946; decommissioned 3 October 1957; redesignated AVT-6 15 May 1959; conversion to command ship 30 March 1963; reclassified as CC-3 1 January 1964; renamed *Arlington* 8 April 1965; redesignated AGMR-2 21 August 1965; commissioned 27 August 1966; decommissioned 27 May 1970; struck 1 December 1977; scrapped 1980.

Remarks: Saipan replaced the *Monterey* CVL-26 as training carrier in 1955; replaced by *Antietam* CVS-36 in 1957. Final displacement was 19,800 tons full load; carried 8 dual 3"/50 and extensive communications facilities.

Operational History

Commissioned eleven months after the end of World War II, the *Saipan* trained student pilots out of Pensacola from September 1946 to April 1947, when her home port changed to Norfolk. Participating in exercises in the Caribbean before being overhauled at Philadelphia, Saipan returned to Pensacola in November 1947. A brief stint training midshipmen followed before the light carrier headed up the east coast to serve with the Operational Development Force. One notable accomplishment with the Operational Development Force occurred in May 1948, when she qualified all the pilots of VF-17A, the Navy's first carrier-based jet squadron, with the McDonnell FH-1 Phantom.

Apart from a deployment to the Mediterranean with the Sixth Fleet in 1951, *Saipan* spent the next few years operating with the Second Fleet from Greenland to the Caribbean, alternating between local operations, midshipmen summer cruises, and overhauls. In September 1953, *Saipan* departed for a world cruise, going through the Panama Canal and on to the west coast, operating briefly out of San Diego before heading on to the Far East in November. *Saipan* monitored the uneasy truce in Korea and transported aircraft and personnel around the Western Pacific. In May 1954 she departed Japanese waters and headed for Norfolk via the Suez Canal, completing her round-the-world-cruise in July.

After participating in relief operations in Haiti following Hurricane Hazel in October, *Saipan* was overhauled in Norfolk before resuming Caribbean operations in April 1955. In June, she returned to Pensacola to support training operations, but was called upon for another hurricane relief operation, this time to Mexico, in September. *Saipan* operated out of Pensacola until April 1957. Departing for Bayonne, New Jersey for inactivation, the ship was decommissioned 3 October 1957 and became part of the Atlantic Reserve Fleet.[2]

CVL-49 *Wright*
Builder: New York Shipbuilding Corporation, Camden, NJ.

Keel laid 21 August 1944; launched 1 September 1944; commissioned 9 February 1947; decommissioned 15 March 1956; redesignated AVT-7 15 March 1959; converted to CC-2; recommissioned 11 May 1963; decommissioned 27 May 1970; struck 1 December 1977; scrapped 1980.

Remarks: Training carrier 1947-48, 1952-54? Final displacement was 19,750 tons full load; carried 4 twin 40 mm and extensive command facilities with flight deck converted to antenna farm.

Operational History
In April 1947 the *Wright* followed the *Saipan* in the training role at Pensacola, spending the next several years operating out of various ports on the east coast conducting training and ASW operations. After completing two

deployments to the Mediterranean with the Sixth Fleet, in 1951 and 1953, and participating in a NATO exercise in northern European waters from August to October 1952, the light carrier was overhauled at the Philadelphia Navy Yard.

Following overhaul, and refresher training off Cuba, *Wright* departed in April 1954 for the Far East via the Panama Canal, San Diego, and Pearl Harbor. Arriving in Yokosuka, Japan, in May, she embarked Marine attack squadron VMA-211 and operated with the Seventh Fleet off Korea and Okinawa before departing for San Diego in October. *Wright* entered the Long Beach Navy Yard in November and remained there until February 1955. Operating off San Diego for a few months, *Wright* joined Task Force 7.3, formed around the flagship *Mount McKinley* (AGC-27), for the Operation Wigwam atomic test carried out in the Pacific. She returned to the west coast, and, after a cruise to Pearl Harbor, reported to Mare Island in July to prepare for inactivation. Shifting to Puget Sound in October, *Wright* began the final phase of the preservation process. Decommissioned there on 15 March 1956, she was assigned to the Bremerton group of the Pacific Reserve Fleet.[3]

Other Roles
In 1962 the *Wright* began conversion to a national emergency command post afloat (NECPA) as the *Wright* (CC-2) and the *Saipan* began a similar conversion the following year. The *Saipan*, however, became a major communications relay ship instead and was redesignated and renamed as the *Arlington*

(AGMR-2). In this role she alternated off the coast of Vietnam with the *Annapolis* (AGMR-1), which had been converted from *Gilbert Islands* (CVE-107), a *Commencement Bay*-class escort carrier. Satellite communications eventually made communications relay ships obsolete and the NECPA role itself was abandoned about 1969. Both former CVLs were decommissioned in 1970.[4]

Notes

The following abbreviations are used in the end notes: DANFS–*Dictionary of American Naval Fighting Ships*; NARA–National Archives and Records Administration; NHC–Naval Historical Center; and WWW–the Internet's World Wide Web. Citations for Norman Friedman refer to his work *U.S. Aircraft Carriers, An Illustrated Design History* except as noted. Similarly, citations for Clark G. Reynolds refer to his work *The Fast Carriers: The Forging of an Air Navy,* except as noted. Due to the wide variation in rendering ship names, they are italicized in the body of the text, but presented in their original format when included in the title of a cited work.

Chapter 1: A Wartime Expedient

1. Nichols, p.386.
2. Nichols, p.386.
3. Friedman, p.162.
4. Friedman, p.162. At the time of her conversion the *Long Island* enjoyed an equal priority with the construction of the *Hornet* CV-8 fleet carrier. The original escort carrier designation AVG (Aircraft Escort Vessel) was first assigned on 31 March 1941. The classification was changed to ACV (Auxiliary Aircraft Carrier) on 20 August 1942 and to CVE (Escort Carrier) on 15 July 1943. The *Mormacland* became the HMS *Archer* under the designation BAVG-1 for British AVG.
5. Friedman, pp.159, 177.
6. Friedman, p.181.
7. Brown, p.62.
8. Friedman, p.182.
9. Brown, pp. 62-63.
10. Friedman, pp.182-3; Ewing, p.123.
11. Freidman, pp.188-9; also "CVLs: The U.S. *Independence* Class," p.272.
12. Friedman, p.169.
13. Friedman, p.182.
14. Friedman, "CVLs: The U.S. *Independence* Class," p.266.
15. Friedman, p.188.
16. Friedman, p.188. *Independence* was completed without these improvements. They were added during her 1944 refit.
17. Freidman, p.188. The ninth 40mm twin mount on the port side forward was authorized 8 February 1943. Six more 20mm guns were authorized 6 August 1943.

18. Pawlowski, p.231. Also "A Short History of the U.S.S. San Jacinto," p. 7 (NHC).
19. Friedman, "CVLs: The U.S. *Independence* Class," p.268.
20.   Friedman, p. 189.
21. History of USS Bataan (CVL-29) (NHC).
22. Belote, p. 203.
23. Belote, pp. 203-204.
24. Belote, p. 204.
25. Pawlowski, p. 199.
26. Pawlowski, p. 203.
27. Brown, p. 62.
28. On 29 June 1944 Carrier Air Groups were standardized for all commands under the following designations: CVBG, large carrier air group; CVG, medium carrier air group; CVLG, light carrier air group; CVEG, escort carrier air group (*Sangamon* class); and VC, escort carrier air group (*Long Island, Charger, Bogue, and Casablanca classes*) (NHC Naval Aviation WWW).
29. Wooldridge, E.T., editor, *Carrier Warfare in the Pacific: An Oral History Collection,* CAPT Arthur R. Hawkins, "The Marianas 'Turkey Shoot'" pp. 188-189.
30. The Japanese lost all four of their fleet carriers assigned to the Carrier Striking Force, the *Akagi, Kaga, Hiryu,* and *Soryu,* while the Americans lost the *Yorktown,* which had been hurriedly repaired at Pearl Harbor following the Coral Sea battle. The Battle of Midway, fought in early June 1942, was a major defeat for the Japanese and marked the turning point in the war.
31. With the arrival of the *Wasp* from the Atlantic and the return of the *Saratoga* from repairs on the West Coast, American carrier strength immediately after the Battle of Midway was superior to that of the Japanese. The Marines landed on Guadalcanal in August and several hard-fought naval engagements took place in the Solomons. The Japanese lost the light carrier *Ryujo* to American carrier aircraft in the Battle of the Eastern Solomons in August. The *Wasp* was sunk by three torpedoes from a Japanese submarine in September. The *Hornet* was sunk by Japanese carrier aircraft during the Battle of Santa Cruz Islands in October.

Chapter 2: The Central Pacific
1. Nimitz instructed Spruance to conduct the battle under the principle of "calculated risk," since so much was at stake at that desperate juncture of the war. Having no aviation background, Spruance had the good sense to rely heavily on the aviation expertise of his inherited chief of staff, Captain Miles R. Browning.
2. Ewing gives details about the various detachments from VF-6 in *Fateful Rendezvous.* By mid-August the shuffle was 24 F6F (6 divisions) to AG-22 on *Independence;* 12 (3 divisions) to AG-23 on *Princeton* and VF-22 went to AG-24 on *Belleau Wood.* O'Hare led the detachment on the *Independence* for the Marcus and Wake strikes. On 19 September *Cowpens* arrived at Pearl Harbor and AirPac divided VF-6 evenly among three CVLs. AG-22 on the *Independence* now had 12 VF-6 and the original 12 from VF-22; AG-25 on the *Cowpens* had 12 VF-6 and 12 VF-25; and the 12 VF-6 with AG-23 on *Princeton* was switched to AG-24 on *Belleau Wood.* These changes went into effect 29 September before the Wake strikes. (The *Princeton* missed the Wake strike because her catapult was being repaired at Pearl Harbor.) Early in October, the *Monterey* dropped off her dive bombers in San Diego and loaded 12 more Hellcats on her way to the forward area. (History of the U.S.S. Monterey, Part I Chronology, NHC).
3. Reynolds, p.83 (citing Towers diary for 9 September 1943) and "USS

Independence," p. 2, (a unit history, NHC). Johnson, in turn was replaced as XO by Commander W.F. Rodes.

4. Reynolds, p. 82 (citing Pownall's Action Report of 4 September 1943). ADM King himself rejected the proposal.

5. Reynolds, pp.83-84 (occupation of Baker Island), Pawlowski, p. 192 and DANFS p. 384 (Hellcat combat). Also USS Princeton Serial 0415, 23 September 1943, Occupation of Baker Island, Operations of USS PRINCETON Air Group in Connection with - Action Report On, covers 24 August-15 September 1943 (NARA). The first Emily intercept was by VF-6 pilots north of Howland Island on 1 September; the second was also by VF-6 pilots 20-50 miles west and southwest of Baker Island on 3 September; the last was by VF-23 pilots south-southeast of Baker Island on 8 September. Quote from Bradshaw, p. 23.

6. Unfortunately for the Marines who landed at Tarawa later in November, the obliques did not show the reefs clearly. Planning for the Gilberts invasion assumed there would be enough water under the amphibious landing craft to clear the reef, and the lack of adequate overhead photography, which might have shown otherwise, did not help. Amphibious tractors ("amphtracs") capable of crossing the reefs were only available because of the dogged insistence of "Howlin' Mad" Smith.

7. The story about LCDR Peters painting wheels on the underside of VF-22 Hellcats is from an undated document "A History of the U.S.S. *Independence* (CVL-22) (unofficial?), p. 2, (NHC). Information from Ewing's *Fateful Rendezvous* (p. 207) about the VF-6 detachments indicated that VF-6 and VF-22 operated together on the *Independence* for the Wake strike and only the Hellcats of LT Leland Johnson's

VF-22 had the fake wheels painted on.

8. Pawlowski, p.209.

9. Pawlowski, p.204. Also U.S.S. Cowpens Serial 0015, 22 October 1943, U.S.S. COWPENS (CVL25) ° Ramming of by U.S.S. ABBOTT (DD629) (NARA).

10. Bradshaw, pp. 26-28.

11. Belote, p.232; Bradshaw, pp. 29-30. Following the attack, the Japanese command at Rabaul ordered the cruisers back to Truk, except for the damaged *Maya,* which could not move and *Agano,* which was not part of the 2nd Fleet. The departing ships missed an attack by Army Air Force B-24s from New Guinea. The Japanese launched a strike of 12 Kate torpedo bombers which missed *Saratoga* and *Princeton,* but caught a PT, an LCI and an LCT, putting torpedoes (which did not explode) through the PT and LCT while losing two aircraft to automatic weapons fire from the American craft.

12. Belote, p.234.

13. Compiled from undated documents: "A History of the U.S.S. *Independence* (CVL-22), p. 2, (unofficial?) and "U.S.S. *Independence*" (both from NHC). The main description of the damage is included in a 4 December 1943 report from the *Independence.* (Action Report - Galvanic, CVL-22/A16-3, Serial No. 0012) (NARA). Also, an undated document received by *Independence* historian Al Hiegel titled "'Evil I' The Gallant Carrier the Japs Could Never Hex," provided many details of the crew's experiences.

14. Bradshaw, pp.34-35.

15. History of the U.S.S. Monterey, pp. 42-43 (NHC).

Chapter 3: Task Force 58

1. Landings on Kwajalein and Majuro, which had been included in the operation to provide a future fleet anchorage,

began on 31 January. Landings on Eniwetok started on 18 February, after the first Task Force 58 strike on Truk.

2. Placing close air support aircraft under the direct control of specially equipped amphibious command ships (AGC) began with Operation Flintlock. The Commander Support Aircraft relieved the carriers of responsibility for control of the Target Combat Air Patrols (TAR-CAP) and selected local targets. The Support Air Control Units ashore were also strengthened.

3. As part of Operation Flintlock, the 4th Marine Division landed on Roi-Namur, in the northern part of the Kwajalein atoll, 31 January; Roi was secured on 1 February and Namur on 2 February. The Majuro atoll, southeast of Kwajalein, was to be used as a fleet anchorage and was occupied 31 January. The landings on Kwajalein Island were carried out by the 7th Infantry Division on 1 February and the island was secured on 5 February. Ebeye was taken next. Kwajalein atoll was secured by 7 February. The Japanese flew a long-range bomber strike against American forces on Roi-Namur 12 February. The attack was carried out by Saipan-based aircraft staged out of Ponape, in the eastern end of the Carolines. Seventh Air Force B-24s hit Ponape between 15 and 26 February to prevent any further attacks.

4. Buracker, pp.191-192.

5. RADM Ginder's Task Group 58.4 remained behind to cover the Eniwetok landings, as Mitscher felt that Ginder's performance was less than satisfactory compared to his other task group commanders. Task Group 58.4 hit Eniwetok 11 and 13 February and returned on 17 February with the escort carriers. The islets were taken 17-22 February and the carriers departed 28 February.

6. After temporary repairs, *Intrepid* pro

ceeded on to Hunters Point Naval Shipyard in Bremerton, Washington.

7. In December 1943, following the Gilberts operations, RADM Radford became Chief of Staff to ComAirPac. He began to formulate a nightfighter policy and issued a training syllabus to each carrier captain. Each *Essex*-class carrier would form at least two "Bat teams" of either one TBF and two Hellcats, or two TBFs and two Hellcats. Every task group would conduct experiments to figure out the best combinations and develop night doctrine. Using the ship's fighter directors and radars, the planes would maintain visual contact with each other to avoid shooting each other down, as had been feared to have happened to Butch O'Hare, although he was probably brought down by a burst from a Betty in the area. On 8 January 1944, each *Essex* class carrier was assigned a Bat team of one TBF and two Hellcats. These teams were later strengthened by the arrival of four-plane night Corsair teams, although *Yorktown* and *Bunker Hill* got teams of four night Hellcats each.

8. Operation Catchpole, the Eniwetok landings, were carried out by the 22nd Marine Regiment who landed on Engebi, at the northern end of Eniwetok atoll, on 17 February; Engebi was secured the next day. The 106th Infantry Regiment (part of the 27th Infantry Division) landed on Eniwetok Island at the southern end of atoll, but the island was not secured until 21 February. Landings on Parry Island, north of Eniwetok Island, began on 22 February and the island was secured that day.

9. The *Lexington,* returning from her repairs on the West Coast, had launched practice strikes against bypassed Mili on 18 March 1944.

10. USS Cabot Unit History, p. 2-5 (NHC).

11. USS Cabot Unit History, p. 2-5 (NHC).

12. During the Palau operations, Ginder worried to the point of becoming ineffective. He was relieved and replaced by Clark upon Task Force 58's return to Majuro.

13. Tillman, pp.21-22, 64. Hills became an ace when he got his fifth kill in September 1944, although he is not technically considered an ace since his first victory was scored with the RCAF.

14. Pawlowski, p. 219.

15. Hawkins, p. 189.

16. Pawlowski, p. 227.

17. ADM Koga, who had replaced Yamamoto as Commander in Chief of the Combined Fleet in April 1943, was lost in April 1944 on an aircraft flight that never reached its destination in the Philippines, probably because of bad weather. ADM Soemu Toyoda, Koga's replacement, was a much more aggressive commander.

18. Ozawa's aircraft included 145 Zero fighters (Zeke model 52), 80 Zero fighter-bombers (Zeke model 32), 99 Judy dive bombers (90 Judy model 33s and 9 Judy model 11s), 87 Jill torpedo bombers (33 Jill model 11s and 54 Jill model 12s), and 12 Kate torpedo bombers. He was also counting on the support of nearly five 500 land-based aircraft from ADM Kurita's First Air Fleet. These aircraft, however, were dispersed by Kurita between Yap and the Palaus.

19. The *Puffer* sank two of the precious tankers. The *Harder* later added to the score by sinking three of the destroyers between 3 and 8 June. The Japanese submarines, on the other hand, did not play a significant part in the coming battle. Deployed along the "NA" line running northeast from Manus in the Admiralty Islands, they did not sink any American ships, but became victims of American antisubmarine hunter-killer groups, which sank 17 of them in the last days of May.

20. Reynolds, p. 173.

21. Tillman, p. 22. This was Strange's second kill. He eventually made ace with a total of five.

22. History of USS Monterey, p. 87 (NHC).

23. Tillman, p. 22. LTJG Vincent A. Reiger claimed three. He eventually made ace with five kills.

24. Pawlowski, p. 219. Also USS Cabot Unit History, p. 2-7 (NHC).

25. Pawlowski, p. 205.

26. Buracker, p. 209.

27. Marine Lt. Gen. Holland M. Smith was forced to commit his floating reserve, the Army's 27th Infantry Division, on 15 June and the landings on Guam, originally scheduled for 18 June, were postponed until 21 July.

28. Mitscher gave neither carrier group commander tactical command: Clark was junior to Harrill, but was all fighter; Harrill would prove to be too timid. By instructing them to cooperate as independent commanders, but to remain "tactically concentrated," Mitscher could ensure that the job would get done.

29. Y'Blood, p. 57.

30. Y'Blood, p. 59.

31. Reynolds, p. 178.

Chapter 4: Philippine Sea

1. Tillman, p. 30. VF-51's sole ace, LT Bob Maxwell, scored six of his seven kills during the "Turkey Shoot." VF-51 claimed a total of 22 kills between 11 June and 25 July.

2. Miller, p. 119. LCDR Earnest Wood and LTJG Van Buren Carter of VF-27 and LTJG F.R. Steiglitz of VF-25.

3. Buracker, p. 209.

4. Just after the *Taiho* launched her aircraft, she was struck by a torpedo from the submarine Albacore, but the damage was not immediately regarded as serious.

5. USS Cabot Unit History, p. 2-8 (NHC).

6. Pawlowski, p. 193.

7. Miller, p. 120.

8. Miller, p. 120. Also, USS Cabot Unit History, p. 2-8 (NHC).

9. Reynolds, p. 197.

10. Reynolds, p. 200.

11. Y'Blood, p. 184.

12. Y'Blood, pp. 184-185.

13. Y'Blood, p. 192

14. Y'Blood, pp. 192-193.

15. Task Group 58.1 was assigned the *Monterey* and *Cabot,* giving Clark six carriers in one formation, something that hadn't been done since the Wake strikes of the previous October.

16. Tillman, p. 31.

17. Tillman, p. 31. Nooy would eventually have a total of 19 kills, tying for fourth place among Hellcat aces.

18. The Tinian landings on 24 July did not need the fast carriers and close air support was provided by artillery and land-based air from Saipan. Organized resistance on Tinian ended on 1 August.

19. In June 1944, Task Force 58 abandoned Majuro and Kwajalein for Eniwetok in the western Marshalls and Manus in the Admiralties and Saipan. Manus was abandoned by the carriers in October 1944 and Saipan in November 1944 in favor of Eniwetok and closer anchorages such as Ulithi.

20. Reynolds, p. 228 (citing Towers diary entry of 5 July 1944). Towers had moved up from being ComAirPac to Deputy CincPac-CincPOA.

21. Reynolds, pp. 228-9; CVL-22/A16-3, Ser. No. 0015, Action Report, 1 October 1944 (NARA); "A History of the U.S.S. Independence," p. 5 (NHC).

22. Article by CDR Turner Caldwell as told to LT Philip Gustafson, "We Put The Flattops On the Night Shift," p. 8. Originally appeared in the 11 August 1945 issue of the *Saturday Evening Post;* reprinted with permission (provided by Al Hiegel).

23. Caldwell, p. 9.

24. Article by CDR Kenneth McCracken, "Night Wings Over The Fleet," p. 15. Written in January 1945 but never released by Navy Public Relations at Pearl Harbor (provided by Al Hiegel)

25. A History of the USS Independence (CVL-22), p. 4 (NHC).

26. Analysis of Air Operations, Night Carrier Operations, U.S.S. Independence, Sept.-Dec., 1944, p.1 (NHC).

Chapter 5: Halsey and the Third Fleet

1. On 18 August, VADM McCain relieved Clark as commander of Task Group 58.1.

2. Within the dual command structure, the Fast Carrier Force Pacific became the First Fast Carrier Force Pacific under Mitscher and the Second Fast Carrier Force Pacific under McCain.

3. "Vice President Bush Calls World War II Experience 'Sobering'," article by JO2 Timothy J Christmann, Naval Aviation News 67 (March-April 1985), pp. 12-15 (WWW NHC).

4. USS Cabot Unit History, p. 2-11 (NHC).

5. USS Cabot Unit History, p. 2-11 (NHC); Pawlowski, p. 220.

6. A *Hornet* pilot shot down over Leyte and sheltered by the natives there, relayed native reports of weak Japanese defenses upon his return.

7. Nimitz did not cancel the 15 September Peleliu landings because the forces were already at sea and he felt that a base in the Palaus was necessary to support the upcoming Leyte invasion. The casualties suffered in taking Peleliu and nearby Anguar, however, far outweighed their limited usefulness in later Philippine operations. Organized resistance on Peleliu did not end until the night of 24-25 November. Anguar was secured by 23 October. The fierce Japanese resistance was a prelude to

later landings at Iwo Jima and Okinawa.
8. Servron 10 moved to Ulithi in October. While Servron 2 operated all repair, salvage, and hospital ships in the combat zone, Servron 8 supplied a ship pool of service vessels at Pearl Harbor and Servron 12 was building harbor facilities at Guam and Saipan.
9. The Visayan Islands form the central part of the Philippines and include Bohol, Cebu, Leyte, Masbate, Negros, Panay, Samar, Romblon, and their adjacent islets.
10. Analysis of Air Operations, Night Carrier Operations, U.S.S. Independence, Sept.-Dec., 1944, p.1 (NHC); Caldwell, p. 8.
11. Analysis of Air Operations, Night Carrier Operations, U.S.S. Independence, Sept.-Dec., 1944, p. 2 (NHC).
12. Morrison, Vol. XII, Leyte June 1944-January 1945, p. 95.
13. Tillman, pp. 50-51; Cabot Unit History, pp. 2-15 to 2-18 (NHC).
14. USS Cabot Unit History, p. 2-17 (NHC).
15. USS Cabot Unit History, p. 2-17 (NHC).
16. USS Cabot Unit History, p. 2-19 (NHC).
17. The designations "northern," "center," and "southern" were chosen by American historians. The actual Japanese organization for the Sho-I "victory" plan was as follows: CinC Combined Fleet, ADM Toyoda at Tokyo; the Advance Force (with 16 submarines) under VADM Miwa in the Inland Sea; Mobile Force under VADM Ozawa; and the Southwest Area Force under VADM Mikawa in Manila. The Southwest Area Force included the Fifth Base Air Force under VADM Teraoka in Manila, the Sixth Base Air Force and Second Air Fleet under VADM Fukudome on Formosa and the Ryukyus, and the Second Striking Force under VADM Shima in the Inland Sea. The Southwest Area Guard Force transport unit under VADM Sakonju was also under VADM

Shima's Second Striking Force. Ozawa's Mobile Force was made up of the Main Body with the aircraft carriers, i.e. the "northern force" and the First Striking Force under VADM Kurita at Lingga Roads in Singapore. Kurita's First Striking Force included Force "A" under Kurita, i.e. the "center force" and Force "C" under VADM Nishimura, i.e. the van of the "southern force." Although Nishimura's and Shima's units both made up the "southern force" they never operated together tactically, having come from different directions to the Surigao Strait.

Chapter 6: Leyte Gulf
1. The submarines *Darter* and *Dace* performed brilliantly, sinking two heavy cruisers and putting a third out of action, although *Darter* ran aground and had to be abandoned, her crew taken off by *Dace*.
2. Tillman, p. 52.
3. Compiled from Buracker, History of the USS Princeton CVL-23 (NARA), and Memo: Sinking of the US PRINCETON 24 October 1944, Operational Excerpts from Action Report of C.O. USS RENO (NARA). Quotes from Buracker.
4. Tillman, pp.54-55. His final score was 10.5 kills.
5. The *Ise* and *Hyuga* were battleships whose aft superstructures had been removed and replaced with a short flight deck. During this battle neither ship carried aircraft; they had been included in the decoy force mainly because of their fourteen inch guns.
6. McCampbell would eventually become the Navy's highest scoring ace, with 36 kills.
7. There were 16 escort carriers available, two had departed for Morotai the day before.
8. The text of the original message read: "Turkey trots to water. From CINCPAC.

Where is, repeat, where is Task Force 34. The world wonders."

9. Unknown to Kurita, the American held airfields on Leyte were still operating on an emergency basis only.

10. *Independence* role compiled from Reynolds and Night Carrier Operations USS Independence Sept-Dec 1944 (NHC).

11. The official histories of the Battle for Leyte Gulf list four separate actions: the strike on Kurita's center force in the Sibuyan Sea, the battle of the Surigao Strait, the battle off Samar between the center force and Sprague's escort carriers, and the battle off Cape Engano, which is sometimes called the Second Battle of the Philippine Sea. The primary sources for this chapter were Reynolds and Morison's "The Two-Ocean War," pp. 421-475.

Chapter 7: Kamikaze

1. Analysis of Air Operations, Night Carrier Operations, U.S.S. Independence, Sept.-Dec., 1944, p. 1 (NHC).

2. USS Cabot Unit History, p. 2-22 (NHC).

3. Pawlowski, p. 121.

4. Pawlowski, p. 201. *Belleau Wood* departed San Francisco on 20 January 1945 in company with the newly commissioned *Randolph,* arriving in Hawaii six days later. She rejoined the fleet 29 January 1945 at Ulithi.

5. RADM Arthur Radford was on standby for a task group command, while RADM Clark cut his leave short to be available if needed.

6. The *Lexington* returned to Ulithi for repair and sailed to rejoin the task force on 11 December.

7. Analysis of Air Operations, Night Carrier Operations, U.S.S. Independence, Sept.-Dec., 1944, p. 3 (NHC).

8. USS Cabot Unit History, pp. 2-4 to 2-29. Also, Pawlowski, pp. 220-221, and DANFS.

9. A second airfield was now in operation with P-38s and P-40s, but Kenney's fliers were kept busy repelling Japanese air attacks. The P-61 Black Widow night fighters proved to be too slow for the Japanese night raiders and a squadron of Marine night Hellcats had to be brought in from the new air base at Palau.

10. The two-week respite at Ulithi had given the fast carrier commanders their first real look at McCain as a task force commander and, although he was personally likable, he was resented by some of the more experienced carrier commanders who felt that he had been forced on them by ADM King.

11. The new Escort Carrier Force Pacific Fleet was commanded by RADM Cal Durgin, who came from the Mediterranean. Felix Stump was in tactical command of the escort carriers at Mindoro.

12. Tillman, p. 58.

13. Pawlowski, p. 209.

14. terHorst, pp. 47-48

15. History of the U.S.S. Monterey, pp.105-106 (NHC).

16. Official History of USS Cowpens (CVL-25) (WWW, USS Cowpens home page http://www.geocities.com/Pentagon/5325/navalhistory.htm. Also Sea Stories http://www.geocities.com/Pentagon/5325/typhooncobra.htm)

17. USS Cabot Unit History, p.2-30 (NHC).

18. A Short History of the U.S.S. San Jacinto, Chapter VI Operations in Support of the Recapture of Mindoro and Luzon (NHC).

19. History of the U.S.S. Monterey, pp.106-107 (NHC). Task Group 30.3 was dissolved upon arrival on 21 December. Also USS Cabot Unit History, p. 2-30 (NHC).

20. A Short History of the U.S.S. San Jacinto, Chapter VI Operations in Support of the Recapture of Mindoro and Luzon (NHC).

21. History of the U.S.S. Monterey, pp.109 (NHC).

22. In a subsequent Court of Inquiry, the "preponderance of responsibility" was placed on Halsey for "errors in judgment under stress of war operations and not as offenses." Poor weather information played its part in the tragedy, but Halsey's sloppy handling of the task force only made the situation worse.

23. The day after Christmas, Montgomery got caught between a motor launch and the hull of an escort carrier that he was visiting and suffered several cracked ribs.

24. During the first month the Marines lost seven pilots and 13 aircraft to operational accidents.

25. The attack on neutral Portuguese port of Macao led to a Court of Inquiry and a formal apology to Portugal.

26. Tillman, p. 61. Craig's wartime total was 11.75 kills.

27. Altogether 143 were killed and 202 wounded, including her captain and executive officer.

28. Monsarrat, pp 130-139.

29. Caldwell, p. 11.

30. Reynolds, p. 330 (quoting Air Intelligence Group Interview of Commander Turner F. Caldwell, Jr. USN, 23 March 1945 (OpNav-16-V-#E0706, 24 May 1945).)

31. The primary source for this chapter was Reynolds, pp. 278-300.

Chapter 8: Okinawa

1. Other new Essex-class carriers in 1945 included: Antietam, commissioned in January, Boxer in April, and Lake Champlain in June. The Kearsarge and Tarawa were launched in May. The large carrier Midway was launched in March followed by the Franklin D. Roosevelt in April. With the war winding down, six more Essex-class and two Midway-class carriers were canceled.

2. Because the Seventh Fleet was occupied in regaining the rest of the Philippines, the Central Pacific forces would provide cover for both the Iwo Jima and Okinawa landings. Iwo was to precede the landings on Okinawa because it was thought to be the easier of the two.

3. Nichols, p. 389.

4. Nichols, p. 393. Also, USS Cabot Unit History, p. 2-36 (NHC).

5. USS Cabot Unit History, p.2-37 (NHC).

6. Tillman, p. 64.

7. Saratoga limped back to Eniwetok and then proceeded to the West Coast for major repairs. She would be out of the war for good.

8. A crew member who had worked for the Otis elevator company used his experience to repair the arresting gear machinery and Randolph did not have to return to the States. Using undamaged equipment from her arresting gear to replace damaged parts, she was repaired in the forward area and rejoined the fleet off Okinawa on 7 April.

9. History of USS Bataan, p. 3 (NHC).

10. USS Cabot Unit History, pp. 2-45 to 2-46 (NHC).

11. Japanese records show 163 aircraft lost out of 193 aircraft launched, with an undetermined number destroyed on the ground.

12. During the Okinawa campaign, after the departure of the Franklin, the only air group left equipped with the 11.75" Tiny Tim rockets was the Intrepid's. Results with the large inaccurate rockets were inconclusive and they were withdrawn from the carriers thereafter.

13. The British hit Miyako Island on 26 and 27 March and withdrew to refuel the next day. The escort carriers covered the

gap until Task Force 57 returned and the Sakishima strikes were resumed 31 March. Task Force 57 experienced its first kamikaze attack when one crashed the *Indefatigable* at the base of her island, but her armored flight deck allowed her to promptly resume flight operations. The British remained on station until 3 April, when Task Group 58.1 relieved them, after which they retired for replenishment.

14. Hudson, p. 84; USS Cabot Unit History pp. 2-49 to 2-50 (NHC).

15. The floating chrysanthemum was the emblem on the banner of Masahige Kusanoki, a great Japanese military hero who sacrificed his forces for the sake of his lord.

16. A Short History of the USS San Jacinto, p. 20 (NHC).

17. Reynolds, p. 31; Tillman, p. 66.

18. USS Cabot Unit History, pp. 2-51 to 2-52 (NHC).

19. The commander of the gunfire force, RADM M.L. Deyo, made plans for a line of 6 battleships, 7 cruisers and 21 destroyers to form a barrier between the advancing Japanese and the American transports. Davison's Task Group 58.2, returning from Ulithi with the repaired carriers *Randolph* and *Enterprise,* was delayed by refueling and missed the battle.

20. On 20 April the *Intrepid* entered Ulithi. Inspection revealed previously undetected damage to her elevators, requiring her to return to Hunters Point for repair. The shipyard workers began to regard the *Intrepid* as "their" carrier.

21. Tillman, p. 67. Mazzocco went on to finish the war as a five kill ace.

22. Reynolds, *The Carrier War,* p.170.

23. Wheeler, p. 166.

24. With the draw down in the intensity of kamikaze attacks later in May, the only other British carrier casualty was the *Indomitable,* which collided with a

destroyer in fog and had to return to Sydney on 20 May.

25. Few realized just how beat up Mitscher was; his medical officer, CAPT Ray Hege, had been killed on the *Bunker Hill.*

26. Davison had been relieved because he missed an important airplane flight.

27. RADM Matt Gardner, without a night carrier, detached ComCarDiv 7 on 7 April.

28. At the Court of Inquiry held on Guam on 15 June, the blame was placed firmly on Halsey and McCain. For morale reasons, Halsey was not relieved of command, but would not get his fifth star during the war.

29. On 20 June, Task Group 12.4 under RADM Ralph Jennings attacked bypassed Wake Island. *Lexington, Hancock* and *Cowpens* participated.

30. The primary source for this chapter was Clark Reynolds's *The Fast Carriers,* pp. 324-50.

Chapter 9: Target Japan

1. In May 1945, the Joint Chiefs of Staff directed that Operation Olympic, the landings on Kyushu in southern Japan, would be scheduled for 1 November 1945. The follow-on landings on the Honshu coast near Tokyo, Operation Coronet, were tentatively set to follow in March 1946. The Navy leadership opposed the landings in principle, feeling that the growing effectiveness of the air and sea blockade would force Japan to surrender, but continued to make preparations as directed.

2. Tillman, p. 80.

3. A similar, smaller, attack had been made unsuccessfully on Okinawa, but the planned target for this attack was actually the B-29 bases in the Marianas.

4. Task Force 38 had planned to refuel and retire to Eniwetok, while the British were to retire to Manus. Because of a

lack of tankers, the British commander, Rawlings, conferred with Halsey to leave *Indefatigable* and several escorts as a token force to represent the British should word of the surrender come through. Task Force 37 departed for Manus the next day.

5. Pawlowski, p. 228.

6. Near the end of the war a number of carriers en route to the Western Pacific conducted training strikes against bypassed Wake Island. The *Wasp* hit Wake on 18 July, followed by the *Cabot* on 1 August and *Intrepid* five days later.

7. Reynolds, pp. 377-378.

8. Reynolds, p. 377.

9. Reynolds, pp.356-357. F4Us operated off *Langley* on 24 August 1945. DANFS, p. 48. *Langley* had arrived in San Francisco, via Ulithi and Pearl Harbor, on 3 June for repairs and modernization. She departed 1 August, arriving at Pearl on 8 August.

10. *Randolph* lost steering control for four minutes and the forward flight deck overhang on the *Wasp* buckled, causing her to be detached and sent home for repairs on 31 August. Bogan was exonerated in his handling of the task group during the storm because of its unpredictable nature. Ted Sherman, who had been riding on *Wasp,* had to shift his flag back to the *Lexington.*

11. There were some command changes as the war closed. As part of the final preparations for the invasion of Japan, the Third Fleet and the Fifth Fleet would, for the first time, operate as separate fleets. Spruance remained in command of the Fifth Fleet and Ted Sherman, long in line to command the fast carriers, became Commander, First Fast Carrier Force and commander of Task Force 58. Sherman received his third star in July while in Washington. On 18 August VADM Sherman hoisted his flag in *Lexington,* shifting to the *Wasp*

two days later. In July, it was decided that VADM Jack Towers, a long-time advocate of the fast carriers who had risen to become Nimitz's deputy, would replace McCain as Commander, Second Fast Carrier Force and commander of Task Force 38. On 22 August, VADM Jack Towers raised his flag in *Shangri-La,* formally relieving McCain as commander of Task Force 38 on 1 September. McCain was bitter over his relief and wanted to leave, but Halsey convinced him to stay on for the formal surrender ceremony. The information about the *Bataan* from the History of the USS Bataan (CVL 29) (NHC) conflicts with information on the NHC home page (under Frequently Asked Questions: "Allied Ships Present in Tokyo Bay During the Surrender Ceremony, 2 September 1945)."

12. Reynolds, *The Carrier War,* p. 170.

Chapter 10: Aftermath

1. Many of the troops from Europe were sent home by ships operated by the War Shipping Administration, which had planned to redeploy them from the European Theater to the Pacific. The end of the war in the Pacific caught many planners off guard and the Navy did not participate in the return of troops until after the Japanese surrender.

2. Participation in Magic Carpet from various unit histories, Pawlowski, and DANFS.

3. "Operation Crossroads" pictorial, *National Geographic,* Vol. XCJ, No. 4, April 1947, Plate XI caption.

4. Eliot, p. 72.

5. "Operation Crossroads" pictorial, *National Geographic,* Vol. XCJ, No. 4, April 1947.

6. "Unzipping The Cabot," (article clipped from unidentified Navy publication, NHC).

7. Friedman p. 337.

8. Hudson, p. 125.

9. Freidman, p. 191.

10. DANFS pp.254-256; History of USS Arlington AGMR-2 (NHC).

11. DANFS, pp. 483-486.

12. Friedman, p. 195.

13. *Bataan* cruise books, second and third Far East cruises (NHC).

14. Hallion, p. 156.

15. Historique du Porte-avions "LA FAYETTE" (History of the "La Fayette" Aircraft Carrier). Information provided by the Marine Nationale Service Historique (French Navy Historical Service) translated from French courtesy of Naval Reserve unit DIA 0166 for the Naval Aviation History Office, NHC.

16. La Carriere du Porte-avions "BOIS BEL-LEAU" (History of the "Bois Belleau" Aircraft Carrier). Information provided by the Marine Nationale Service Historique (French Navy Historical Service) translated from French courtesy of Naval Reserve unit DIA 0166 for the Naval Aviation History Office, NHC.

17. NavShips Tech News, December 1967, pp. 29-30.

18. WWW (http://www.uss-salem.org/navhist/carriers/spain.htm#r01) Note: she was apparently designated R01, under the NATO system, when transferred, but was identified as PH-01 when commissioned in Spanish service.

19. WWW (http://www.uss-salem.org/features/cabot/), February 1999.

20. WWW (Associated Press, via CNN.com)/

21. Friedman, p. 191.

22. Friedman, p. 191.

23. Nichols pp. 386-388.

Sources and Bibliography

Sources

The information in this book was compiled from several sources. Norman Friedman's *U.S. Aircraft Carriers, An Illustrated Design History* provided most of the information about the *Independence* class design and technical characteristics. Clark G. Reynolds's *The Fast Carriers: The Forging of an Air Navy* was a very valuable source for World War II carrier operations and command relationships. Other major sources for World War II included Norman Polmar's *Aircraft Carriers: A Graphic History of Carrier Aviation and Its Influence on World Events* and Samuel Eliot Morison's multivolume *History of United States Naval Operations in World War II*, along with his one volume summary *The Two Ocean War*. Information on individual ships came from Gareth Pawlowski's *Flat-Tops and Fledglings: A History of American Aircraft Carriers* and the *Dictionary of American Naval Fighting Ships*.

The files on individual ships located in the Ships History Branch of the Naval Historical Center as well as the World War II operational archives at the National Archives provided details not available from other sources. Various veterans' groups and individuals have also provided information from their files. Several of these groups also have information available on the Internet's World Wide Web. Where cited, these additional materials are included in the end notes.

Bibliography

Belote, James H. and William M. Belote. *Titans of the Sea*. New York, NY: Harper & Row, 1975.

Bradshaw, Thomas I., and Marsha L. Clark. *The Sinking of the U.S.S. Princeton (CVL–23)*. Austin, TX: Eakin Press, 1990.

Brown, David K. *Aircraft Carriers: WW2 Fact Files*. New York, NY: Arco Publishing, Inc., 1977.

Buracker, William H. *"Saga of the Carrier Princton"*. National Geographic Society, Washington DC: *National Geographic*, Vol. LXXXVIII, August 1945.

Dictionary of American Naval Fighting Ships. U.S. Government Printing Office, Washington, D.C.: Naval Historical Center, Department of the Navy.
Volume I, Part A, Historical Sketches - Letter A, 1991.
Volume I, Historical Sketches - A and B, 1961.
Volume II, Historical Sketches - C through F, 1963.
Volume III, Historical Sketches - G through K, 1968.
Volume IV, Historical Sketches - L and M, 1969.
Volume V, Historical Sketches - N through Q, 1970.
Volume VI, Historical Sketches - R and S, 1976.
Volume VII, Historical Sketches - T through V, 1981.
Volume VIII, Historical Sketches - W through Z, 1981.

Eliot, John L. "Bikini's Nuclear Graveyard." National Geographic Society, Washington DC: *National Geographic* Vol. 181, No. 6, June 1992

Ewing, Steve and John B. Lundstrom. *Fateful Rendezvous.* Annapolis, MD: Naval Institute Press, 1997.

Friedman, Norman. "CVLs: The U.S. *Independence* Class." Warship International, London, UK: *Warship Volume II*, Conway Maritime Press, Ltd., 1978.
U.S. Aircraft Carriers, An Illustrated Design History. Annapolis, MD: Naval Institute Press, 1983.

Hallion, Richard P. *The Naval Air War in Korea.* Baltimore, MD: The Nautical & Aviation Publishing Company, 1986.

Hammel, Eric. *Aces Against Japan, The American Aces Speak*, Volume 1. Novato, CA: Presidio Press, 1992.

Hudson, J. Ed. *A History of the USS* Cabot CVL-28): *A Fast Carrier in World War II.* Self published, 1986

Miller, Thomas G., Jr. "Anatomy of an Air Battle." American Aviation Historical Society, Santa Ana, CA: *A.A.H.S. Journal*, Summer 1970.

Monsarrat, John. *Angel On The Yardarm: The Beginnings of Fleet Radar Defense and the Kamikaze Threat.* Newport, RI: Naval War College Press, 1985.

Morison, Samuel Eliot. *History of United States Naval Operations in World War II.* Boston, MA: Little, Brown and Company.
Volume VI, Breaking the Bismarks Barrier, 22 July 1942-1 May 1944, 1950.
Volume VII, Aleutians, Gilberts and Marshalls, June 1942-April 1944, 1951.
Volume VIII, New Guinea and the Marianas, March 1944-August 1944, 1953.
Volume XII, Leyte, June 1944-January 1945, 1958.
Volume XIII, The Liberation of the Philippines: Luzon, Mindanao, the Visayas 1944-45, 1959.
Volume XIV, Victory in the Pacific, 1945, 1960.
Volume XV, Supplement and General Index, 1962.
_____.*The Two Ocean War.* Boston, MA: Little, Brown and Company, 1963.

Nichols, David. *Ernie's War: The Best of Ernie Pyle's World War II Dispatches.* New York, NY: Random House, Inc., 1986.

Pawlowski, Gareth L. *Flat-Tops and Fledglings, A History of American Aircraft Carriers.* Cranburg, NJ: A.S. Barnes and Co., Inc., 1971.

Phillips, Christopher. *Steichen at War.* New York, NY: Henry N. Adams, Inc., 1987.

Polmar, Norman. *Aircraft Carriers: A Graphic History of Carrier Aviation and Its Influence on World Events.* Garden City, NY: Doubleday & Company, Inc., 1969.

Reynolds, Clark G., *The Carrier War.* Alexandria, VA: Time-Life Books, Inc., 1982.
_____. *The Fast Carriers: The Forging of an Air Navy.* Huntington, NY: Robert E. Krieger Publishing Company, 1978 (original edition 1968).

Silverstone, Paul H. *U.S. Warships of World War II.* Garden City, NY: Doubleday & Company, Inc., 1968.

Sowinski, Larry and Tom Walkowiak. *United States Navy Camouflage of the WW2 Era. 2,* Philadelphia, PA: The Floating Drydock, 1977.

Swanborough, Gordon and Bowers, Peter M. *United States Naval Aircraft Since 1911.* (3rd ed.), Annapolis, MD: Naval Institute Press, 1990.

terHorst, Jerald F. *Gerald Ford and the Future of the Presidency.* New York, NY: Joseph Okpaku Publishing Company, Inc., 1974.

Terzibaschitsch, Stefan. *Aircraft Carriers of the U.S. Navy.* Annapolis, MD: Naval Institute Press, 1989.

Tillman, Barrett. *Hellcat Aces of World War 2.* London, UK: Osprey Aerospace, 1996.

_____. *Hellcat: The F6F in World War II* Annapolis, MD, Naval Institute Press, 1979.

_____. *The Forgotten Flattops.* Association of Shipmates, CVL-24, P.O. Box 846, Annandale, VA.

United States Naval Aviation 1910-1990. U.S. Government Printing Office, Washington, DC: NAVAIR 00-80P-1, 1991.

Wheeler, Keith. The Road to Tokyo. Alexandria. VA: Time-Life Books, Inc., 1979.

Wooldridge, E.T., editor, *Carrier Warfare in the Pacific: An Oral History Collection.* Washington, DC: Smithsonian Institution Press, 1993.

Hawkins, Arthur R., CAPT, "The Marianas 'Turkey Shoot'." pp. 188-189.

_____. "Shoot Them Down in a Friendly Fashion." pp. 272-275.

Y'Blood, William T., *Red Sun Setting: The Battle of the Philippine Sea* Annapolis, MD: Naval Institute Press, 1981.

Glossary

AAA - Antiaircraft artillery. (Also AA.)

ACI - Air Combat Intelligence officer

Air boss - Nickname for the air officer; head of the air department.

Air group - The complement of aircraft aboard a carrier.

Angels - Fighter direction brevity code for altitude in thousands of feet, e.g. "angels twenty" is 20,000 feet.

Armor belt - A layer of specially treated steel armor, usually from the waterline to the main deck and extending most of the length of the hull designed to protect a ships vital machinery and magazines from shellfire.

ASP - Antisubmarine patrol.

ASW - Antisubmarine warfare.

Bandit - Fighter direction brevity code for an enemy aircraft.

Betty - Japanese Navy Mitsubishi G4M long-range, land-based, twin-engine bomber frequently used as a torpedo bomber.

Black Shoes - Non-aviation Naval officers.

Blister - A bulge below the waterline of a warship hull designed to protect against torpedoes. Blisters are sometimes added to a ship to increase buoyancy.

Bogey - Fighter direction brevity code for an unknown aircraft.

Break - The position in the landing pattern directly over the point of intended touchdown where individual members of a formation break out of formation and turn to the downwind leg for separate landing approaches.

Brown Shoes - Naval aviation officers.

Bulkhead - Nautical term for a wall; also a vertical panel in an aircraft.

Buster - A fighter direction brevity code used during intercept telling the pilot to use full military power.

CAG - Carrier air group. Also, the commander of the air group is known as "CAG."

Caliber - In smaller weapons, caliber refers to the diameter or the bore in hundredths of an inch, i.e. a "fifty caliber" machine gun has a bore diameter of .50 inches. In larger naval weapons, caliber refers to the length of the barrel, i.e., a 5"/38 gun has a barrel length of 190 inches (the bore in inches times the calibers).

Camber - The slight upward curve of a ship's deck, designed to let water run off.

CAP - Combat air patrol.

CarDiv - Carrier Division. A Carrier Division was an administrative or "type" command, not an operational "task" command. During World War II, a CarDiv was commanded by a Rear Admiral, with three to four carriers assigned. (CarDivs were renamed Carrier Groups "CarGru" in 1973. One or two carriers belong to a group.)

Charlie - Radio transmission meaning "return to the ship for recovery." (The signal flag for the letter "C" is flown when flight operations are being conducted.)

CIC - Combat Information Center.

Collier - Ship designed to carry coal as fuel.

Conning tower - The armored pilot house of a warship. The *Independence* class didn't have such armor.

Dinah - Japanese Army Mitsubishi Ki-46 twin-engine high altitude reconnaissance aircraft.

Displacement - The weight of a ship is equal to the weight of the water it displaces, hence the term used to indicate the size of a warship. Merchant ship "tonnage" refers to a ship's volume, from the ancient word "tun," a cask used to store cargo.

Division - Unit of aircraft. Four fighters made up a division. Also, unit of a department in a ship's organization made up of varying numbers of men.

Echelon - Two or more aircraft in a formation lined up with equal spacing in a line from the flight leader.

Emily - Japanese Navy Kawanishi H8K1 Type 2 large four-engine flying boat.

FDC - Fighter Direction Center.

FDO - Fighter Direction Officer.

Feet wet - Fighter direction brevity code to indicate that a pilot had left land and was now over water. (Feet dry indicated crossing the shore from the sea.)

Flush deck - A ship designed with a single main deck from bow to stern.

Frank - Japanese Army Ki-84 high altitude interceptor fighter.

"G" - Unit of force of gravity.

GP bombs - General purpose explosive bombs.

High-side run - A fighter attack pattern using a dive from the side.

Jill - Japanese Navy Nakajima B6N Tenzan carrier torpedo bomber.

Judy - Japanese Navy Yokosuka D4Y Suisei carrier dive bomber.

Kate - Japanese Navy Nakajima B5N carrier torpedo and level bomber.

Lily - Kawasaki Ki-48-IIa twin-engine bomber.

LSO - Landing Signals Officer.

Mainmount - One of the main landing gear wheels on an aircraft.

Maru - Japanese term for "ship."

Mavis - Kawanishi H6K5 Type 97 large four-engine flying boat.

Nell - Mitsubishi G3M2 Type 96 twin-engine bomber.

Oscar - Japanese Army Ki-43 fighter.

Overhead - A steep diving attack run from directly above a target; aboard ship, the ceiling.

Porpoise - Broach of a torpedo when dropped from an aircraft.

PriFly - Primary Flight Control; station located on the island from where the air boss controls flight operations. The flight deck is divided into areas–Fly 1 forward, Fly 2 amidships, and Fly 3 aft.

Revetment - Horseshoe-shaped embankment around an aircraft parking spot for protection from horizontal blast.

Saddle position - Astern of another aircraft in position for attack.

Sally - Mitsubishi Ki-21-IIa twin-engine bomber.

Scramble - Launch aircraft as fast as possible.

Scuttlebutt - Rumor, gossip. Also, a water fountain. In the days of sailing ships, a large keg (a "butt") with a hole in it (a "scuttle") was where sailors gathered to drink water and converse, hence, the two meanings.

Section - A formation of aircraft that is part of a division. For fighters, two aircraft make up a section and two sections make a division.

Sheer - The amount of rise from level of a ship's deck along the lengthwise lines of the hull.

Slipstream - Turbulent air caused by an aircraft propeller.

Split-S - A violent half-roll to an inverted position, followed by a vertical dive.

Sponson - A projecting structure from a ship hull, often used to mount weapons.

Tojo - Japanese Army Nakajima Ki-44 radial-engine fighter.

Tony - Japanese Army Kawasaki Ki-61 in-line engine fighter.

Torpecker - Slang term for torpedo plane.

Underway replenishment - Refueling and resupply at sea where the receiving ship steams alongside the supply ship. During most of World War II, only refueling underway from oilers was possible, but by 1945, ammunition and other stores were being transferred.

Val - Japanese Navy Aichi D3A carrier dive bomber.

Vultures Row - Area of the carriers island where those not on watch can observe flight operations.

Wave-off - Direction to discontinue a landing approach and go around.

Yak - Russian propeller driven fighters of World War II vintage encountered early in the Korean War. These were the Yak-3, Yak-7, or the Yak-9, which generally have a similar appearance.

Zeke - Japanese Navy Mitsubishi A6M Zero carrier fighter.

Zoom - A steep climb started from high speed for maximum altitude gain.

Index

ACI (Air Combat Intelligence) officer, 56
Aircraft, American:
  Boeing B-29 Superfortress, 38, 85-86, 89,
    92, 102, 104
  Consolidated B-24 Liberator, 36, 99
  Consolidated PBY Catalina, 71
  Curtiss SB2C Helldiver, 15, 25, 38, 48-49,
    95
  Douglas SBD Dauntless, 15-16, 9, 23-25,
    48, 50, 85
  Douglas TBD Devastator, 15
  Grumman AF-2S/W Guardian, 107, 109
  Grumman F4F (FM) Wildcat, 15, 63
  Grumman F6F Hellcat, 15-16, 19, 20-24, 26,
    29, 33, 38-40, 44-48, 52, 60, 65, 67-68, 73,
    76, 78, 82, 88, 95, 101, 111
  Grumman F8F Bearcat, 101
  Grumman F9F Panther, 109
  Grumman S2F (S-2) Tracker, 115
  Grumman TBF (TBM) Avenger,
    15-16, 19-21, 23-25, 27, 34-35, 38-39,
    48-49, 52, 56, 69, 73, 81, 88, 93, 95, 97, 111
  Lockheed P-38 Lightning, 76-77, 98
  Martin PBM Mariner, 58, 93
  North American B-25 Mitchell, 17
  Republic F-84 Thunderjet, 108
  Republic P-47 Thunderbolt, 96
  Vought F4U Corsair, 25, 38, 95, 101,
    108-109, 111-112
Aircraft, Japanese:

The following abbreviations are used in the index:

Naval ranks:
  FADM, Fleet Admiral
  ADM, Admiral
  VADM, Vice Admiral
  RADM, Rear Admiral
  COMO, Commodore
  CAPT, Captain
  CDR, Commander
  LCDR, Lieutenant Commander
  LT, Lieutenant
  LTJG, Lieutenant (junior grade)
  ENS, Ensign

Other abbreviations:
  USAAF, United States Army Air
    Forces
  USA, United States Army
  IJN, Imperial Japanese Navy
  RN, Royal Navy

Geographic references: for islands and atolls of the Pacific, the island group follows in parentheses, e.g., Saipan (Marianas) indicates that Saipan is in the Marianas Islands.

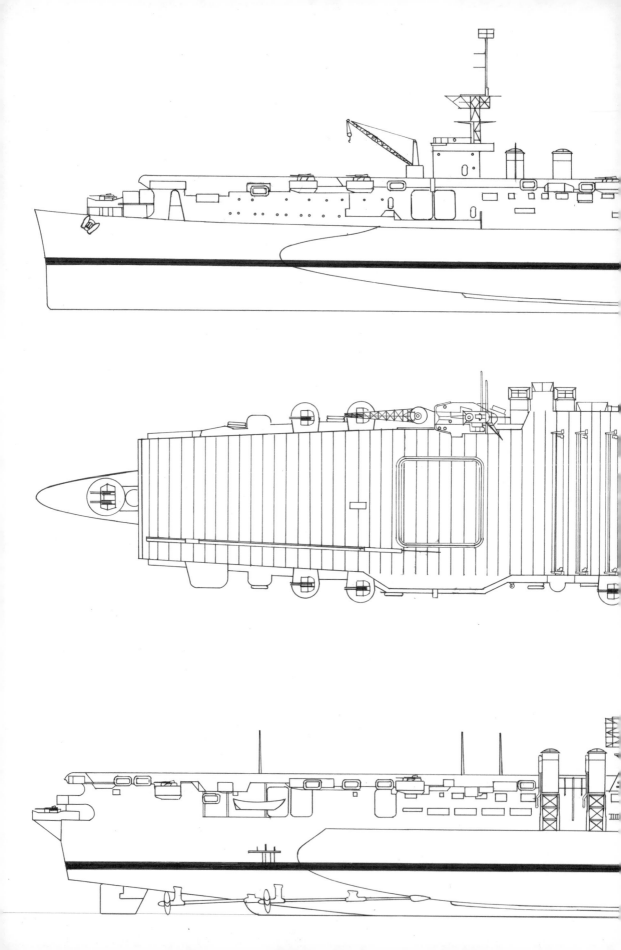